Amazon Virtual Private Cloud Network Administrator Guide

A catalogue record for this book is available from the Hong Kong Public Libraries.

Published in Hong Kong by Samurai Media Limited.

Email: info@samuraimedia.org

ISBN 9789888407675

Contents

Welcome

Welcome to the *Amazon VPC Network Administrator Guide*. This guide is for customers who plan to use an AWS managed IPsec VPN connection with their virtual private cloud (VPC). The topics in this guide help you configure your customer gateway, which is the device on your side of the VPN connection.

The VPN connection lets you bridge your VPC and IT infrastructure, and extend your existing security and management policies to EC2 instances in your VPC as if they were running within your own infrastructure.

For more information, see the following topics:

- Your Customer Gateway
- Example: Check Point Device with Border Gateway Protocol
- Example: Check Point Device without Border Gateway Protocol
- Example: Cisco ASA Device
- Example: Cisco IOS Device
- Example: Cisco IOS Device without Border Gateway Protocol
- Example: Cisco ASA Device with a Virtual Tunnel Interface and Border Gateway Protocol
- Example: Cisco ASA Device with a Virtual Tunnel Interface (without Border Gateway Protocol)
- Example: Dell SonicWALL SonicOS Device Without Border Gateway Protocol
- Example: Dell SonicWALL Device
- Example: Juniper J-Series JunOS Device
- Example: Juniper SRX JunOS Device
- Example: Juniper ScreenOS Device
- Example: Netgate PfSense Device without Border Gateway Protocol
- Example: Palo Alto Networks Device
- Example: Yamaha Device
- Example: Generic Customer Gateway Using Border Gateway Protocol
- Example: Generic Customer Gateway without Border Gateway Protocol
- Configuring Windows Server 2008 R2 as a Customer Gateway
- Configuring Windows Server 2012 R2 as a Customer Gateway

Your Customer Gateway

Topics

- What Is a Customer Gateway?
- Overview of Setting Up a VPN Connection
- AWS VPN CloudHub and Redundant Customer Gateways
- Configuring Multiple VPN Connections to Your VPC
- Customer Gateway Devices We've Tested
- Requirements for Your Customer Gateway
- Configuring a Firewall Between the Internet and Your Customer Gateway

What Is a Customer Gateway?

An Amazon VPC VPN connection links your data center (or network) to your Amazon VPC virtual private cloud (VPC). A *customer gateway* is the anchor on your side of that connection. It can be a physical or software appliance. The anchor on the AWS side of the VPN connection is called a *virtual private gateway*.

The following diagram shows your network, the customer gateway, the VPN connection that goes to the virtual private gateway, and the VPC. There are two lines between the customer gateway and virtual private gateway because the VPN connection consists of two tunnels to provide increased availability for the Amazon VPC service. If there's a device failure within AWS, your VPN connection automatically fails over to the second tunnel so that your access isn't interrupted. From time to time, AWS also performs routine maintenance on the virtual private gateway, which may briefly disable one of the two tunnels of your VPN connection. Your VPN connection automatically fails over to the second tunnel while this maintenance is performed. When you configure your customer gateway, it's therefore important that you configure both tunnels.

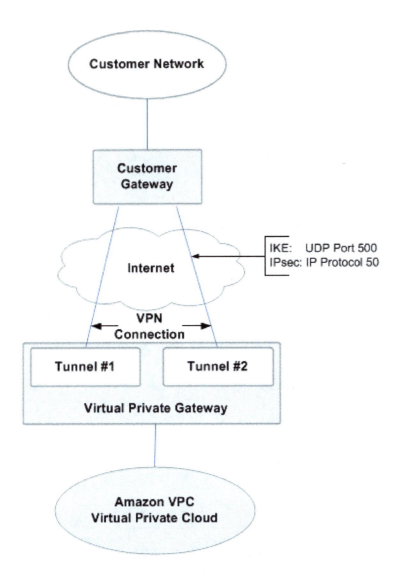

You can create additional VPN connections to other VPCs using the same customer gateway device. You can reuse the same customer gateway IP address for each of those VPN connections.

When you create a VPN connection, the VPN tunnel comes up when traffic is generated from your side of the VPN connection. The virtual private gateway is not the initiator; your customer gateway must initiate the tunnels.

For more information about the components of a VPN connection, see VPN Connections in the *Amazon VPC User Guide*.

To protect against a loss of connectivity if your customer gateway becomes unavailable, you can set up a second VPN connection. For more information, see Using Redundant VPN Connections to Provide Failover.

Your Role

Throughout this guide, we refer to your company's *integration team*, which is the person (or persons) at your company working to integrate your infrastructure with Amazon VPC. This team (which may or may not consist of you) must use the AWS Management Console to create a VPN connection and get the information that you need to configure your customer gateway. Your company might have a separate team for each task (an integration team that uses the AWS Management Console, and a separate network engineering group that has access to network devices and configures the customer gateway). This guide assumes that you're someone in the network engineering group who receives information from your company's integration team so you can then configure the customer gateway device.

Overview of Setting Up a VPN Connection

The process of setting up the VPN connection in AWS is covered in the *Amazon VPC User Guide*. One task in the overall process is to configure the customer gateway. To create the VPN connection, AWS needs information about the customer gateway, and you must configure the customer gateway device itself.

To set up a VPN connection, follow these general steps:

1. Designate an appliance to act as your customer gateway. For more information, see Customer Gateway Devices We've Tested and Requirements for Your Customer Gateway.

2. Get the necessary Network Information, and provide this information to the team that will create the VPN connection in AWS.

3. Create the VPN connection in AWS and get the configuration file for your customer gateway. For more information, see Setting Up an AWS VPN Connection in the *Amazon VPC User Guide*.

4. Configure your customer gateway using the information from the configuration file. Examples are provided in this guide.

5. Generate traffic from your side of the VPN connection to bring up the VPN tunnel.

Network Information

To create a VPN connection in AWS, you need the following information.

Item	Comments
Customer gateway vendor (for example, Cisco), platform (for example, ISR Series Routers), and software version (for example, IOS 12.4)	This information is used to generate a configuration file for the customer gateway.
The internet-routable IP address for the customer gateway device's external interface.	The value must be static. Your customer gateway may reside behind a device performing network address translation (NAT). For a NAT configuration, traffic sent across a VPN tunnel must not be translated to the customer gateway IP address.
(Optional) Border Gateway Protocol (BGP) Autonomous System Number (ASN) of the customer gateway.	You can use an existing ASN assigned to your network. If you don't have one, you can use a private ASN in the 64512–65534 range. Otherwise, we assume that the BGP ASN for the customer gateway is 65000.
(Optional) The ASN for the Amazon side of the BGP session.	Specified when creating a virtual private gateway. If you do not specify a value, the default ASN applies. For more information, see Virtual Private Gateway.

Item	Comments
(Optional) Tunnel information for each VPN tunnel	You can specify the following tunnel information for the VPN connection: [See the AWS documentation website for more details] For more information, see Configuring the VPN Tunnels for Your VPN Connection.

The configuration file for your customer gateway includes the values that you specify for the above items. It also contains any additional values required for setting up the VPN tunnels, including the outside IP address for the virtual private gateway. This value is static unless you recreate the VPN connection in AWS.

AWS VPN CloudHub and Redundant Customer Gateways

You can establish multiple VPN connections to a single virtual private gateway from multiple customer gateways. This configuration can be used in different ways; you can have redundant customer gateways between your data center and your VPC, or you can have multiple locations connected to the AWS VPN CloudHub.

If you have redundant customer gateways, each customer gateway advertises the same prefix (for example, 0.0.0.0/0) to the virtual private gateway. We use BGP routing to determine the path for traffic. If one customer gateway fails, the virtual private gateway directs all traffic to the working customer gateway.

If you use the AWS VPN CloudHub configuration, multiple sites can access your VPC or securely access each other using a simple hub-and-spoke model. You configure each customer gateway to advertise a site-specific prefix (such as 10.0.0.0/24, 10.0.1.0/24) to the virtual private gateway. The virtual private gateway routes traffic to the appropriate site and advertises the reachability of one site to all other sites.

To configure the AWS VPN CloudHub, use the Amazon VPC console to create multiple customer gateways, each with the public IP address of the gateway. You must use a unique Border Gateway Protocol (BGP) Autonomous System Number (ASN) for each. Then create a VPN connection from each customer gateway to a common virtual private gateway. Use the instructions that follow to configure each customer gateway to connect to the virtual private gateway.

To enable instances in your VPC to reach the virtual private gateway (and then your customer gateways), you must configure routes in your VPC routing tables. For complete instructions, see VPN Connections in the *Amazon VPC User Guide*. For AWS VPN CloudHub, you can configure an aggregate route in your VPC routing table (for example, 10.0.0.0/16), and use more specific prefixes between customer gateways and the virtual private gateway.

Configuring Multiple VPN Connections to Your VPC

You can create up to ten VPN connections for your VPC. You can use multiple VPN connections to link your remote offices to the same VPC. For example, if you have offices in Los Angeles, Chicago, New York, and Miami, you can link each of these offices to your VPC. You can also use multiple VPN connections to establish redundant customer gateways from a single location.

Note
If you need more than ten VPN connections, complete the Request to Increase Amazon VPC Limits form to request an increased limit.

When you create multiple VPN connections, the virtual private gateway sends network traffic to the appropriate VPN connection using statically assigned routes or BGP route advertisements, depending upon how the VPN connection was configured. Statically assigned routes are preferred over BGP advertised routes in cases where identical routes exist in the virtual private gateway.

When you have customer gateways at multiple geographic locations, each customer gateway should advertise a unique set of IP ranges specific to the location. When you establish redundant customer gateways at a single location, both gateways should advertise the same IP ranges.

The virtual private gateway receives routing information from all customer gateways and calculates the set of preferred paths using the BGP best path selection algorithm. The rules of that algorithm, as it applies to VPC, are:

1. The most specific IP prefix is preferred (for example, 10.0.0.0/24 is preferable to 10.0.0.0/16). For more information, see Route Priority in the *Amazon VPC User Guide*.

2. When the prefixes are the same, statically configured VPN connections, if they exist, are preferred. For matching prefixes where each VPN connection uses BGP, the AS PATH is compared and the prefix with the shortest AS PATH is preferred. Alternatively, you can prepend AS_PATH, so that the path is less preferred.

3. When the AS PATHs are the same length, the path origin is compared. Prefixes with an Interior Gateway Protocol (IGP) origin are preferred to Exterior Gateway Protocol (EGP) origins, which are preferred to unknown origins.

The following diagram shows the configuration of multiple VPNs.

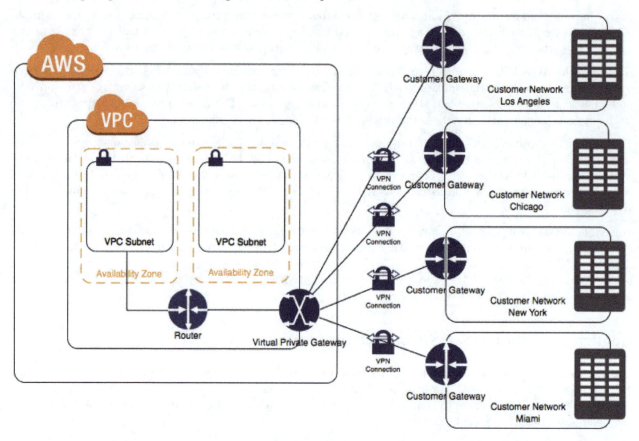

Customer Gateway Devices We've Tested

Your customer gateway can be a physical or software appliance.

For information about the specific routers that we've tested, see **What customer gateway devices are known to work with Amazon VPC?** in the Connectivity section of the Amazon VPC FAQ.

This guide presents information about how to configure the following devices:

- Check Point Security Gateway running R77.10 (or later) software
- Cisco ASA running Cisco ASA 8.2 (or later) software
- Cisco IOS running Cisco IOS 12.4 (or later) software
- Dell SonicWALL running SonicOS 5.9 (or later) software
- Fortinet Fortigate 40+ Series running FortiOS 4.0 (or later) software
- Juniper J-Series running JunOS 9.5 (or later) software
- Juniper SRX running JunOS 11.0 (or later) software
- Juniper SSG running ScreenOS 6.1, or 6.2 (or later) software
- Juniper ISG running ScreenOS 6.1, or 6.2 (or later) software
- Netgate pfSense running OS 2.2.5 (or later) software.
- Palo Alto Networks PANOS 4.1.2 (or later) software
- Yamaha RT107e, RTX1200, RTX1210, RTX1500, RTX3000 and SRT100 routers
- Microsoft Windows Server 2008 R2 (or later) software
- Microsoft Windows Server 2012 R2 (or later) software
- Zyxel Zywall Series 4.20 (or later) software for statically routed VPN connections, or 4.30 (or later) software for dynamically routed VPN connections

If you have one of these devices, but configure it for IPsec in a different way than presented in this guide, feel free to alter our suggested configuration to match your particular needs.

Requirements for Your Customer Gateway

There are four main parts to the configuration of your customer gateway. Throughout this guide, we use a symbol for each of these parts to help you understand what you need to do. The following table shows the four parts and the corresponding symbols.

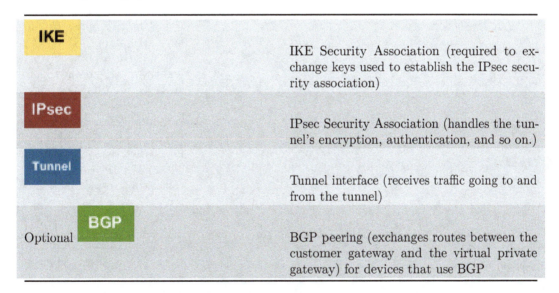

IKE	IKE Security Association (required to exchange keys used to establish the IPsec security association)
IPsec	IPsec Security Association (handles the tunnel's encryption, authentication, and so on.)
Tunnel	Tunnel interface (receives traffic going to and from the tunnel)
Optional **BGP**	BGP peering (exchanges routes between the customer gateway and the virtual private gateway) for devices that use BGP

If you have a device that isn't in the preceding list of tested devices, this section describes the requirements the device must meet for you to use it with Amazon VPC. The following table lists the requirement the customer gateway must adhere to, the related RFC (for reference), and comments about the requirement. For an example of the configuration information if your device isn't one of the tested Cisco or Juniper devices, see Example: Generic Customer Gateway Using Border Gateway Protocol.

Each VPN connection consists of 2 separate tunnels. Each tunnel contains an IKE Security Association, an IPsec Security Association, and a BGP Peering. You are limited to 1 unique Security Association (SA) pair per tunnel (1 inbound and 1 outbound), and therefore 2 unique SA pairs in total for 2 tunnels (4 SAs). Some devices use policy-based VPN and will create as many SAs as ACL entries. Therefore, you may need to consolidate your rules and then filter so you don't permit unwanted traffic.

The VPN tunnel comes up when traffic is generated from your side of the VPN connection. The AWS endpoint is not the initiator; your customer gateway must initiate the tunnels.

Requirement	RFC	Comments
Establish IKE Security Association using pre-shared keys **IKE**	RFC 2409	The IKE Security Association is established first between the virtual private gateway and customer gateway using the pre-shared key as the authenticator. Upon establishment, IKE negotiates an ephemeral key to secure future IKE messages. Proper establishment of an IKE Security Association requires complete agreement among the parameters, including encryption and authentication parameters. When you create a VPN connection in AWS, you can specify your own pre-shared key for each tunnel, or you can let AWS generate one for you. For more information, see Configuring the VPN Tunnels for Your VPN Connection.
Establish IPsec Security Associations in Tunnel mode **IPsec**	RFC 4301	Using the IKE ephemeral key, keys are established between the virtual private gateway and customer gateway to form an IPsec Security Association (SA). Traffic between gateways is encrypted and decrypted using this SA. The ephemeral keys used to encrypt traffic within the IPsec SA are automatically rotated by IKE on a regular basis to ensure confidentiality of communications.
Utilize the AES 128-bit encryption or AES 256-bit encryption function	RFC 3602	The encryption function is used to ensure privacy among both IKE and IPsec Security Associations.
Utilize the SHA-1 or SHA-256 hashing function	RFC 2404	This hashing function is used to authenticate both IKE and IPsec Security Associations.
Utilize Diffie-Hellman Perfect Forward Secrecy. The following groups are supported: [See the AWS documentation website for more details]	RFC 2409	IKE uses Diffie-Hellman to establish ephemeral keys to secure all communication between customer gateways and virtual private gateways.

Requirement	RFC	Comments
Utilize IPsec Dead Peer Detection	RFC 3706	The use of Dead Peer Detection enables the VPN devices to rapidly identify when a network condition prevents delivery of packets across the internet. When this occurs, the gateways delete the Security Associations and attempt to create new associations. During this process, the alternate IPsec tunnel is utilized if possible.
Bind tunnel to logical interface **Tunnel** (route-based VPN)	None	Your gateway must support the ability to bind the IPsec tunnel to a logical interface. The logical interface contains an IP address used to establish BGP peering to the virtual private gateway. This logical interface should perform no additional encapsulation (for example, GRE, IP in IP). Your interface should be set to a 1399 byte Maximum Transmission Unit (MTU).
Fragment IP packets before encryption	RFC 4459	When packets are too large to be transmitted, they must be fragmented. We will not reassemble fragmented encrypted packets. Therefore, your VPN device must fragment packets *before* encapsulating with the VPN headers. The fragments are individually transmitted to the remote host, which reassembles them. For more information about fragmentation, see the IP fragmentation Wikipedia article.
(Optional) Establish BGP **BGP** peerings	RFC 4271	BGP is used to exchange routes between the customer gateway and virtual private gateway for devices that use BGP. All BGP traffic is encrypted and transmitted via the IPsec Security Association. BGP is required for both gateways to exchange the IP prefixes reachable through the IPsec SA.

We recommend you use the techniques listed in the following table to minimize problems related to the amount of data that can be transmitted through the IPsec tunnel. Because the connection encapsulates packets with additional network headers (including IPsec), the amount of data that can be transmitted in a single packet is reduced.

Technique	RFC	Comments
Adjust the maximum segment size of TCP packets entering the VPN tunnel	RFC 4459	TCP packets are often the most prevalent type of packet across IPsec tunnels. Some gateways have the ability to change the TCP Maximum Segment Size parameter. This causes the TCP endpoints (clients, servers) to reduce the amount of data sent with each packet. This is an ideal approach, as the packets arriving at the VPN devices are small enough to be encapsulated and transmitted.
Reset the "Don't Fragment" flag on packets	RFC 791	Some packets carry a flag, known as the Don't Fragment (DF) flag, that indicates that the packet should not be fragmented. If the packets carry the flag, the gateways generate an ICMP Path MTU Exceeded message. In some cases, applications do not contain adequate mechanisms for processing these ICMP messages and reducing the amount of data transmitted in each packet. Some VPN devices have the ability to override the DF flag and fragment packets unconditionally as required. If your customer gateway has this ability, we recommend that you use it as appropriate.

If you have a firewall between your customer gateway and the Internet, see Configuring a Firewall Between the Internet and Your Customer Gateway.

Configuring a Firewall Between the Internet and Your Customer Gateway

To use this service, you must have an internet-routable IP address to use as the endpoint for the IPsec tunnels connecting your customer gateway to the virtual private gateway. If a firewall is in place between the Internet and your gateway, the rules in the following tables must be in place to establish the IPsec tunnels. The virtual private gateway addresses are in the configuration information that you'll get from the integration team.

Inbound (from the Internet)

Input Rule I1

Source IP	
Dest IP	
Protocol	
Source Port	
Destination	
Input Rule I2	
Source IP	
Dest IP	
Protocol	
Source Port	
Destination Port	
Input Rule I3	
Source IP	
Dest IP	
Protocol	
Input Rule I4	
Source IP	
Dest IP	
Protocol	

Outbound (to the Internet)

Output Rule O1	
Source IP	
Dest IP	
Protocol	
Source Port	
Destination Port	
Output Rule O2	
Source IP	
Dest IP	
Protocol	
Source Port	
Destination Port	
Output Rule O3	
Source IP	
Dest IP	
Protocol	
Output Rule O4	
Source IP	
Dest IP	
Protocol	

Rules I1, I2, O1, and O2 enable the transmission of IKE packets. Rules I3, I4, O3, and O4 enable the transmission of IPsec packets containing the encrypted network traffic.

If you are using NAT traversal (NAT-T) on your device, then you must include rules that allow UDP access over port 4500. Check if your device is advertising NAT-T.

Example: Check Point Device with Border Gateway Protocol

This section has example configuration information provided by your integration team if your customer gateway is a Check Point Security Gateway device running R77.10 or above, and using the Gaia operating system.

Topics

- High-Level View of the Customer Gateway
- Configuration File
- Configuring the Check Point Device
- How to Test the Customer Gateway Configuration

High-Level View of the Customer Gateway

The following diagram shows the general details of your customer gateway. Note that the VPN connection consists of two separate tunnels. Using redundant tunnels ensures continuous availability in the case that a device fails.

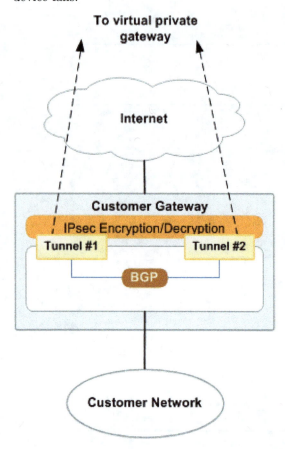

Configuration File

Your integration team will provide you with a configuration file with the values you need in order to configure each tunnel and the IKE and IPsec settings for your VPN device. The configuration file includes instructions on how to use the Gaia web portal and Check Point SmartDashboard to configure your device. The same steps are provided in the next section.

The following is an extract of an example configuration file. The file contains two sections: `IPSec Tunnel #1` and `IPSec Tunnel #2`. You must use the values provided in each section to configure each tunnel.

```
 1  ! Amazon Web Services
 2  ! Virtual Private Cloud
 3
 4  ! AWS uses unique identifiers to manipulate the configuration of
 5  ! a VPN connection. Each VPN connection is assigned an identifier and is
 6  ! associated with two other identifiers, namely the
 7  ! customer gateway identifier and virtual private gateway identifier.
 8  !
 9  ! Your VPN connection ID        : vpn-12345678
10  ! Your virtual private gateway ID : vgw-12345678
11  ! Your customer gateway ID      : cgw-12345678
12  !
13  !
14  ! This configuration consists of two tunnels. Both tunnels must be
15  ! configured on your customer gateway.
16  !
17
18  ! -----------------------------------------------------------------------
19  ! IPSec Tunnel #1
20  ! -----------------------------------------------------------------------
21  ! #1: Tunnel Interface Configuration
22
23   ...
24
25  ! -----------------------------------------------------------------------
26  ! -----------------------------------------------------------------------
27  ! IPSec Tunnel #2
28  ! -----------------------------------------------------------------------
29  ! #1: Tunnel Interface Configuration
30
31   ...
```

Configuring the Check Point Device

The following procedures demonstrate how to configure the VPN tunnels, network objects, and security for your VPN connection. You must replace the example values in the procedures with the values that are provided in the configuration file.

Note
For more information, go to the Amazon Web Services (AWS) VPN BGP article on the Check Point Support Center.

Topics

- Step 1: Configure the Tunnel Interfaces
- Step 2: Configure BGP
- Step 3: Create Network Objects
- Step 4: Create a VPN Community and Configure IKE and IPsec
- Step 5: Configure the Firewall
- Step 6: Enable Dead Peer Detection and TCP MSS Clamping

Step 1: Configure the Tunnel Interfaces

The first step to create the VPN tunnels and provide the private (inside) IP addresses of the customer gateway and virtual private gateway for each tunnel. For the first tunnel, use the information provided under the IPSec Tunnel #1 section of the configuration file. For the second tunnel, use the values provided in the IPSec Tunnel #2 section of the configuration file.

To configure the tunnel interface

1. Connect to your security gateway over SSH. If you're using the non-default shell, change to clish by running the following command: clish

2. Set the customer gateway ASN (the ASN that was provided when the customer gateway was created in AWS) by running the following command:

```
1 set as 65000
```

3. Create the tunnel interface for the first tunnel, using the information provided under the IPSec Tunnel #1 section of the configuration file. Provide a unique name for your tunnel, such as AWS_VPC_Tunnel_1.

```
1 add vpn tunnel 1 type numbered local 169.254.44.234 remote 169.254.44.233 peer
    AWS_VPC_Tunnel_1
2 set interface vpnt1 state on
3 set interface vpnt1 mtu 1436
```

4. Repeat these commands to create the second tunnel, using the information provided under the IPSec Tunnel #2 section of the configuration file. Provide a unique name for your tunnel, such as AWS_VPC_Tunnel_2.

```
1 add vpn tunnel 1 type numbered local 169.254.44.38 remote 169.254.44.37 peer
    AWS_VPC_Tunnel_2
2 set interface vpnt2 state on
3 set interface vpnt2 mtu 1436
```

5. Set the virtual private gateway ASN:

```
1 set bgp external remote-as 7224 on
```

6. Configure the BGP for the first tunnel, using the information provided IPSec Tunnel #1 section of the configuration file:

```
1 set bgp external remote-as 7224 peer 169.254.44.233 on
2 set bgp external remote-as 7224 peer 169.254.44.233 holdtime 30
3 set bgp external remote-as 7224 peer 169.254.44.233 keepalive 10
```

7. Configure the BGP for the second tunnel, using the information provided IPSec Tunnel #2 section of the configuration file:

```
1 set bgp external remote-as 7224 peer 169.254.44.37 on
2 set bgp external remote-as 7224 peer 169.254.44.37 holdtime 30
3 set bgp external remote-as 7224 peer 169.254.44.37 keepalive 10
```

8. Save the configuration:

```
1 save config
```

Step 2: Configure BGP

In this step, you create a BGP policy that allows the import of routes that are advertised by AWS, and then configure your customer gateway to advertise its local routes to AWS.

To create a BGP policy

1. In the Gaia WebUI, choose **Advanced Routing, Inbound Route Filters**. Choose **Add**, and select **Add BGP Policy (Based on AS)**.

2. For **Add BGP Policy**, select a value between 512 and 1024 in the first field, and enter the virtual private gateway ASN in the second field; for example, 7224.

3. Choose **Save**.

The following steps are for distributing local interface routes. You can also redistribute routes from different sources; for example, static routes, or routes obtained through dynamic routing protocols. For more information, go to the Gaia Advanced Routing R77 Versions Administration Guide.

To advertise local routes

1. In the Gaia WebUI, choose **Advanced Routing**,** Routing Redistribution**. Choose **Add Redistribution From** and select **Interface**.

2. For **To Protocol**, select the virtual private gateway ASN; for example, 7224.

3. For **Interface**, select an internal interface. Choose **Save**.

Step 3: Create Network Objects

In this step, you create a network object for each VPN tunnel, specifying the public (outside) IP addresses for the virtual private gateway. You later add these network objects as satellite gateways for your VPN community. You also need to create an empty group to act as a placeholder for the VPN domain.

To define a new network object

1. Open the Check Point SmartDashboard.

2. For **Groups**, open the context menu and choose **Groups, Simple Group**. You can use the same group for each network object.

3. For **Network Objects**, open the context (right-click) menu and choose **New, Interoperable Device**.

4. For **Name**, enter the name you provided for your tunnel in step 1, for example, `AWS_VPC_Tunnel_1` or `AWS_VPC_Tunnel_2`.

5. For **IPv4 Address**, enter the outside IP address of the virtual private gateway provided in the configuration file, for example, `54.84.169.196`. Save your settings and close the dialog box.

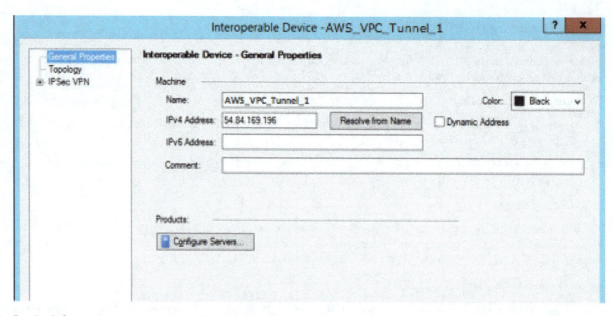

6. In the left category pane, choose **Topology**.

7. In the **VPN Domain** section, choose **Manually defined**, and browse to and select the empty simple group that you created in step 2. Choose **OK**.

8. Repeat these steps to create a second network object, using the information under the `IPSec Tunnel #2` section of the configuration file.

9. Go to your gateway network object, open your gateway or cluster object, and choose **Topology**.

10. In the **VPN Domain** section, choose **Manually defined**, and browse to and select the empty simple group that you created in step 2. Choose **OK Note**
You can keep any existing VPN domain that you've configured; however, ensure that the hosts and networks that are used or served by the new VPN connection are not declared in that VPN domain, especially if the VPN domain is automatically derived.

Note
If you're using clusters, then edit the topology and define the interfaces as cluster interfaces. Use the IP addresses specified in the configuration file.

Step 4: Create a VPN Community and Configure IKE and IPsec

In this step, you create a VPN community on your Check Point gateway, to which you add the network objects (interoperable devices) for each tunnel. You also configure the Internet Key Exchange (IKE) and IPsec settings.

To create and configure the VPN community, IKE, and IPsec settings

1. From your gateway properties, choose **IPSec VPN** in the category pane.

2. Choose **Communities, New, Star Community**.

3. Provide a name for your community (for example, `AWS_VPN_Star`), and then choose **Center Gateways** in the category pane.

4. Choose **Add**, and add your gateway or cluster to the list of participant gateways.

5. In the category pane, choose **Satellite Gateways, Add**, and add the interoperable devices you created earlier (`AWS_VPC_Tunnel_1` and `AWS_VPC_Tunnel_2`) to the list of participant gateways.

6. In the category pane, choose **Encryption**. In the **Encryption Method** section, choose **IKEv1 for IPv4 and IKEv2 for IPv6**. In the **Encryption Suite** section, choose **Custom, Custom Encryption**.

Note

You must select the **IKEv1 for IPv4 and IKEv2 for IPv6** option for IKEv1 functionality; however, IKEv2 and IPv6 are currently not supported.

7. In the dialog box, configure the encryption properties as follows, and choose **OK** when you're done:

   - IKE Security Association (Phase 1) Properties:
     - **Perform key exchange encryption with**: AES-128
     - **Perform data integrity with**: SHA1
   - IPsec Security Association (Phase 2) Properties:
     - **Perform IPsec data encryption with**: AES-128
     - **Perform data integrity with**: SHA-1

8. In the category pane, choose **Tunnel Management**. Choose **Set Permanent Tunnels, On all tunnels in the community**. In the **VPN Tunnel Sharing** section, choose **One VPN tunnel per Gateway pair**.

9. In the category pane, expand **Advanced Settings**, and choose **Shared Secret**.

10. Select the peer name for the first tunnel, choose **Edit**, and enter the pre-shared key as specified in the configuration file in the `IPSec Tunnel #1` section.

11. Select the peer name for the second tunnel, choose **Edit**, and enter the pre-shared key as specified in the configuration file in the `IPSec Tunnel #2` section.

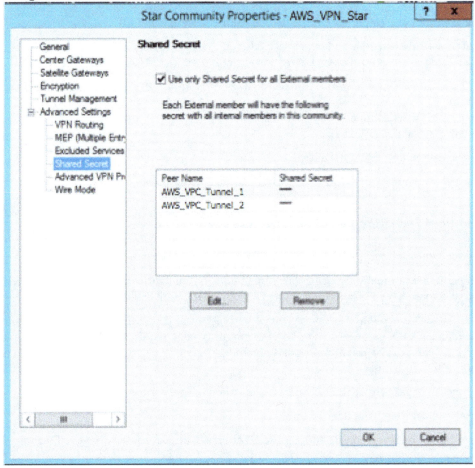

12. Still in the **Advanced Settings** category, choose **Advanced VPN Properties**, configure the properties as follows, and choose **OK** when you're done:

    - IKE (Phase 1):

- Use **Diffie-Hellman group**: `Group 2 (1024 bit)`
- **Renegotiate IKE security associations every** 480 **minutes**
- IPsec (Phase 2):
  - Choose **Use Perfect Forward Secrecy**
  - Use **Diffie-Hellman group**: `Group 2 (1024 bit)`
  - **Renegotiate IPsec security associations every** 3600 **seconds**

Step 5: Configure the Firewall

In this step, you configure a policy with firewall rules and directional match rules that allow communication between the VPC and the local network. You then install the policy on your gateway.

To create firewall rules

1. In the SmartDashboard, choose **Global Properties** for your gateway. In the category pane, expand **VPN**, and choose **Advanced**.

2. Choose **Enable VPN Directional Match in VPN Column**, and choose **OK**.

3. In the SmartDashboard, choose **Firewall**, and create a policy with the following rules:

   - Allow the VPC subnet to communicate with the local network over the required protocols.
   - Allow the local network to communicate with the VPC subnet over the required protocols.

4. Open the context menu for the cell in the VPN column, and choose **Edit Cell**.

5. In the **VPN Match Conditions** dialog box, choose **Match traffic in this direction only**. Create the following directional match rules by choosing **Add** for each, and choose **OK** when you're done:

   - `internal_clear` > VPN community (The VPN star community you created earlier, for example, `AWS_VPN_Star`)
   - VPN community > VPN community
   - VPN community > `internal_clear`

6. In the SmartDashboard, choose **Policy**, **Install**.

7. In the dialog box, choose your gateway and choose **OK** to install the policy.

Step 6: Enable Dead Peer Detection and TCP MSS Clamping

Your Check Point gateway can use Dead Peer Detection (DPD) to identify when an IKE association is down.

To configure DPD for a permanent tunnel, the permanent tunnel must be configured in the AWS VPN community (refer to Step 8 in Step 4: Create a VPN Community and Configure IKE and IPsec).

By default, the `tunnel_keepalive_method` property for a VPN gateway is set to `tunnel_test`. You must change the value to `dpd`. Each VPN gateway in the VPN community that requires DPD monitoring must be configured with the `tunnel_keepalive_method` property, including any 3rd party VPN gateway (you cannot configure different monitoring mechanisms for the same gateway).

You can update the `tunnel_keepalive_method` property using the GuiDBedit tool.

To modify the tunnel_keepalive_method property

1. Open the Check Point SmartDashboard, and choose **Security Management Server**, **Domain Management Server**.

2. Choose **File, Database Revision Control...** and create a revision snapshot.

3. Close all SmartConsole windows, such as the SmartDashboard, SmartView Tracker, and SmartView Monitor.

4. Start the GuiBDedit tool. For more information, see the Check Point Database Tool article on the Check Point Support Center.

5. Choose **Security Management Server, Domain Management Server**.

6. In the upper left pane, choose **Table, Network Objects, network_objects**.

7. In the upper right pane, select the relevant **Security Gateway, Cluster** object.

8. Press CTRL+F, or use the **Search** menu to search for the following: `tunnel_keepalive_method`.

9. In the lower pane, open the context menu for `tunnel_keepalive_method`, and select **Edit...**. Choose **dpd** and choose **OK**.

10. Repeat steps 7 - 9 for each gateway that's part of the AWS VPN Community.

11. Choose **File, Save All**.

12. Close the GuiDBedit tool.

13. Open the Check Point SmartDashboard, and choose **Security Management Server, Domain Management Server**.

14. Install the policy on the relevant **Security Gateway, Cluster** object.

For more information, see the New VPN features in R77.10 article on the Check Point Support Center.

TCP MSS clamping reduces the maximum segment size of TCP packets to prevent packet fragmentation.

To enable TCP MSS clamping

1. Navigate to the following directory: `C:\Program Files (x86)\CheckPoint\SmartConsole\R77.10\PROGRAM\`.

2. Open the Check Point Database Tool by running the `GuiDBEdit.exe` file.

3. Choose **Table, Global Properties, properties**.

4. For `fw_clamp_tcp_mss`, choose **Edit**. Change the value to `true` and choose **OK**.

How to Test the Customer Gateway Configuration

You can test the gateway configuration for each tunnel.

To test the customer gateway configuration for each tunnel

1. On your customer gateway, determine whether the BGP status is `Active`.

   It takes approximately 30 seconds for a BGP peering to become active.

2. Ensure that the customer gateway is advertising a route to the virtual private gateway. The route may be the default route (`0.0.0.0/0`) or a more specific route you prefer.

When properly established, your BGP peering should be receiving one route from the virtual private gateway corresponding to the prefix that your VPC integration team specified for the VPC (for example, `10.0.0.0/24`). If the BGP peering is established, you are receiving a prefix, and you are advertising a prefix, your tunnel is configured correctly. Make sure that both tunnels are in this state.

Next you must test the connectivity for each tunnel by launching an instance into your VPC, and pinging the instance from your home network. Before you begin, make sure of the following:

- Use an AMI that responds to ping requests. We recommend that you use one of the Amazon Linux AMIs.
- Configure your instance's security group and network ACL to enable inbound ICMP traffic.
- Ensure that you have configured routing for your VPN connection: your subnet's route table must contain a route to the virtual private gateway. For more information, see Enable Route Propagation in Your Route Table in the *Amazon VPC User Guide*.

To test the end-to-end connectivity of each tunnel

1. Launch an instance of one of the Amazon Linux AMIs into your VPC. The Amazon Linux AMIs are listed in the launch wizard when you launch an instance from the Amazon EC2 Console. For more information, see the Amazon VPC Getting Started Guide.

2. After the instance is running, get its private IP address (for example, `10.0.0.4`). The console displays the address as part of the instance's details.

3. On a system in your home network, use the ping command with the instance's IP address. Make sure that the computer you ping from is behind the customer gateway. A successful response should be similar to the following.

```
1 ping 10.0.0.4
```

```
1 Pinging 10.0.0.4 with 32 bytes of data:
2
3 Reply from 10.0.0.4: bytes=32 time<1ms TTL=128
4 Reply from 10.0.0.4: bytes=32 time<1ms TTL=128
5 Reply from 10.0.0.4: bytes=32 time<1ms TTL=128
6
7 Ping statistics for 10.0.0.4:
8 Packets: Sent = 3, Received = 3, Lost = 0 (0% loss),
9
10 Approximate round trip times in milliseconds:
11 Minimum = 0ms, Maximum = 0ms, Average = 0ms
```

Note

If you ping an instance from your customer gateway router, ensure that you are sourcing ping messages from an internal IP address, not a tunnel IP address. Some AMIs don't respond to ping messages from tunnel IP addresses.

1. (Optional) To test tunnel failover, you can temporarily disable one of the tunnels on your customer gateway, and repeat the above step. You cannot disable a tunnel on the AWS side of the VPN connection.

On the Check Point gateway side, you can verify the tunnel status by running the following command from the command line tool in expert mode:

```
1 vpn tunnelutil
```

In the options that display, choose 1 to verify the IKE associations and 2 to verify the IPsec associations.

You can also use the Check Point Smart Tracker Log to verify that packets over the connection are being encrypted. For example, the following log indicates that a packet to the VPC was sent over tunnel 1 and was encrypted.

Log Info

Product	🔳 Security Gateway/Management
Date	4Nov2015
Time	9:42:01
Number	21254
Type	📄 Log
Origin	cpgw-997695

Traffic

Source	🔲 Management_PC (192.168.1.116)
Destination	🔲 10.28.13.28
Service	---
Protocol	ICMP icmp
Interface	📥 eth0
Source Port	---

Policy

Policy Name	Standard
Policy Date	Tue Nov 03 11:33:45 2015
Policy Management	cpgw-997695

Rule

Action	🔒 Encrypt
Rule	4
Current Rule Number	4-Standard
Rule Name	---
User	---

More

Rule UID	{0AA18015-FF7B-4650-B0CE-3989E658CF04}
Community	AWS_VPN_Star
Encryption Scheme	📧 IKE
Data Encryption Methods	ESP: AES-128 + SHA1 + PFS (group 2)
VPN Peer Gateway	AWS_VPC_Tunnel_1 (54.84.169.196)
Subproduct	🔵 VPN
VPN Feature	VPN
Product Family	🖥 Network
Information	service_id: icmp-proto ICMP: Echo Request ICMP Type: 8 ICMP Code: 0

Example: Check Point Device without Border Gateway Protocol

This section has example configuration information provided by your integration team if your customer gateway is a Check Point Security Gateway device running R77.10 or above, and using the Gaia operating system.

Topics

- High-Level View of the Customer Gateway
- Configuration File
- Configuring the Check Point Device
- How to Test the Customer Gateway Configuration

High-Level View of the Customer Gateway

The following diagram shows the general details of your customer gateway. Note that the VPN connection consists of two separate tunnels. Using redundant tunnels ensures continuous availability in the case that a device fails.

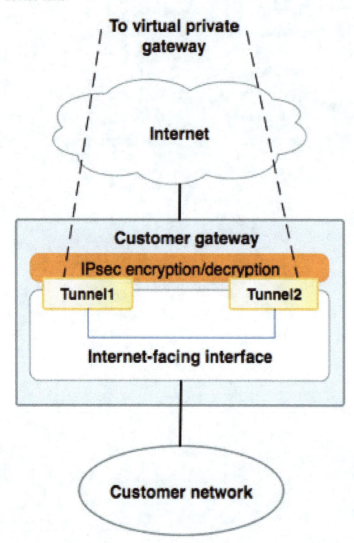

Configuration File

Your integration team will provide you with a configuration file with the values you need in order to configure each tunnel and the IKE and IPsec settings for your VPN device. The configuration file includes instructions on how to use the Gaia web portal and Check Point SmartDashboard to configure your device. The same steps are provided in the next section.

The following is an extract of an example configuration file. The file contains two sections: `IPSec Tunnel #1` and `IPSec Tunnel #2`. You must use the values provided in each section to configure each tunnel.

```
1  ! Amazon Web Services
2  ! Virtual Private Cloud
3
4  ! AWS uses unique identifiers to manipulate the configuration of
5  ! a VPN connection. Each VPN connection is assigned an identifier and is
6  ! associated with two other identifiers, namely the
7  ! customer gateway identifier and virtual private gateway identifier.
8  !
9  ! Your VPN connection ID          : vpn-12345678
10 ! Your virtual private gateway ID : vgw-12345678
11 ! Your customer gateway ID        : cgw-12345678
12 !
13 !
14 ! This configuration consists of two tunnels. Both tunnels must be
15 ! configured on your customer gateway.
16 !
17
18 ! -------------------------------------------------------------------
19 ! IPSec Tunnel #1
20 ! -------------------------------------------------------------------
21 ! #1: Tunnel Interface Configuration
22
23   ...
24
25 ! -------------------------------------------------------------------
26 ! -------------------------------------------------------------------
27 ! IPSec Tunnel #2
28 ! -------------------------------------------------------------------
29 ! #1: Tunnel Interface Configuration
30
31 ...
```

Configuring the Check Point Device

The following procedures demonstrate how to configure the VPN tunnels, network objects, and security for your VPN connection. You must replace the example values in the procedures with the values that are provided in the configuration file.

Note

For more information, go to the Check Point Security Gateway IPsec VPN to Amazon Web Services VPC article on the Check Point Support Center.

Topics

- Step 1: Configure Tunnel Interface
- Step 2: Configure the Static Route

- Step 3: Create Network Objects
- Step 4: Create a VPN Community and Configure IKE and IPsec
- Step 5: Configure the Firewall
- Step 6: Enable Dead Peer Detection and TCP MSS Clamping

Step 1: Configure Tunnel Interface

The first step is to create the VPN tunnels and provide the private (inside) IP addresses of the customer gateway and virtual private gateway for each tunnel. To create the first tunnel, use the information provided under the `IPSec Tunnel #1` section of the configuration file. To create the second tunnel, use the values provided in the `IPSec Tunnel #2` section of the configuration file.

To configure the tunnel interface

1. Open the Gaia portal of your Check Point Security Gateway device.

2. Choose **Network Interfaces**, **Add**, **VPN tunnel**.

3. In the dialog box, configure the settings as follows, and choose **OK** when you are done:

    - For **VPN Tunnel ID**, enter any unique value, such as 1.
    - For **Peer**, enter a unique name for your tunnel, such as `AWS_VPC_Tunnel_1` or `AWS_VPC_Tunnel_2`.
    - Ensure that **Numbered** is selected, and for **Local Address**, enter the IP address specified for `CGW Tunnel IP` in the configuration file, for example, `169.254.44.234`.
    - For **Remote Address**, enter the IP address specified for `VGW Tunnel IP` in the configuration file, for example, `169.254.44.233`.

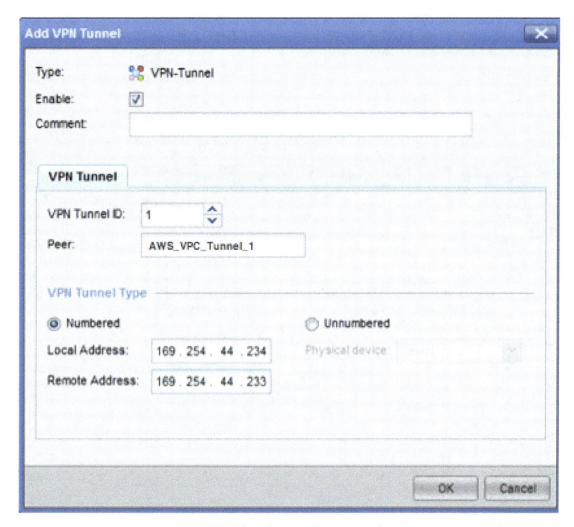

4. Connect to your security gateway over SSH. If you're using the non-default shell, change to clish by running the following command: `clish`

5. For tunnel 1, run the following command:

```
1 set interface vpnt1 mtu 1436
```

For tunnel 2, run the following command:

```
1 set interface vpnt2 mtu 1436
```

6. Repeat these steps to create a second tunnel, using the information under the `IPSec Tunnel #2` section of the configuration file.

Step 2: Configure the Static Route

In this step, you'll specify the static route to the subnet in the VPC for each tunnel to enable you to send traffic over the tunnel interfaces. The second tunnel enables failover in case there is an issue with the first tunnel — if an issue is detected, the policy-based static route is removed from the routing table, and the second route is activated. You must also enable the Check Point gateway to ping the other end of the tunnel to check if the tunnel is up.

To configure the static routes

1. In the Gaia portal, choose **IPv4 Static Routes, Add.**

2. Specify the CIDR of your subnet, for example, `10.28.13.0/24`.

3. Choose **Add Gateway**, **IP Address**.

4. Enter the IP address specified for `VGW Tunnel IP` in the configuration file (for example, `169.254.44.233`), and specify a priority of 1.

5. Select **Ping**.

6. Repeat steps 3 and 4 for the second tunnel, using the `VGW Tunnel IP` value under the `IPSec Tunnel #2` section of the configuration file. Specify a priority of 2.

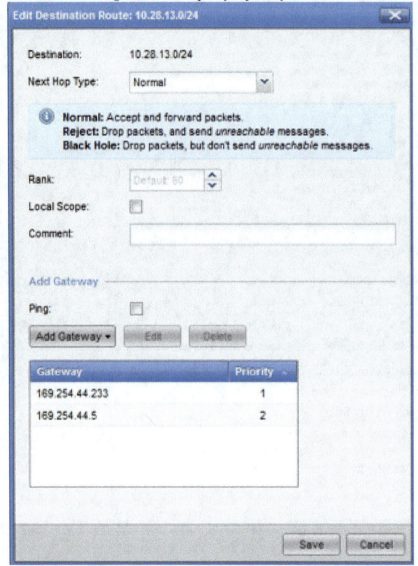

7. Choose **Save**.

If you're using a cluster, repeat the steps above for the other members of the cluster.

Step 3: Create Network Objects

In this step, you create a network object for each VPN tunnel, specifying the public (outside) IP addresses for the virtual private gateway. You later add these network objects as satellite gateways for your VPN community. You also need to create an empty group to act as a placeholder for the VPN domain.

To define a new network object

1. Open the Check Point SmartDashboard.

2. For **Groups**, open the context menu and choose **Groups**, **Simple Group**. You can use the same group for each network object.

3. For **Network Objects**, open the context (right-click) menu and choose **New, Interoperable Device**.

4. For **Name**, enter the name you provided for your tunnel, for example, AWS_VPC_Tunnel_1 or AWS_VPC_Tunnel_2.

5. For **IPv4 Address**, enter the outside IP address of the virtual private gateway provided in the configuration file, for example, 54.84.169.196. Save your settings and close the dialog box.

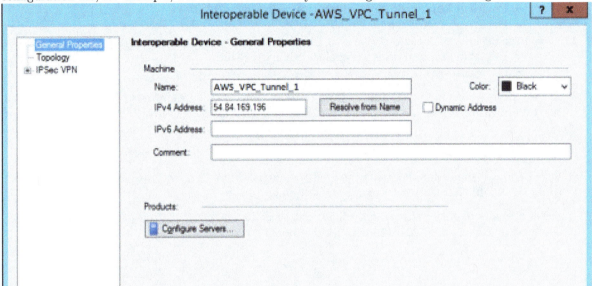

6. In the SmartDashboard, open your gateway properties and in the category pane, choose **Topology**.

7. To retrieve the interface configuration, choose **Get Topology**.

8. In the **VPN Domain** section, choose **Manually defined**, and browse to and select the empty simple group that you created in step 2. Choose **OK**. **Note**
   You can keep any existing VPN domain that you've configured; however, ensure that the hosts and networks that are used or served by the new VPN connection are not declared in that VPN domain, especially if the VPN domain is automatically derived.

9. Repeat these steps to create a second network object, using the information under the IPSec Tunnel #2 section of the configuration file.

Note
If you're using clusters, then edit the topology and define the interfaces as cluster interfaces. Use the IP addresses specified in the configuration file.

Step 4: Create a VPN Community and Configure IKE and IPsec

In this step, you create a VPN community on your Check Point gateway, to which you add the network objects (interoperable devices) for each tunnel. You also configure the Internet Key Exchange (IKE) and IPsec settings.

To create and configure the VPN community, IKE, and IPsec settings

1. From your gateway properties, choose **IPSec VPN** in the category pane.

2. Choose **Communities, New, Star Community**.

3. Provide a name for your community (for example, `AWS_VPN_Star`), and then choose **Center Gateways** in the category pane.

4. Choose **Add**, and add your gateway or cluster to the list of participant gateways.

5. In the category pane, choose **Satellite Gateways**, **Add**, and add the interoperable devices you created earlier (`AWS_VPC_Tunnel_1` and `AWS_VPC_Tunnel_2`) to the list of participant gateways.

6. In the category pane, choose **Encryption**. In the **Encryption Method** section, choose **IKEv1 only**. In the **Encryption Suite** section, choose **Custom**, **Custom Encryption**.

7. In the dialog box, configure the encryption properties as follows, and choose **OK** when you're done:
   - IKE Security Association (Phase 1) Properties:
     - **Perform key exchange encryption with**: AES-128
     - **Perform data integrity with**: SHA1
   - IPsec Security Association (Phase 2) Properties:
     - **Perform IPsec data encryption with**: AES-128
     - **Perform data integrity with**: SHA-1

8. In the category pane, choose **Tunnel Management**. Choose **Set Permanent Tunnels**, **On all tunnels in the community**. In the **VPN Tunnel Sharing** section, choose **One VPN tunnel per Gateway pair**.

9. In the category pane, expand **Advanced Settings**, and choose **Shared Secret**.

10. Select the peer name for the first tunnel, choose **Edit**, and enter the pre-shared key as specified in the configuration file in the `IPSec Tunnel #1` section.

11. Select the peer name for the second tunnel, choose **Edit**, and enter the pre-shared key as specified in the configuration file in the `IPSec Tunnel #2` section.

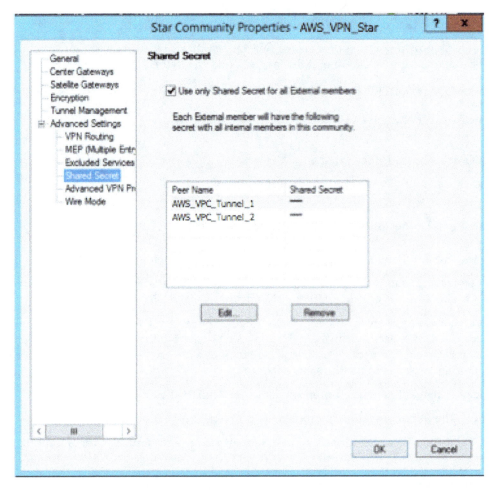

12. Still in the **Advanced Settings** category, choose **Advanced VPN Properties**, configure the properties as follows, and choose **OK** when you're done:

- IKE (Phase 1):
    - **Use Diffie-Hellman group**: Group 2
    - **Renegotiate IKE security associations every 480 minutes**
- IPsec (Phase 2):
    - Choose **Use Perfect Forward Secrecy**
    - **Use Diffie-Hellman group**: Group 2
    - **Renegotiate IPsec security associations every 3600 seconds**

Step 5: Configure the Firewall

In this step, you configure a policy with firewall rules and directional match rules that allow communication between the VPC and the local network. You then install the policy on your gateway.

To create firewall rules

1. In the SmartDashboard, choose **Global Properties** for your gateway. In the category pane, expand **VPN**, and choose **Advanced**.

2. Choose **Enable VPN Directional Match in VPN Column**, and save your changes.

3. In the SmartDashboard, choose **Firewall**, and create a policy with the following rules:

    - Allow the VPC subnet to communicate with the local network over the required protocols.
    - Allow the local network to communicate with the VPC subnet over the required protocols.

4. Open the context menu for the cell in the VPN column, and choose **Edit Cell**.

5. In the **VPN Match Conditions** dialog box, choose **Match traffic in this direction only**. Create the following directional match rules by choosing **Add** for each, and choose **OK** when you're done:

   - `internal_clear` > VPN community (The VPN star community you created earlier, for example, `AWS_VPN_Star`)
   - VPN community > VPN community
   - VPN community > `internal_clear`

6. In the SmartDashboard, choose **Policy, Install**.

7. In the dialog box, choose your gateway and choose **OK** to install the policy.

Step 6: Enable Dead Peer Detection and TCP MSS Clamping

Your Check Point gateway can use Dead Peer Detection (DPD) to identify when an IKE association is down.

To configure DPD for a permanent tunnel, the permanent tunnel must be configured in the AWS VPN community (refer to Step 8 in Step 4: Create a VPN Community and Configure IKE and IPsec).

By default, the `tunnel_keepalive_method` property for a VPN gateway is set to `tunnel_test`. You must change the value to `dpd`. Each VPN gateway in the VPN community that requires DPD monitoring must be configured with the `tunnel_keepalive_method` property, including any 3rd party VPN gateway (you cannot configure different monitoring mechanisms for the same gateway).

You can update the `tunnel_keepalive_method` property using the GuiDBedit tool.

To modify the tunnel_keepalive_method property

1. Open the Check Point SmartDashboard, and choose **Security Management Server, Domain Management Server**.

2. Choose **File, Database Revision Control...** and create a revision snapshot.

3. Close all SmartConsole windows, such as the SmartDashboard, SmartView Tracker, and SmartView Monitor.

4. Start the GuiBDedit tool. For more information, see the Check Point Database Tool article on the Check Point Support Center.

5. Choose **Security Management Server, Domain Management Server**.

6. In the upper left pane, choose **Table, Network Objects, network_objects**.

7. In the upper right pane, select the relevant **Security Gateway, Cluster** object.

8. Press CTRL+F, or use the **Search** menu to search for the following: `tunnel_keepalive_method`.

9. In the lower pane, open the context menu for `tunnel_keepalive_method`, and select **Edit...**. Choose **dpd** and choose **OK**.

10. Repeat steps 7 - 9 for each gateway that's part of the AWS VPN Community.

11. Choose **File, Save All**.

12. Close the GuiDBedit tool.

13. Open the Check Point SmartDashboard, and choose **Security Management Server, Domain Management Server**.

14. Install the policy on the relevant **Security Gateway, Cluster** object.

For more information, see the New VPN features in R77.10 article on the Check Point Support Center.

TCP MSS clamping reduces the maximum segment size of TCP packets to prevent packet fragmentation.

To enable TCP MSS clamping

1. Navigate to the following directory: `C:\Program Files (x86)\CheckPoint\SmartConsole\R77.10\PROGRAM\`.

2. Open the Check Point Database Tool by running the `GuiDBEdit.exe` file.

3. Choose **Table**, **Global Properties**, **properties**.

4. For `fw_clamp_tcp_mss`, choose **Edit**. Change the value to `true` and choose **OK**.

How to Test the Customer Gateway Configuration

You can test the gateway configuration for each tunnel.

To test the customer gateway configuration for each tunnel

1. Ensure that the customer gateway has a static route to your VPC, as suggested in the configuration templates provided by AWS.

2. Ensure that a static route has been added to the VPN connection so that traffic can get back to your customer gateway. For example, if your local subnet prefix is `198.10.0.0/16`, you need to add a static route with that CIDR range to your VPN connection. Make sure that both tunnels have a static route to your VPC.

Next you must test the connectivity for each tunnel by launching an instance into your VPC, and pinging the instance from your home network. Before you begin, make sure of the following:

- Use an AMI that responds to ping requests. We recommend that you use one of the Amazon Linux AMIs.
- Configure your instance's security group and network ACL to enable inbound ICMP traffic.
- Ensure that you have configured routing for your VPN connection - your subnet's route table must contain a route to the virtual private gateway. For more information, see Enable Route Propagation in Your Route Table in the *Amazon VPC User Guide*.

To test the end-to-end connectivity of each tunnel

1. Launch an instance of one of the Amazon Linux AMIs into your VPC. The Amazon Linux AMIs are listed in the launch wizard when you launch an instance from the AWS Management Console. For more information, see the Amazon VPC Getting Started Guide.

2. After the instance is running, get its private IP address (for example, `10.0.0.4`). The console displays the address as part of the instance's details.

3. On a system in your home network, use the ping command with the instance's IP address. Make sure that the computer you ping from is behind the customer gateway. A successful response should be similar to the following.

```
1 ping 10.0.0.4
```

```
1 Pinging 10.0.0.4 with 32 bytes of data:
2
3 Reply from 10.0.0.4: bytes=32 time<1ms TTL=128
4 Reply from 10.0.0.4: bytes=32 time<1ms TTL=128
5 Reply from 10.0.0.4: bytes=32 time<1ms TTL=128
6
7 Ping statistics for 10.0.0.4:
8 Packets: Sent = 3, Received = 3, Lost = 0 (0% loss),
9
```

```
10 Approximate round trip times in milliseconds:
11 Minimum = 0ms, Maximum = 0ms, Average = 0ms
```

Note

If you ping an instance from your customer gateway router, ensure that you are sourcing ping messages from an internal IP address, not a tunnel IP address. Some AMIs don't respond to ping messages from tunnel IP addresses.

1. (Optional) To test tunnel failover, you can temporarily disable one of the tunnels on your customer gateway, and repeat the above step. You cannot disable a tunnel on the AWS side of the VPN connection.

On the Check Point gateway side, you can verify the tunnel status by running the following command from the command line tool in expert mode:

```
1 vpn tunnelutil
```

In the options that display, choose 1 to verify the IKE associations and 2 to verify the IPsec associations.

You can also use the Check Point Smart Tracker Log to verify that packets over the connection are being encrypted. For example, the following log indicates that a packet to the VPC was sent over tunnel 1 and was encrypted.

Log Info	
Product	🔳 Security Gateway/Management
Date	4Nov2015
Time	9:42:01
Number	21254
Type	📄 Log
Origin	cpgw-997695

Traffic	
Source	🖥 Management_PC (192.168.1.116)
Destination	🖥 10.28.13.28
Service	---
Protocol	🔳 icmp
Interface	🔳 eth0
Source Port	---

Policy	
Policy Name	Standard
Policy Date	Tue Nov 03 11:33:45 2015
Policy Management	cpgw-997695

Rule	
Action	🔒 Encrypt
Rule	4
Current Rule Number	4-Standard
Rule Name	---
User	---

More	
Rule UID	{0AA18015-FF7B-4650-B0CE-3989E658CF04}
Community	AWS_VPN_Star
Encryption Scheme	🔳 IKE
Data Encryption Methods	ESP: AES-128 + SHA1 + PFS (group 2)
VPN Peer Gateway	AWS_VPC_Tunnel_1 (54.84.169.196)
Subproduct	🔳 VPN
VPN Feature	VPN
Product Family	🔳 Network
Information	service_id: icmp-proto ICMP: Echo Request ICMP Type: 8 ICMP Code: 0

Example: Cisco ASA Device

Topics

- A High-Level View of the Customer Gateway
- An Example Configuration
- How to Test the Customer Gateway Configuration

In this section we walk you through an example of the configuration information provided by your integration team if your customer gateway is a Cisco ASA device running Cisco ASA 8.2+ software.

The diagram shows the high-level layout of the customer gateway. You should use the real configuration information that you receive from your integration team and apply it to your customer gateway.

A High-Level View of the Customer Gateway

The following diagram shows the general details of your customer gateway. Note that the VPN connection consists of two separate tunnels. Using redundant tunnels ensures continuous availability in the case that a device fails.

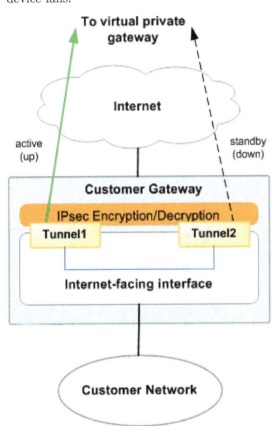

Please note that some Cisco ASAs only support Active/Standby mode. When you use these Cisco ASAs, you can have only one active tunnel at a time. The other standby tunnel becomes active if the first tunnel becomes unavailable. With this redundancy, you should always have connectivity to your VPC through one of the tunnels.

An Example Configuration

The configuration in this section is an example of the configuration information your integration team should provide. The example configuration contains a set of information for each of the tunnels that you must configure.

The example configuration includes example values to help you understand how configuration works. For example, we provide example values for the VPN connection ID (vpn-12345678) and virtual private gateway ID (vgw-12345678), and placeholders for the AWS endpoints (*AWS_ENDPOINT_1* and *AWS_ENDPOINT_2*). You'll replace these example values with the actual values from the configuration information that you receive.

In addition, you must:

- Configure the outside interface.
- Ensure that the Crypto ISAKMP Policy Sequence number is unique.
- Ensure that the Crypto List Policy Sequence number is unique.
- Ensure that the Crypto IPsec Transform Set and the Crypto ISAKMP Policy Sequence are harmonious with any other IPsec tunnels configured on the device.
- Ensure that the SLA monitoring number is unique.
- Configure all internal routing that moves traffic between the customer gateway and your local network.

Important

The following configuration information is an example of what you can expect your integration team to provide. Many of the values in the following example will be different from the actual configuration information that you receive. You must use the actual values and not the example values shown here, or your implementation will fail.

```
1  ! Amazon Web Services
2  ! Virtual Private Cloud
3  !
4  ! AWS utilizes unique identifiers to manipulate the configuration of
5  ! a VPN Connection. Each VPN Connection is assigned an identifier and is
6  ! associated with two other identifiers, namely the
7  ! Customer Gateway Identifier and Virtual Private Gateway Identifier.
8  !
9  ! Your VPN Connection ID                 : vpn-12345678
10 ! Your Virtual Private Gateway ID        : vgw-12345678
11 ! Your Customer Gateway ID               : cgw-12345678
12 !
13 ! This configuration consists of two tunnels. Both tunnels must be
14 ! configured on your Customer Gateway. Only a single tunnel will be up at a
15 ! time to the VGW.
16 !
17 ! You may need to populate these values throughout the config based on your setup:
18 ! outside_interface - External interface of the ASA
19 ! outside_access_in - Inbound ACL on the external interface
20 ! amzn_vpn_map - Outside crypto map
21 ! vpc_subnet and vpc_subnet_mask - VPC address range
22 ! local_subnet and local_subnet_mask - Local subnet address range
23 ! sla_monitor_address - Target address that is part of acl-amzn to run SLA monitoring
24 !
25 ! -------------------------------------------------------------------
26 ! IPSec Tunnels
27 ! -------------------------------------------------------------------
28 ! #1: Internet Key Exchange (IKE) Configuration
29 !
30 ! A policy is established for the supported ISAKMP encryption,
31 ! authentication, Diffie-Hellman, lifetime, and key parameters.
32 !
```

```
33 ! Note that there are a global list of ISAKMP policies, each identified by
34 ! sequence number. This policy is defined as #201, which may conflict with
35 ! an existing policy using the same or lower number depending on
36 ! the encryption type. If so, we recommend changing the sequence number to
37 ! avoid conflicts and overlap.
38 !
39 ! Please note, these sample configurations are for the minimum requirement of AES128, SHA1, and
       DH Group 2.
40 ! You will need to modify these sample configuration files to take advantage of AES256, SHA256,
       or other DH groups like 2, 14-18, 22, 23, and 24.
41 ! The address of the external interface for your customer gateway must be a static address.
42 ! Your customer gateway may reside behind a device performing network address translation (NAT).
43 ! To ensure that NAT traversal (NAT-T) can function, you must adjust your firewall rules to
       unblock UDP port 4500. If not behind NAT, we recommend disabling NAT-T.
44 !
45 crypto isakmp identity address
46 crypto isakmp enable outside_interface
47 crypto isakmp policy 201
48    encryption aes
49    authentication pre-share
50    group 2
51    lifetime 28800
52    hash sha
53 exit
54 !
55 ! The tunnel group sets the Pre Shared Key used to authenticate the
56 ! tunnel endpoints.
57 !
58 tunnel-group AWS_ENDPOINT_1 type ipsec-l2l
59 tunnel-group AWS_ENDPOINT_1 ipsec-attributes
60    pre-shared-key password_here
61 !
62 ! This option enables IPSec Dead Peer Detection, which causes periodic
63 ! messages to be sent to ensure a Security Association remains operational.
64 !
65    isakmp keepalive threshold 10 retry 10
66 exit
67 !
68 tunnel-group AWS_ENDPOINT_2 type ipsec-l2l
69 tunnel-group AWS_ENDPOINT_2 ipsec-attributes
70    pre-shared-key password_here
71 !
72 ! This option enables IPSec Dead Peer Detection, which causes periodic
73 ! messages to be sent to ensure a Security Association remains operational.
74 !
75    isakmp keepalive threshold 10 retry 10
76 exit
77
78 ! ------------------------------------------------------------------------------
79 ! #2: Access List Configuration
80 !
81 ! Access lists are configured to permit creation of tunnels and to send applicable traffic over
       them.
82 ! This policy may need to be applied to an inbound ACL on the outside interface that is used to
```

```
        manage control-plane traffic.
83  ! This is to allow VPN traffic into the device from the Amazon endpoints.
84  !
85  access-list outside_access_in extended permit ip host AWS_ENDPOINT_1 host YOUR_UPLINK_ADDRESS
86  access-list outside_access_in extended permit ip host AWS_ENDPOINT_2 host YOUR_UPLINK_ADDRESS
87  !
88  ! The following access list named acl-amzn specifies all traffic that needs to be routed to the
        VPC. Traffic will
89  ! be encrypted and transmitted through the tunnel to the VPC. Association with the IPSec
        security association
90  ! is done through the "crypto map" command.
91  !
92  ! This access list should contain a static route corresponding to your VPC CIDR and allow
        traffic from any subnet.
93  ! If you do not wish to use the "any" source, you must use a single access-list entry for
        accessing the VPC range.
94  ! If you specify more than one entry for this ACL without using "any" as the source, the VPN
        will function erratically.
95  ! The any rule is also used so the security association will include the ASA outside interface
        where the SLA monitor
96  ! traffic will be sourced from.
97  ! See section #4 regarding how to restrict the traffic going over the tunnel
98  !
99  !
100 access-list acl-amzn extended permit ip any vpc_subnet vpc_subnet_mask
101
102 !------------------------------------------------------------------------------
103 ! #3: IPSec Configuration
104 !
105 ! The IPSec transform set defines the encryption, authentication, and IPSec
106 ! mode parameters.
107 ! Please note, you may use these additionally supported IPSec parameters for encryption like
        AES256 and other DH groups like 2, 5, 14-18, 22, 23, and 24.
108 !
109 crypto ipsec ikev1 transform-set transform-amzn esp-aes esp-sha-hmac
110
111 ! The crypto map references the IPSec transform set and further defines
112 ! the Diffie-Hellman group and security association lifetime. The mapping is created
113 ! as #1, which may conflict with an existing crypto map using the same
114 ! number. If so, we recommend changing the mapping number to avoid conflicts.
115 !
116 crypto map amzn_vpn_map 1 match address acl-amzn
117 crypto map amzn_vpn_map 1 set pfs group2
118 crypto map amzn_vpn_map 1 set peer AWS_ENDPOINT_1 AWS_ENDPOINT_2
119 crypto map amzn_vpn_map 1 set transform-set transform-amzn
120 crypto map amzn_vpn_map 1 set security-association lifetime seconds 3600
121 !
122 ! Only set this if you do not already have an outside crypto map, and it is not applied:
123 !
124 crypto map amzn_vpn_map interface outside_interface
125 !
126 ! Additional parameters of the IPSec configuration are set here. Note that
127 ! these parameters are global and therefore impact other IPSec
128 ! associations.
```

```
129  !
130  ! This option instructs the firewall to clear the "Don't Fragment"
131  ! bit from packets that carry this bit and yet must be fragmented, enabling
132  ! them to be fragmented.
133  !
134  crypto ipsec df-bit clear-df outside_interface
135  !
136  ! This configures the gateway's window for accepting out of order
137  ! IPSec packets. A larger window can be helpful if too many packets
138  ! are dropped due to reordering while in transit between gateways.
139  !
140  crypto ipsec security-association replay window-size 128
141  !
142  ! This option instructs the firewall to fragment the unencrypted packets
143  ! (prior to encryption).
144  !
145  crypto ipsec fragmentation before-encryption outside_interface
146  !
147  ! This option causes the firewall to reduce the Maximum Segment Size of
148  ! TCP packets to prevent packet fragmentation.
149  sysopt connection tcpmss 1379
150  !
151  ! In order to keep the tunnel in an active or always up state, the ASA needs to send traffic to
         the subnet
152  ! defined in acl-amzn. SLA monitoring can be configured to send pings to a destination in the
         subnet and
153  ! will keep the tunnel active. This traffic needs to be sent to a target that will return a
         response.
154  ! This can be manually tested by sending a ping to the target from the ASA sourced from the
         outside interface.
155  ! A possible destination for the ping is an instance within the VPC. For redundancy multiple SLA
         monitors
156  ! can be configured to several instances to protect against a single point of failure.
157  !
158  ! The monitor is created as #1, which may conflict with an existing monitor using the same
159  ! number. If so, we recommend changing the sequence number to avoid conflicts.
160  !
161  sla monitor 1
162     type echo protocol ipIcmpEcho sla_monitor_address interface outside_interface
163     frequency 5
164  exit
165  sla monitor schedule 1 life forever start-time now
166  !
167  ! The firewall must allow icmp packets to use "sla monitor"
168  icmp permit any outside_interface
169
170  !-------------------------------------------------------------------------------
171  ! #4: VPN Filter
172  ! The VPN Filter will restrict traffic that is permitted through the tunnels. By default all
         traffic is denied.
173  ! The first entry provides an example to include traffic between your VPC Address space and your
         office.
174  ! You may need to run 'clear crypto isakmp sa', in order for the filter to take effect.
175  !
```

```
176 ! access-list amzn-filter extended permit ip vpc_subnet vpc_subnet_mask local_subnet
       local_subnet_mask
177 access-list amzn-filter extended deny ip any any
178 group-policy filter internal
179 group-policy filter attributes
180 vpn-filter value amzn-filter
181 tunnel-group AWS_ENDPOINT_1 general-attributes
182 default-group-policy filter
183 exit
184 tunnel-group AWS_ENDPOINT_2 general-attributes
185 default-group-policy filter
186 exit
187
188 !--------------------------------------------------------------------------
189 ! #5: NAT Exemption
190 ! If you are performing NAT on the ASA you will have to add a nat exemption rule.
191 ! This varies depending on how NAT is set up.  It should be configured along the lines of:
192 ! object network obj-SrcNet
193 !    subnet 0.0.0.0 0.0.0.0
194 ! object network obj-amzn
195 !    subnet vpc_subnet vpc_subnet_mask
196 ! nat (inside,outside) 1 source static obj-SrcNet obj-SrcNet destination static obj-amzn obj-
       amzn
197 ! If using version 8.2 or older, the entry would need to look something like this:
198 ! nat (inside) 0 access-list acl-amzn
199 ! Or, the same rule in acl-amzn should be included in an existing no nat ACL.
```

How to Test the Customer Gateway Configuration

When using Cisco ASA as a customer gateway, only one tunnel will be in the UP state. The second tunnel should be configured, but will only be used if the first tunnel goes down. The second tunnel cannot be in the UP state when the first tunnel is in the UP state. Your console will display that only one tunnel is up and it will show the second tunnel as down. This is expected behavior for Cisco ASA customer gateway tunnels because ASA as a customer gateway only supports a single tunnel being up at one time.

You can test the gateway configuration for each tunnel.

To test the customer gateway configuration for each tunnel

- Ensure that a static route has been added to the VPN connection so that traffic can get back to your customer gateway. For example, if your local subnet prefix is 198.10.0.0/16, you need to add a static route with that CIDR range to your VPN connection. Make sure that both tunnels have a static route to your VPC.

Next you must test the connectivity for each tunnel by launching an instance into your VPC, and pinging the instance from your home network. Before you begin, make sure of the following:

- Use an AMI that responds to ping requests. We recommend that you use one of the Amazon Linux AMIs.
- Configure your instance's security group and network ACL to enable inbound ICMP traffic.
- Ensure that you have configured routing for your VPN connection - your subnet's route table must contain a route to the virtual private gateway. For more information, see Enable Route Propagation in Your Route Table in the *Amazon VPC User Guide*.

To test the end-to-end connectivity of each tunnel

1. Launch an instance of one of the Amazon Linux AMIs into your VPC. The Amazon Linux AMIs are listed in the launch wizard when you launch an instance from the AWS Management Console. For more

information, see the Amazon VPC Getting Started Guide.

2. After the instance is running, get its private IP address (for example, 10.0.0.4). The console displays the address as part of the instance's details.

3. On a system in your home network, use the ping command with the instance's IP address. Make sure that the computer you ping from is behind the customer gateway. A successful response should be similar to the following.

```
1 ping 10.0.0.4
```

```
1 Pinging 10.0.0.4 with 32 bytes of data:
2
3 Reply from 10.0.0.4: bytes=32 time<1ms TTL=128
4 Reply from 10.0.0.4: bytes=32 time<1ms TTL=128
5 Reply from 10.0.0.4: bytes=32 time<1ms TTL=128
6
7 Ping statistics for 10.0.0.4:
8 Packets: Sent = 3, Received = 3, Lost = 0 (0% loss),
9
10 Approximate round trip times in milliseconds:
11 Minimum = 0ms, Maximum = 0ms, Average = 0ms
```

Note
If you ping an instance from your customer gateway router, ensure that you are sourcing ping messages from an internal IP address, not a tunnel IP address. Some AMIs don't respond to ping messages from tunnel IP addresses.

1. (Optional) To test tunnel failover, you can temporarily disable one of the tunnels on your customer gateway, and repeat the above step. You cannot disable a tunnel on the AWS side of the VPN connection.

If your tunnels do not test successfully, see Troubleshooting Cisco ASA Customer Gateway Connectivity.

Example: Cisco ASA Device with a Virtual Tunnel Interface and Border Gateway Protocol

Topics

- A High-Level View of the Customer Gateway
- Example Configuration
- How to Test the Customer Gateway Configuration

In this section we walk you through an example of the configuration information provided by your integration team if your customer gateway is a Cisco ASA device running Cisco ASA 9.7.1+ software.

A High-Level View of the Customer Gateway

The following diagram shows the general details of your customer gateway. Note that the VPN connection consists of two separate tunnels. Using redundant tunnels ensures continuous availability in the case that a device fails.

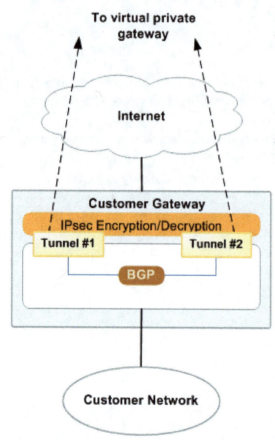

Cisco ASAs from version 9.7.1 and later support Active/Active mode. When you use these Cisco ASAs, you can have both tunnels active at the same time. With this redundancy, you should always have connectivity to your VPC through one of the tunnels.

Example Configuration

The configuration in this section is an example of the configuration information your integration team should provide. The example configuration contains a set of information for each of the tunnels that you must configure.

The example configuration includes example values to help you understand how configuration works. For example, we provide example values for the VPN connection ID (vpn-12345678) and virtual private gateway ID (vgw-12345678), and placeholders for the AWS endpoints (*AWS_ENDPOINT_1* and *AWS_ENDPOINT_2*). You'll replace these example values with the actual values from the configuration information that you receive.

In addition, you must do the following:

- Configure the outside interface.
- Ensure that the Crypto ISAKMP Policy Sequence number is unique.
- Ensure that the Crypto IPsec Transform Set and the Crypto ISAKMP Policy Sequence are harmonious with any other IPsec tunnels configured on the device.
- Configure all internal routing that moves traffic between the customer gateway and your local network.

Important

The following configuration information is an example of what you can expect your integration team to provide. Many of the values in the following example will be different from the actual configuration information that you receive. You must use the actual values and not the example values shown here, or your implementation will fail.

```
1  ! Amazon Web Services
2  ! Virtual Private Cloud
3
4  ! AWS utilizes unique identifiers to manipulate the configuration of
5  ! a VPN Connection. Each VPN Connection is assigned an identifier and is
6  ! associated with two other identifiers, namely the
7  ! Customer Gateway Identifier and Virtual Private Gateway Identifier.
8  !
9  ! Your VPN Connection ID              : vpn-12345678
10 ! Your Virtual Private Gateway ID     : vgw-12345678
11 ! Your Customer Gateway ID         : cgw-12345678
12 !
13 !
14 ! This configuration consists of two tunnels. Both tunnels must be
15 ! configured on your Customer Gateway.
16 !
17
18 ! -------------------------------------------------------------------
19 ! IPSec Tunnel #1
20 ! -------------------------------------------------------------------
21 ! #1: Internet Key Exchange (IKE) Configuration
22 !
23 ! A policy is established for the supported ISAKMP encryption,
24 ! authentication, Diffie-Hellman, lifetime, and key parameters.
25 ! Please note, these sample configurations are for the minimum requirement of AES128, SHA1, and
       DH Group 2.
26 ! You will need to modify these sample configuration files to take advantage of AES256, SHA256,
       or other DH groups like 2, 14-18, 22, 23, and 24.
27 ! The address of the external interface for your customer gateway must be a static address.
28 ! Your customer gateway may reside behind a device performing network address translation (NAT).
29 ! To ensure that NAT traversal (NAT-T) can function, you must adjust your firewall !rules to
       unblock UDP port 4500. If not behind NAT, we recommend disabling NAT-T.
30 !
31 ! Note that there are a global list of ISAKMP policies, each identified by
```

```
32  ! sequence number. This policy is defined as #200, which may conflict with
33  ! an existing policy using the same number. If so, we recommend changing
34  ! the sequence number to avoid conflicts.
35  !
36
37  crypto ikev1 enable 'outside_interface'
38
39  crypto ikev1 policy 200
40    encryption aes
41    authentication pre-share
42    group 2
43    lifetime 28800
44    hash sha
45
46  ! ------------------------------------------------------------------------
47  ! #2: IPSec Configuration
48  !
49  ! The IPSec transform set defines the encryption, authentication, and IPSec
50  ! mode parameters.
51  ! Please note, you may use these additionally supported IPSec parameters for encryption like
       AES256 and other DH groups like 2, 5, 14-18, 22, 23, and 24.
52  !
53  crypto ipsec ikev1 transform-set ipsec-prop-vpn-12345678-0 esp-aes   esp-sha-hmac
54
55
56  ! The IPSec profile references the IPSec transform set and further defines
57  ! the Diffie-Hellman group and security association lifetime.
58  !
59  crypto ipsec profile ipsec-vpn-12345678-0
60    set pfs group2
61    set security-association lifetime seconds 3600
62    set ikev1 transform-set ipsec-prop-vpn-12345678-0
63  exit
64
65  ! Additional parameters of the IPSec configuration are set here. Note that
66  ! these parameters are global and therefore impact other IPSec
67  ! associations.
68  ! This option instructs the router to clear the "Don't Fragment"
69  ! bit from packets that carry this bit and yet must be fragmented, enabling
70  ! them to be fragmented.
71  !
72  !You will need to replace the outside_interface with the interface name of your ASA Firewall.
73
74  crypto ipsec df-bit clear-df 'outside_interface'
75
76
77
78  ! This option causes the firewall to reduce the Maximum Segment Size of
79  ! TCP packets to prevent packet fragmentation.
80
81  sysopt connection tcpmss 1379
82
83
84  ! This configures the gateway's window for accepting out of order
```

```
85  ! IPSec packets. A larger window can be helpful if too many packets
86  ! are dropped due to reordering while in transit between gateways.
87  !
88  crypto ipsec security-association replay window-size 128
89
90  ! This option instructs the router to fragment the unencrypted packets
91  ! (prior to encryption).
92  !You will need to replace the outside_interface with the interface name of your ASA Firewall.
93  !
94  crypto ipsec fragmentation before-encryption 'outside_interface'
95
96
97
98  ! -----------------------------------------------------------------------
99
100
101 ! The tunnel group sets the Pre Shared Key used to authenticate the
102 ! tunnel endpoints.
103 !
104 tunnel-group 13.54.43.86 type ipsec-l2l
105 tunnel-group 13.54.43.86 ipsec-attributes
106    ikev1 pre-shared-key pre-shared-key
107 !
108 ! This option enables IPSec Dead Peer Detection, which causes semi-periodic
109 ! messages to be sent to ensure a Security Association remains operational.
110 !
111    isakmp keepalive threshold 10 retry 10
112 exit
113
114 ! -----------------------------------------------------------------------
115 ! #3: Tunnel Interface Configuration
116 !
117 ! A tunnel interface is configured to be the logical interface associated
118 ! with the tunnel. All traffic routed to the tunnel interface will be
119 ! encrypted and transmitted to the VPC. Similarly, traffic from the VPC
120 ! will be logically received on this interface.
121 !
122 ! Association with the IPSec security association is done through the
123 ! "tunnel protection" command.
124 !
125 ! The address of the interface is configured with the setup for your
126 ! Customer Gateway.  If the address changes, the Customer Gateway and VPN
127 ! Connection must be recreated with Amazon VPC.
128 !
129 !You will need to replace the outside_interface with the interface name of your ASA Firewall.
130
131
132
133 interface Tunnel1
134    nameif Tunnel-int-vpn-12345678-0
135    ip address 169.254.33.198 255.255.255.252
136    tunnel source interface 'outside_interface'
137    tunnel destination 13.54.43.86
138    tunnel mode ipsec ipv4
```

```
139    tunnel protection ipsec profile ipsec-vpn-12345678-0
140    no shutdown
141 exit
142
143 ! ---------------------------------------------------------------------
144
145 ! #4: Border Gateway Protocol (BGP) Configuration
146 !
147 ! BGP is used within the tunnel to exchange prefixes between the
148 ! Virtual Private Gateway and your Customer Gateway. The Virtual Private Gateway
149 ! will announce the prefix corresponding to your VPC.
150 !
151 ! Your Customer Gateway may announce a default route (0.0.0.0/0),
152 ! which can be done with the 'network' and 'default-originate' statements.
153 !
154 ! The BGP timers are adjusted to provide more rapid detection of outages.
155 !
156 ! The local BGP Autonomous System Number (ASN) (65343) is configured
157 ! as part of your Customer Gateway. If the ASN must be changed, the
158 ! Customer Gateway and VPN Connection will need to be recreated with AWS.
159 !
160 router bgp 65343
161    address-family ipv4 unicast
162       neighbor 169.254.33.197 remote-as 7224
163       neighbor 169.254.33.197 timers 10 30 30
164       neighbor 169.254.33.197 default-originate
165       neighbor 169.254.33.197 activate
166
167 ! To advertise additional prefixes to Amazon VPC, copy the 'network' statement
168 ! and identify the prefix you wish to advertise. Make sure the prefix is present
169 ! in the routing table of the device with a valid next-hop.
170       network 0.0.0.0
171       no auto-summary
172 no synchronization
173    exit-address-family
174 exit
175 !
176
177 ! ---------------------------------------------------------------------
178 ! IPSec Tunnel #2
179 ! ---------------------------------------------------------------------
180 ! #1: Internet Key Exchange (IKE) Configuration
181 !
182 ! A policy is established for the supported ISAKMP encryption,
183 ! authentication, Diffie-Hellman, lifetime, and key parameters.
184 ! Please note, these sample configurations are for the minimum requirement of AES128, SHA1, and
        DH Group 2.
185 ! You will need to modify these sample configuration files to take advantage of AES256, SHA256,
        or other DH groups like 2, 14-18, 22, 23, and 24.
186 ! The address of the external interface for your customer gateway must be a static address.
187 ! Your customer gateway may reside behind a device performing network address translation (NAT).
188 ! To ensure that NAT traversal (NAT-T) can function, you must adjust your firewall !rules to
        unblock UDP port 4500. If not behind NAT, we recommend disabling NAT-T.
189 !
```

```
190 ! Note that there are a global list of ISAKMP policies, each identified by
191 ! sequence number. This policy is defined as #201, which may conflict with
192 ! an existing policy using the same number. If so, we recommend changing
193 ! the sequence number to avoid conflicts.
194 !
195
196 crypto ikev1 enable 'outside_interface'
197
198 crypto ikev1 policy 201
199    encryption aes
200    authentication pre-share
201    group 2
202    lifetime 28800
203    hash sha
204
205 ! ----------------------------------------------------------------------
206 ! #2: IPSec Configuration
207 !
208 ! The IPSec transform set defines the encryption, authentication, and IPSec
209 ! mode parameters.
210 ! Please note, you may use these additionally supported IPSec parameters for encryption like
         AES256 and other DH groups like 2, 5, 14-18, 22, 23, and 24.
211 !
212 crypto ipsec ikev1 transform-set ipsec-prop-vpn-12345678-1 esp-aes   esp-sha-hmac
213
214
215 ! The IPSec profile references the IPSec transform set and further defines
216 ! the Diffie-Hellman group and security association lifetime.
217 !
218 crypto ipsec profile ipsec-vpn-12345678-1
219    set pfs group2
220    set security-association lifetime seconds 3600
221    set ikev1 transform-set ipsec-prop-vpn-12345678-1
222 exit
223
224 ! Additional parameters of the IPSec configuration are set here. Note that
225 ! these parameters are global and therefore impact other IPSec
226 ! associations.
227 ! This option instructs the router to clear the "Don't Fragment"
228 ! bit from packets that carry this bit and yet must be fragmented, enabling
229 ! them to be fragmented.
230 !
231 !You will need to replace the outside_interface with the interface name of your ASA Firewall.
232
233 crypto ipsec df-bit clear-df 'outside_interface'
234
235
236
237 ! This option causes the firewall to reduce the Maximum Segment Size of
238 ! TCP packets to prevent packet fragmentation.
239
240 sysopt connection tcpmss 1379
241
242
```

```
243  ! This configures the gateway's window for accepting out of order
244  ! IPSec packets. A larger window can be helpful if too many packets
245  ! are dropped due to reordering while in transit between gateways.
246  !
247  crypto ipsec security-association replay window-size 128
248
249  ! This option instructs the router to fragment the unencrypted packets
250  ! (prior to encryption).
251  !You will need to replace the outside_interface with the interface name of your ASA Firewall.
252  !
253  crypto ipsec fragmentation before-encryption 'outside_interface'
254
255
256
257  ! ------------------------------------------------------------------------
258
259
260  ! The tunnel group sets the Pre Shared Key used to authenticate the
261  ! tunnel endpoints.
262  !
263  tunnel-group 52.65.137.78 type ipsec-l2l
264  tunnel-group 52.65.137.78 ipsec-attributes
265     ikev1 pre-shared-key pre-shared-key
266  !
267  ! This option enables IPSec Dead Peer Detection, which causes semi-periodic
268  ! messages to be sent to ensure a Security Association remains operational.
269  !
270     isakmp keepalive threshold 10 retry 10
271  exit
272
273  ! ------------------------------------------------------------------------
274  ! #3: Tunnel Interface Configuration
275  !
276  ! A tunnel interface is configured to be the logical interface associated
277  ! with the tunnel. All traffic routed to the tunnel interface will be
278  ! encrypted and transmitted to the VPC. Similarly, traffic from the VPC
279  ! will be logically received on this interface.
280  !
281  ! Association with the IPSec security association is done through the
282  ! "tunnel protection" command.
283  !
284  ! The address of the interface is configured with the setup for your
285  ! Customer Gateway.  If the address changes, the Customer Gateway and VPN
286  ! Connection must be recreated with Amazon VPC.
287  !
288  !You will need to replace the outside_interface with the interface name of your ASA Firewall.
289
290
291
292  interface Tunnel2
293     nameif Tunnel-int-vpn-12345678-1
294     ip address 169.254.33.194 255.255.255.252
295     tunnel source interface 'outside_interface'
296     tunnel destination 52.65.137.78
```

```
297    tunnel mode ipsec ipv4
298    tunnel protection ipsec profile ipsec-vpn-12345678-1
299    no shutdown
300 exit
301
302 ! -----------------------------------------------------------------------
303
304 ! #4: Border Gateway Protocol (BGP) Configuration
305 !
306 ! BGP is used within the tunnel to exchange prefixes between the
307 ! Virtual Private Gateway and your Customer Gateway. The Virtual Private Gateway
308 ! will announce the prefix corresponding to your VPC.
309 !
310 ! Your Customer Gateway may announce a default route (0.0.0.0/0),
311 ! which can be done with the 'network' and 'default-originate' statements.
312 !
313 ! The BGP timers are adjusted to provide more rapid detection of outages.
314 !
315 ! The local BGP Autonomous System Number (ASN) (65343) is configured
316 ! as part of your Customer Gateway. If the ASN must be changed, the
317 ! Customer Gateway and VPN Connection will need to be recreated with AWS.
318 !
319 router bgp 65343
320    address-family ipv4 unicast
321      neighbor 169.254.33.193 remote-as 7224
322      neighbor 169.254.33.193 timers 10 30 30
323      neighbor 169.254.33.193 default-originate
324      neighbor 169.254.33.193 activate
325
326 ! To advertise additional prefixes to Amazon VPC, copy the 'network' statement
327 ! and identify the prefix you wish to advertise. Make sure the prefix is present
328 ! in the routing table of the device with a valid next-hop.
329      network 0.0.0.0
330      no auto-summary
331      no synchronization
332    exit-address-family
333 exit
334 !
```

How to Test the Customer Gateway Configuration

When using Cisco ASA as a customer gateway in routed mode, both tunnels will be in the UP state.

You can test the gateway configuration for each tunnel.

To test the customer gateway configuration for each tunnel

- Ensure that routes are advertised with BGP correctly and showing in routing table so that traffic can get back to your customer gateway. For example, if your local subnet prefix is 198.10.0.0/16, you must advertise it through BGP. Make sure that both tunnels are configured with BGP routing.

Next you must test the connectivity for each tunnel by launching an instance into your VPC, and pinging the instance from your home network. Before you begin, make sure of the following:

- Use an AMI that responds to ping requests. We recommend that you use one of the Amazon Linux AMIs.
- Configure your instance's security group and network ACL to enable inbound ICMP traffic.

- Ensure that you have configured routing for your VPN connection - your subnet's route table must contain a route to the virtual private gateway. For more information, see Enable Route Propagation in Your Route Table in the *Amazon VPC User Guide*.

To test the end-to-end connectivity of each tunnel

1. Launch an instance of one of the Amazon Linux AMIs into your VPC. The Amazon Linux AMIs are listed in the launch wizard when you launch an instance from the AWS Management Console. For more information, see the Amazon VPC Getting Started Guide.

2. After the instance is running, get its private IP address (for example, 10.0.0.4). The console displays the address as part of the instance's details.

3. On a system in your home network, use the ping command with the instance's IP address. Make sure that the computer you ping from is behind the customer gateway. A successful response should be similar to the following.

```
1 ping 10.0.0.4
```

```
1 Pinging 10.0.0.4 with 32 bytes of data:
2
3 Reply from 10.0.0.4: bytes=32 time<1ms TTL=128
4 Reply from 10.0.0.4: bytes=32 time<1ms TTL=128
5 Reply from 10.0.0.4: bytes=32 time<1ms TTL=128
6
7 Ping statistics for 10.0.0.4:
8 Packets: Sent = 3, Received = 3, Lost = 0 (0% loss),
9
10 Approximate round trip times in milliseconds:
11 Minimum = 0ms, Maximum = 0ms, Average = 0ms
```

Note

If you ping an instance from your customer gateway router, ensure that you are sourcing ping messages from an internal IP address, not a tunnel IP address. Some AMIs don't respond to ping messages from tunnel IP addresses.

1. (Optional) To test tunnel failover, you can temporarily disable one of the tunnels on your customer gateway, and repeat the above step. You cannot disable a tunnel on the AWS side of the VPN connection.

If your tunnels do not test successfully, see Troubleshooting Cisco ASA Customer Gateway Connectivity.

Example: Cisco ASA Device with a Virtual Tunnel Interface (without Border Gateway Protocol)

Topics

- A High-Level View of the Customer Gateway
- Example Configuration
- How to Test the Customer Gateway Configuration

In this section we walk you through an example of the configuration information provided by your integration team if your customer gateway is a Cisco ASA device running Cisco ASA 9.7.1+ software and if you want to configure a statically-routed VPN connection.

A High-Level View of the Customer Gateway

The following diagram shows the general details of your customer gateway. Note that the VPN connection consists of two separate tunnels. Using redundant tunnels ensures continuous availability in the case that a device fails.

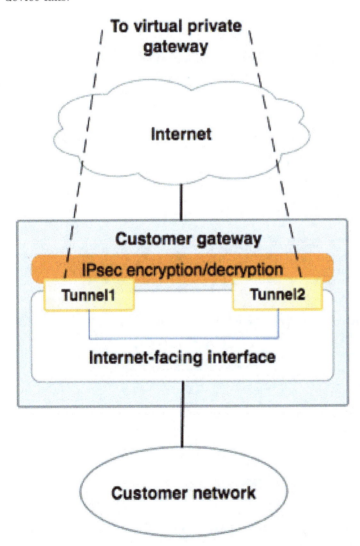

Cisco ASAs from version 9.7.1 and later support Active/Active mode. When you use these Cisco ASAs, you can have both tunnels active at the same time. With this redundancy, you should always have connectivity to your VPC through one of the tunnels.

Example Configuration

The configuration in this section is an example of the configuration information your integration team should provide. The example configuration contains a set of information for each of the tunnels that you must configure.

The example configuration includes example values to help you understand how configuration works. For example, we provide example values for the VPN connection ID (vpn-12345678) and virtual private gateway ID (vgw-12345678), and placeholders for the AWS endpoints (*AWS_ENDPOINT_1* and *AWS_ENDPOINT_2*). You'll replace these example values with the actual values from the configuration information that you receive.

In addition, you must do the following:

- Configure the outside interface.
- Ensure that the Crypto ISAKMP Policy Sequence number is unique.
- Ensure that the Crypto IPsec Transform Set and the Crypto ISAKMP Policy Sequence are harmonious with any other IPsec tunnels configured on the device.
- Configure all internal routing that moves traffic between the customer gateway and your local network.

Important

The following configuration information is an example of what you can expect your integration team to provide. Many of the values in the following example will be different from the actual configuration information that you receive. You must use the actual values and not the example values shown here, or your implementation will fail.

```
1  ! Amazon Web Services
2  ! Virtual Private Cloud
3
4  ! AWS utilizes unique identifiers to manipulate the configuration of
5  ! a VPN Connection. Each VPN Connection is assigned an identifier and is
6  ! associated with two other identifiers, namely the
7  ! Customer Gateway Identifier and Virtual Private Gateway Identifier.
8  !
9  ! Your VPN Connection ID            : vpn-12345678
10 ! Your Virtual Private Gateway ID   : vgw-12345678
11 ! Your Customer Gateway ID    : cgw-12345678
12 !
13 !
14 ! This configuration consists of two tunnels. Both tunnels must be
15 ! configured on your Customer Gateway.
16 !
17
18 ! -----------------------------------------------------------------------
19 ! IPSec Tunnel #1
20 ! -----------------------------------------------------------------------
21 ! #1: Internet Key Exchange (IKE) Configuration
22 !
23 ! A policy is established for the supported ISAKMP encryption,
24 ! authentication, Diffie-Hellman, lifetime, and key parameters.
25 ! Please note, these sample configurations are for the minimum requirement of AES128, SHA1, and
       DH Group 2.
26 ! You will need to modify these sample configuration files to take advantage of AES256, SHA256,
       or other DH groups like 2, 14-18, 22, 23, and 24.
27 ! The address of the external interface for your customer gateway must be a static address.
```

```
28 ! Your customer gateway may reside behind a device performing network address translation (NAT).
29 ! To ensure that NAT traversal (NAT-T) can function, you must adjust your firewall !rules to
       unblock UDP port 4500. If not behind NAT, we recommend disabling NAT-T.
30 !
31 ! Note that there are a global list of ISAKMP policies, each identified by
32 ! sequence number. This policy is defined as #200, which may conflict with
33 ! an existing policy using the same number. If so, we recommend changing
34 ! the sequence number to avoid conflicts.
35 !
36
37 crypto ikev1 enable 'outside_interface'
38
39 crypto ikev1 policy 200
40    encryption aes
41    authentication pre-share
42    group 2
43    lifetime 28800
44    hash sha
45
46 ! ----------------------------------------------------------------------
47 ! #2: IPSec Configuration
48 !
49 ! The IPSec transform set defines the encryption, authentication, and IPSec
50 ! mode parameters.
51 ! Please note, you may use these additionally supported IPSec parameters for encryption like
       AES256 and other DH groups like 2, 5, 14-18, 22, 23, and 24.
52 !
53 crypto ipsec ikev1 transform-set ipsec-prop-vpn-12345678-0 esp-aes   esp-sha-hmac
54
55
56 ! The IPSec profile references the IPSec transform set and further defines
57 ! the Diffie-Hellman group and security association lifetime.
58 !
59 crypto ipsec profile ipsec-vpn-12345678-0
60    set pfs group2
61    set security-association lifetime seconds 3600
62    set ikev1 transform-set ipsec-prop-vpn-12345678-0
63 exit
64
65 ! Additional parameters of the IPSec configuration are set here. Note that
66 ! these parameters are global and therefore impact other IPSec
67 ! associations.
68 ! This option instructs the router to clear the "Don't Fragment"
69 ! bit from packets that carry this bit and yet must be fragmented, enabling
70 ! them to be fragmented.
71 !
72 !You will need to replace the outside_interface with the interface name of your ASA Firewall.
73
74 crypto ipsec df-bit clear-df 'outside_interface'
75
76
77
78 ! This option causes the firewall to reduce the Maximum Segment Size of
79 ! TCP packets to prevent packet fragmentation.
```

```
80
81 sysopt connection tcpmss 1379
82
83
84 ! This configures the gateway's window for accepting out of order
85 ! IPSec packets. A larger window can be helpful if too many packets
86 ! are dropped due to reordering while in transit between gateways.
87 !
88 crypto ipsec security-association replay window-size 128
89
90 ! This option instructs the router to fragment the unencrypted packets
91 ! (prior to encryption).
92 !You will need to replace the outside_interface with the interface name of your ASA Firewall.
93 !
94 crypto ipsec fragmentation before-encryption 'outside_interface'
95
96
97
98 ! -------------------------------------------------------------------------
99
100
101 ! The tunnel group sets the Pre Shared Key used to authenticate the
102 ! tunnel endpoints.
103 !
104 tunnel-group 13.54.43.86 type ipsec-l2l
105 tunnel-group 13.54.43.86 ipsec-attributes
106    ikev1 pre-shared-key pre-shared-key
107 !
108 ! This option enables IPSec Dead Peer Detection, which causes semi-periodic
109 ! messages to be sent to ensure a Security Association remains operational.
110 !
111    isakmp keepalive threshold 10 retry 10
112 exit
113
114 ! -------------------------------------------------------------------------
115 ! #3: Tunnel Interface Configuration
116 !
117 ! A tunnel interface is configured to be the logical interface associated
118 ! with the tunnel. All traffic routed to the tunnel interface will be
119 ! encrypted and transmitted to the VPC. Similarly, traffic from the VPC
120 ! will be logically received on this interface.
121 !
122 ! Association with the IPSec security association is done through the
123 ! "tunnel protection" command.
124 !
125 ! The address of the interface is configured with the setup for your
126 ! Customer Gateway.  If the address changes, the Customer Gateway and VPN
127 ! Connection must be recreated with Amazon VPC.
128 !
129 !You will need to replace the outside_interface with the interface name of your ASA Firewall.
130
131
132
133 interface Tunnel1
```

```
134   nameif Tunnel-int-vpn-12345678-0
135   ip address 169.254.33.198 255.255.255.252
136   tunnel source interface 'outside_interface'
137   tunnel destination 13.54.43.86
138   tunnel mode ipsec ipv4
139   tunnel protection ipsec profile ipsec-vpn-12345678-0
140   no shutdown
141 exit
142
143 ! --------------------------------------------------------------------
144 ! #4 Static Route Configuration
145 !
146 ! Your Customer Gateway needs to set a static route for the prefix corresponding to your
147 ! VPC to send traffic over the tunnel interface.
148 ! An example for a VPC with the prefix 10.0.0.0/16 is provided below:
149 ! route Tunnel-int-vpn-12345678-0 10.0.0.0 255.255.0.0 169.254.33.197 100
150
151
152 ! --------------------------------------------------------------------
153 ! IPSec Tunnel #2
154 ! --------------------------------------------------------------------
155 ! #1: Internet Key Exchange (IKE) Configuration
156 !
157 ! A policy is established for the supported ISAKMP encryption,
158 ! authentication, Diffie-Hellman, lifetime, and key parameters.
159 ! Please note, these sample configurations are for the minimum requirement of AES128, SHA1, and
         DH Group 2.
160 ! You will need to modify these sample configuration files to take advantage of AES256, SHA256,
         or other DH groups like 2, 14-18, 22, 23, and 24.
161 ! The address of the external interface for your customer gateway must be a static address.
162 ! Your customer gateway may reside behind a device performing network address translation (NAT).
163 ! To ensure that NAT traversal (NAT-T) can function, you must adjust your firewall !rules to
         unblock UDP port 4500. If not behind NAT, we recommend disabling NAT-T.
164 !
165 ! Note that there are a global list of ISAKMP policies, each identified by
166 ! sequence number. This policy is defined as #201, which may conflict with
167 ! an existing policy using the same number. If so, we recommend changing
168 ! the sequence number to avoid conflicts.
169 !
170
171 crypto ikev1 enable 'outside_interface'
172
173 crypto ikev1 policy 201
174   encryption aes
175   authentication pre-share
176   group 2
177   lifetime 28800
178   hash sha
179
180 ! --------------------------------------------------------------------
181 ! #2: IPSec Configuration
182 !
183 ! The IPSec transform set defines the encryption, authentication, and IPSec
184 ! mode parameters.
```

```
185 ! Please note, you may use these additionally supported IPSec parameters for encryption like
       AES256 and other DH groups like 2, 5, 14-18, 22, 23, and 24.
186 !
187 crypto ipsec ikev1 transform-set ipsec-prop-vpn-12345678-1 esp-aes  esp-sha-hmac
188
189
190 ! The IPSec profile references the IPSec transform set and further defines
191 ! the Diffie-Hellman group and security association lifetime.
192 !
193 crypto ipsec profile ipsec-vpn-12345678-1
194   set pfs group2
195   set security-association lifetime seconds 3600
196   set ikev1 transform-set ipsec-prop-vpn-12345678-1
197 exit
198
199 ! Additional parameters of the IPSec configuration are set here. Note that
200 ! these parameters are global and therefore impact other IPSec
201 ! associations.
202 ! This option instructs the router to clear the "Don't Fragment"
203 ! bit from packets that carry this bit and yet must be fragmented, enabling
204 ! them to be fragmented.
205 !
206 !You will need to replace the outside_interface with the interface name of your ASA Firewall.
207
208 crypto ipsec df-bit clear-df 'outside_interface'
209
210
211
212 ! This option causes the firewall to reduce the Maximum Segment Size of
213 ! TCP packets to prevent packet fragmentation.
214
215 sysopt connection tcpmss 1379
216
217
218 ! This configures the gateway's window for accepting out of order
219 ! IPSec packets. A larger window can be helpful if too many packets
220 ! are dropped due to reordering while in transit between gateways.
221 !
222 crypto ipsec security-association replay window-size 128
223
224 ! This option instructs the router to fragment the unencrypted packets
225 ! (prior to encryption).
226 !You will need to replace the outside_interface with the interface name of your ASA Firewall.
227 !
228 crypto ipsec fragmentation before-encryption 'outside_interface'
229
230
231
232 ! -------------------------------------------------------------------------
233
234
235 ! The tunnel group sets the Pre Shared Key used to authenticate the
236 ! tunnel endpoints.
237 !
```

```
238 tunnel-group 52.65.137.78 type ipsec-121
239 tunnel-group 52.65.137.78 ipsec-attributes
240    ikev1 pre-shared-key pre-shared-key
241 !
242 ! This option enables IPSec Dead Peer Detection, which causes semi-periodic
243 ! messages to be sent to ensure a Security Association remains operational.
244 !
245    isakmp keepalive threshold 10 retry 10
246 exit
247
248 ! --------------------------------------------------------------------------
249 ! #3: Tunnel Interface Configuration
250 !
251 ! A tunnel interface is configured to be the logical interface associated
252 ! with the tunnel. All traffic routed to the tunnel interface will be
253 ! encrypted and transmitted to the VPC. Similarly, traffic from the VPC
254 ! will be logically received on this interface.
255 !
256 ! Association with the IPSec security association is done through the
257 ! "tunnel protection" command.
258 !
259 ! The address of the interface is configured with the setup for your
260 ! Customer Gateway.  If the address changes, the Customer Gateway and VPN
261 ! Connection must be recreated with Amazon VPC.
262 !
263 !You will need to replace the outside_interface with the interface name of your ASA Firewall.
264
265
266
267 interface Tunnel2
268    nameif Tunnel-int-vpn-12345678-1
269    ip address 169.254.33.194 255.255.255.252
270    tunnel source interface 'outside_interface'
271    tunnel destination 52.65.137.78
272    tunnel mode ipsec ipv4
273    tunnel protection ipsec profile ipsec-vpn-12345678-1
274    no shutdown
275 exit
276
277 ! --------------------------------------------------------------------------
278 ! #4 Static Route Configuration
279 !
280 ! Your Customer Gateway needs to set a static route for the prefix corresponding to your
281 ! VPC to send traffic over the tunnel interface.
282 ! An example for a VPC with the prefix 10.0.0.0/16 is provided below:
283 ! route Tunnel-int-vpn-12345678-1 10.0.0.0 255.255.0.0 169.254.33.193 200
```

How to Test the Customer Gateway Configuration

When using Cisco ASA as a customer gateway in routed mode, both tunnels will be in the UP state.

You can test the gateway configuration for each tunnel.

To test the customer gateway configuration for each tunnel

- Ensure that a static route has been added to the VPN connection so that traffic can get back to your customer gateway. For example, if your local subnet prefix is 198.10.0.0/16, you need to add a static route with that CIDR range to your VPN connection. Make sure that both tunnels have a static route to your VPC.

Next you must test the connectivity for each tunnel by launching an instance into your VPC, and pinging the instance from your home network. Before you begin, make sure of the following:

- Use an AMI that responds to ping requests. We recommend that you use one of the Amazon Linux AMIs.
- Configure your instance's security group and network ACL to enable inbound ICMP traffic.
- Ensure that you have configured routing for your VPN connection - your subnet's route table must contain a route to the virtual private gateway. For more information, see Enable Route Propagation in Your Route Table in the *Amazon VPC User Guide.*

To test the end-to-end connectivity of each tunnel

1. Launch an instance of one of the Amazon Linux AMIs into your VPC. The Amazon Linux AMIs are listed in the launch wizard when you launch an instance from the AWS Management Console. For more information, see the Amazon VPC Getting Started Guide.

2. After the instance is running, get its private IP address (for example, 10.0.0.4). The console displays the address as part of the instance's details.

3. On a system in your home network, use the ping command with the instance's IP address. Make sure that the computer you ping from is behind the customer gateway. A successful response should be similar to the following.

```
1 ping 10.0.0.4
```

```
1 Pinging 10.0.0.4 with 32 bytes of data:
2
3 Reply from 10.0.0.4: bytes=32 time<1ms TTL=128
4 Reply from 10.0.0.4: bytes=32 time<1ms TTL=128
5 Reply from 10.0.0.4: bytes=32 time<1ms TTL=128
6
7 Ping statistics for 10.0.0.4:
8 Packets: Sent = 3, Received = 3, Lost = 0 (0% loss),
9
10 Approximate round trip times in milliseconds:
11 Minimum = 0ms, Maximum = 0ms, Average = 0ms
```

Note
If you ping an instance from your customer gateway router, ensure that you are sourcing ping messages from an internal IP address, not a tunnel IP address. Some AMIs don't respond to ping messages from tunnel IP addresses.

1. (Optional) To test tunnel failover, you can temporarily disable one of the tunnels on your customer gateway, and repeat the above step. You cannot disable a tunnel on the AWS side of the VPN connection.

If your tunnels do not test successfully, see Troubleshooting Cisco ASA Customer Gateway Connectivity.

Example: Cisco IOS Device

Topics

- A High-Level View of the Customer Gateway
- A Detailed View of the Customer Gateway and an Example Configuration
- How to Test the Customer Gateway Configuration

In this section we walk you through an example of the configuration information provided by your integration team if your customer gateway is a Cisco IOS device running Cisco IOS 12.4 (or later) software.

Two diagrams illustrate the example configuration. The first diagram shows the high-level layout of the customer gateway, and the second diagram shows details from the example configuration. You should use the real configuration information that you receive from your integration team and apply it to your customer gateway.

A High-Level View of the Customer Gateway

The following diagram shows the general details of your customer gateway. Note that the VPN connection consists of two separate tunnels. Using redundant tunnels ensures continuous availability in the case that a device fails.

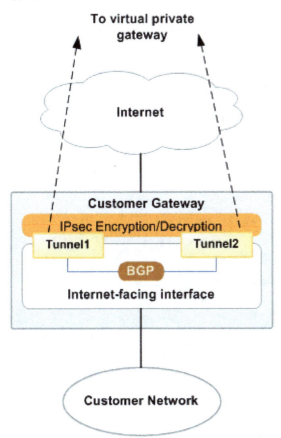

A Detailed View of the Customer Gateway and an Example Configuration

The diagram in this section illustrates an example Cisco IOS customer gateway. Following the diagram is a corresponding example of the configuration information your integration team should provide. The example

configuration contains a set of information for each of the tunnels that you must configure.

In addition, the example configuration refers to these items that you must provide:

- *YOUR_UPLINK_ADDRESS*—The IP address for the Internet-routable external interface on the customer gateway. The address must be static, and may be behind a device performing network address translation (NAT). To ensure that NAT traversal (NAT-T) can function, you must adjust your firewall rules to unblock UDP port 4500.
- *YOUR_BGP_ASN*—The customer gateway's BGP ASN (we use 65000 by default)

The example configuration includes several example values to help you understand how configuration works. For example, we provide example values for the VPN connection ID (vpn-44a8938f), virtual private gateway ID (vgw-8db04f81), the IP addresses (72.21.209.*, 169.254.255.*), and the remote ASN (7224). You'll replace these example values with the actual values from the configuration information that you receive.

In addition, you must:

- Configure the outside interface
- Configure the tunnel interface IDs (referred to as *Tunnel1* and *Tunnel2* in the example configuration).
- Ensure that the Crypto ISAKMP Policy Sequence number is unique.
- Ensure that the Crypto IPsec Transform Set and the Crypto ISAKMP Policy Sequence are harmonious with any other IPsec tunnels configured on the device.
- Configure all internal routing that moves traffic between the customer gateway and your local network.

In the following diagram and example configuration, you must replace the items in red italics with values that apply to your particular configuration.

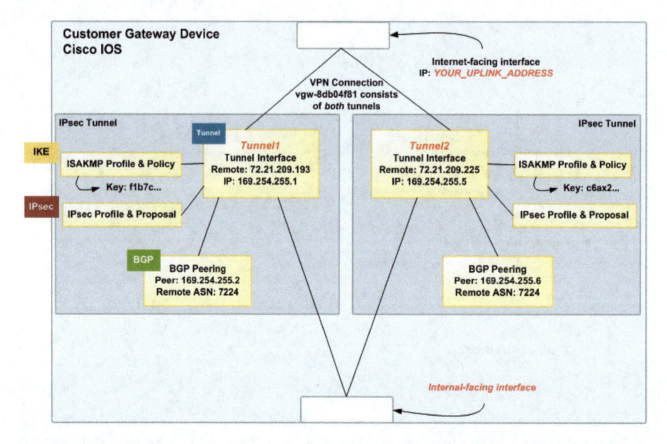

Warning

The following configuration information is an example of what you can expect your integration team to provide. Many of the values in the following example will be different from the actual configuration information that you receive. You must use the actual values and not the example values shown here, or your implementation will fail.

```
1  ! Amazon Web Services
2  ! Virtual Private Cloud
3
4  ! AWS utilizes unique identifiers to manipulate the configuration of
5  ! a VPN Connection. Each VPN Connection is assigned an identifier
6  ! and is associated with two other identifiers, namely the
7  ! Customer Gateway Identifier and Virtual Private Gateway Identifier.
8  !
9  ! Your VPN Connection ID            : vpn-44a8938f
10 ! Your Virtual Private Gateway ID   : vgw-8db04f81
11 ! Your Customer Gateway ID          : cgw-b4dc3961
12 !
13 !
14 ! This configuration consists of two tunnels. Both tunnels must be
15 ! configured on your Customer Gateway.
16 !
17 ! -------------------------------------------------------------------
18 ! IPsec Tunnel #1
19 ! -------------------------------------------------------------------
20 ![\[Image NOT FOUND\]](http://docs.aws.amazon.com/AmazonVPC/latest/NetworkAdminGuide/images/IKE.
      png)
21 ! #1: Internet Key Exchange (IKE) Configuration
22 !
23 ! A policy is established for the supported ISAKMP encryption,
24 ! authentication, Diffie-Hellman, lifetime, and key parameters.
25 !
26 ! Please note, these sample configurations are for the minimum requirement of AES128, SHA1, and
      DH Group 2.
27 ! You will need to modify these sample configuration files to take advantage of AES256, SHA256,
      or other DH groups like 2, 14-18, 22, 23, and 24.
28 ! The address of the external interface for your customer gateway must be a static address.
29 ! Your customer gateway may reside behind a device performing network address translation (NAT).
30 ! To ensure that NAT traversal (NAT-T) can function, you must adjust your firewall rules to
      unblock UDP port 4500. If not behind NAT, we recommend disabling NAT-T.
31 !
32 ! Note that there are a global list of ISAKMP policies, each identified by
33 ! sequence number. This policy is defined as #200, which may conflict with
34 ! an existing policy using the same number. If so, we recommend changing
35 ! the sequence number to avoid conflicts.
36 !
37 crypto isakmp policy 200
38    encryption aes 128
39    authentication pre-share
40    group 2
41    lifetime 28800
42    hash sha
43 exit
44
45 ! The ISAKMP keyring stores the Pre Shared Key used to authenticate the
46 ! tunnel endpoints.
47 !
48 crypto keyring keyring-vpn-44a8938f-0
49    local-address YOUR_UPLINK_ADDRESS
50    pre-shared-key address 72.21.209.225 key plain-text-password1
```

```
51 exit
52
53 ! An ISAKMP profile is used to associate the keyring with the particular
54 ! endpoint.
55 !
56 crypto isakmp profile isakmp-vpn-44a8938f-0
57    local-address YOUR_UPLINK_ADDRESS
58    match identity address 72.21.209.225
59    keyring keyring-vpn-44a8938f-0
60 exit
61
62 ![\[Image NOT FOUND\]](http://docs.aws.amazon.com/AmazonVPC/latest/NetworkAdminGuide/images/
      IPsec.png)
63 ! #2: IPsec Configuration
64 !
65 ! The IPsec transform set defines the encryption, authentication, and IPsec
66 ! mode parameters.
67 ! Please note, you may use these additionally supported IPSec parameters for encryption like
      AES256 and other DH groups like 2, 5, 14-18, 22, 23, and 24.
68 !
69 crypto ipsec transform-set ipsec-prop-vpn-44a8938f-0 esp-aes 128 esp-sha-hmac
70    mode tunnel
71 exit
72
73 ! The IPsec profile references the IPsec transform set and further defines
74 ! the Diffie-Hellman group and security association lifetime.
75 !
76 crypto ipsec profile ipsec-vpn-44a8938f-0
77    set pfs group2
78    set security-association lifetime seconds 3600
79    set transform-set ipsec-prop-vpn-44a8938f-0
80 exit
81
82 ! Additional parameters of the IPsec configuration are set here. Note that
83 ! these parameters are global and therefore impact other IPsec
84 ! associations.
85 ! This option instructs the router to clear the "Don't Fragment"
86 ! bit from packets that carry this bit and yet must be fragmented, enabling
87 ! them to be fragmented.
88 !
89 crypto ipsec df-bit clear
90
91 ! This option enables IPsec Dead Peer Detection, which causes periodic
92 ! messages to be sent to ensure a Security Association remains operational.
93 !
94 crypto isakmp keepalive 10 10 on-demand
95
96 ! This configures the gateway's window for accepting out of order
97 ! IPsec packets. A larger window can be helpful if too many packets
98 ! are dropped due to reordering while in transit between gateways.
99 !
100 crypto ipsec security-association replay window-size 128
101
102 ! This option instructs the router to fragment the unencrypted packets
```

```
103  ! (prior to encryption).
104  !
105  crypto ipsec fragmentation before-encryption
106
107  ![\[Image NOT FOUND\]](http://docs.aws.amazon.com/AmazonVPC/latest/NetworkAdminGuide/images/
        Tunnel.png)
108  ! #3: Tunnel Interface Configuration
109  !
110  ! A tunnel interface is configured to be the logical interface associated
111  ! with the tunnel. All traffic routed to the tunnel interface will be
112  ! encrypted and transmitted to the VPC. Similarly, traffic from the VPC
113  ! will be logically received on this interface.
114  !
115  ! Association with the IPsec security association is done through the
116  ! "tunnel protection" command.
117  !
118  ! The address of the interface is configured with the setup for your
119  ! Customer Gateway.  If the address changes, the Customer Gateway and VPN
120  ! Connection must be recreated with Amazon VPC.
121  !
122  interface Tunnel1
123     ip address 169.254.255.2 255.255.255.252
124     ip virtual-reassembly
125     tunnel source YOUR_UPLINK_ADDRESS
126     tunnel destination 72.21.209.225
127     tunnel mode ipsec ipv4
128     tunnel protection ipsec profile ipsec-vpn-44a8938f-0
129     ! This option causes the router to reduce the Maximum Segment Size of
130     ! TCP packets to prevent packet fragmentation.
131     ip tcp adjust-mss 1387
132     no shutdown
133  exit
134
135  ![\[Image NOT FOUND\]](http://docs.aws.amazon.com/AmazonVPC/latest/NetworkAdminGuide/images/BGP.
        png)
136  ! #4: Border Gateway Protocol (BGP) Configuration
137  !
138  ! BGP is used within the tunnel to exchange prefixes between the
139  ! Virtual Private Gateway and your Customer Gateway. The Virtual Private Gateway
140  ! will announce the prefix corresponding to your VPC.
141  !
142  ! Your Customer Gateway may announce a default route (0.0.0.0/0),
143  ! which can be done with the 'network' statement and
144  ! 'default-originate' statements.
145  !
146  ! The BGP timers are adjusted to provide more rapid detection of outages.
147  !
148  ! The local BGP Autonomous System Number (ASN) (YOUR_BGP_ASN) is configured
149  ! as part of your Customer Gateway. If the ASN must be changed, the
150  ! Customer Gateway and VPN Connection will need to be recreated with AWS.
151  !
152  router bgp YOUR_BGP_ASN
153     neighbor 169.254.255.1 remote-as 7224
154     neighbor 169.254.255.1 activate
```

```
155    neighbor 169.254.255.1 timers 10 30 30
156    address-family ipv4 unicast
157        neighbor 169.254.255.1 remote-as 7224
158        neighbor 169.254.255.1 timers 10 30 30
159        neighbor 169.254.255.1 default-originate
160        neighbor 169.254.255.1 activate
161        neighbor 169.254.255.1 soft-reconfiguration inbound
162 ! To advertise additional prefixes to Amazon VPC, copy the 'network' statement
163 ! and identify the prefix you wish to advertise. Make sure the prefix is present
164 ! in the routing table of the device with a valid next-hop.
165        network 0.0.0.0
166    exit
167 exit
168
169
170 ! --------------------------------------------------------------------------
171 ! IPsec Tunnel #2
172 ! --------------------------------------------------------------------------
173 ![\[Image NOT FOUND\]](http://docs.aws.amazon.com/AmazonVPC/latest/NetworkAdminGuide/images/IKE.
       png)
174 ! #1: Internet Key Exchange (IKE) Configuration
175 !
176 ! A policy is established for the supported ISAKMP encryption,
177 ! authentication, Diffie-Hellman, lifetime, and key parameters.
178 ! Please note, these sample configurations are for the minimum requirement of AES128, SHA1, and
       DH Group 2.
179 ! You will need to modify these sample configuration files to take advantage of AES256, SHA256,
       or other DH groups like 2, 14-18, 22, 23, and 24.
180 ! The address of the external interface for your customer gateway must be a static address.
181 ! Your customer gateway may reside behind a device performing network address translation (NAT).
182 ! To ensure that NAT traversal (NAT-T) can function, you must adjust your firewall rules to
       unblock UDP port 4500. If not behind NAT, we recommend disabling NAT-T.
183 !
184 ! Note that there are a global list of ISAKMP policies, each identified by
185 ! sequence number. This policy is defined as #201, which may conflict with
186 ! an existing policy using the same number. If so, we recommend changing
187 ! the sequence number to avoid conflicts.
188 !
189 crypto isakmp policy 201
190    encryption aes 128
191    authentication pre-share
192    group 2
193    lifetime 28800
194    hash sha
195 exit
196
197 ! The ISAKMP keyring stores the Pre Shared Key used to authenticate the
198 ! tunnel endpoints.
199 !
200 crypto keyring keyring-vpn-44a8938f-1
201    local-address YOUR_UPLINK_ADDRESS
202    pre-shared-key address 72.21.209.193 key plain-text-password2
203 exit
204
```

```
205 ! An ISAKMP profile is used to associate the keyring with the particular
206 ! endpoint.
207 !
208 crypto isakmp profile isakmp-vpn-44a8938f-1
209     local-address YOUR_UPLINK_ADDRESS
210     match identity address 72.21.209.193
211     keyring keyring-vpn-44a8938f-1
212 exit
213
214 ![\[Image NOT FOUND\]](http://docs.aws.amazon.com/AmazonVPC/latest/NetworkAdminGuide/images/
        IPsec.png)
215 ! #2: IPsec Configuration
216 !
217 ! The IPsec transform set defines the encryption, authentication, and IPsec
218 ! mode parameters.
219 ! Please note, you may use these additionally supported IPSec parameters for encryption like
        AES256 and other DH groups like 2, 5, 14-18, 22, 23, and 24.
220 !
221 crypto ipsec transform-set ipsec-prop-vpn-44a8938f-1 esp-aes 128 esp-sha-hmac
222     mode tunnel
223 exit
224
225 ! The IPsec profile references the IPsec transform set and further defines
226 ! the Diffie-Hellman group and security association lifetime.
227 !
228 crypto ipsec profile ipsec-vpn-44a8938f-1
229     set pfs group2
230     set security-association lifetime seconds 3600
231     set transform-set ipsec-prop-vpn-44a8938f-1
232 exit
233
234 ! Additional parameters of the IPsec configuration are set here. Note that
235 ! these parameters are global and therefore impact other IPsec
236 ! associations.
237 ! This option instructs the router to clear the "Don't Fragment"
238 ! bit from packets that carry this bit and yet must be fragmented, enabling
239 ! them to be fragmented.
240 !
241 crypto ipsec df-bit clear
242
243 ! This option enables IPsec Dead Peer Detection, which causes periodic
244 ! messages to be sent to ensure a Security Association remains operational.
245 !
246 crypto isakmp keepalive 10 10 on-demand
247
248 ! This configures the gateway's window for accepting out of order
249 ! IPsec packets. A larger window can be helpful if too many packets
250 ! are dropped due to reordering while in transit between gateways.
251 !
252 crypto ipsec security-association replay window-size 128
253
254 ! This option instructs the router to fragment the unencrypted packets
255 ! (prior to encryption).
256 !
```

```
257 crypto ipsec fragmentation before-encryption
258
259 ![\[Image NOT FOUND\]](http://docs.aws.amazon.com/AmazonVPC/latest/NetworkAdminGuide/images/
        Tunnel.png)
260 ! #3: Tunnel Interface Configuration
261 !
262 ! A tunnel interface is configured to be the logical interface associated
263 ! with the tunnel. All traffic routed to the tunnel interface will be
264 ! encrypted and transmitted to the VPC. Similarly, traffic from the VPC
265 ! will be logically received on this interface.
266 !
267 ! Association with the IPsec security association is done through the
268 ! "tunnel protection" command.
269 !
270 ! The address of the interface is configured with the setup for your
271 ! Customer Gateway.  If the address changes, the Customer Gateway and VPN
272 ! Connection must be recreated with Amazon VPC.
273 !
274 interface Tunnel2
275    ip address 169.254.255.6 255.255.255.252
276    ip virtual-reassembly
277    tunnel source YOUR_UPLINK_ADDRESS
278    tunnel destination 72.21.209.193
279    tunnel mode ipsec ipv4
280    tunnel protection ipsec profile ipsec-vpn-44a8938f-1
281    ! This option causes the router to reduce the Maximum Segment Size of
282    ! TCP packets to prevent packet fragmentation.
283    ip tcp adjust-mss 1387
284    no shutdown
285 exit
286
287 ![\[Image NOT FOUND\]](http://docs.aws.amazon.com/AmazonVPC/latest/NetworkAdminGuide/images/BGP.
        png)
288 ! #4: Border Gateway Protocol (BGP) Configuration
289 !
290 ! BGP is used within the tunnel to exchange prefixes between the
291 ! Virtual Private Gateway and your Customer Gateway. The Virtual Private Gateway
292 ! will announce the prefix corresponding to your Cloud.
293 !
294 ! Your Customer Gateway may announce a default route (0.0.0.0/0),
295 ! which can be done with the 'network' statement and
296 ! 'default-originate' statements.
297 !
298 ! The BGP timers are adjusted to provide more rapid detection of outages.
299 !
300 ! The local BGP Autonomous System Number (ASN) (YOUR_BGP_ASN) is configured
301 ! as part of your Customer Gateway. If the ASN must be changed, the
302 ! Customer Gateway and VPN Connection will need to be recreated with AWS.
303 !
304 router bgp YOUR_BGP_ASN
305    neighbor 169.254.255.5 remote-as 7224
306    neighbor 169.254.255.5 activate
307    neighbor 169.254.255.5 timers 10 30 30
308    address-family ipv4 unicast
```

```
309        neighbor 169.254.255.5 remote-as 7224
310        neighbor 169.254.255.5 timers 10 30 30
311        neighbor 169.254.255.5 default-originate
312        neighbor 169.254.255.5 activate
313        neighbor 169.254.255.5 soft-reconfiguration inbound
314  ! To advertise additional prefixes to Amazon VPC, copy the 'network' statement
315  ! and identify the prefix you wish to advertise. Make sure the prefix is present
316  ! in the routing table of the device with a valid next-hop.
317        network 0.0.0.0
318    exit
319  exit
```

How to Test the Customer Gateway Configuration

You can test the gateway configuration for each tunnel.

To test the customer gateway configuration for each tunnel

1. On your customer gateway, determine whether the BGP status is `Active`.

   It takes approximately 30 seconds for a BGP peering to become active.

2. Ensure that the customer gateway is advertising a route to the virtual private gateway. The route may be the default route (`0.0.0.0/0`) or a more specific route you prefer.

When properly established, your BGP peering should be receiving one route from the virtual private gateway corresponding to the prefix that your VPC integration team specified for the VPC (for example, `10.0.0.0/24`). If the BGP peering is established, you are receiving a prefix, and you are advertising a prefix, your tunnel is configured correctly. Make sure that both tunnels are in this state.

Next you must test the connectivity for each tunnel by launching an instance into your VPC, and pinging the instance from your home network. Before you begin, make sure of the following:

- Use an AMI that responds to ping requests. We recommend that you use one of the Amazon Linux AMIs.
- Configure your instance's security group and network ACL to enable inbound ICMP traffic.
- Ensure that you have configured routing for your VPN connection: your subnet's route table must contain a route to the virtual private gateway. For more information, see Enable Route Propagation in Your Route Table in the *Amazon VPC User Guide.*

To test the end-to-end connectivity of each tunnel

1. Launch an instance of one of the Amazon Linux AMIs into your VPC. The Amazon Linux AMIs are listed in the launch wizard when you launch an instance from the Amazon EC2 Console. For more information, see the Amazon VPC Getting Started Guide.

2. After the instance is running, get its private IP address (for example, `10.0.0.4`). The console displays the address as part of the instance's details.

3. On a system in your home network, use the ping command with the instance's IP address. Make sure that the computer you ping from is behind the customer gateway. A successful response should be similar to the following.

```
1 ping 10.0.0.4
```

```
1 Pinging 10.0.0.4 with 32 bytes of data:
2
3 Reply from 10.0.0.4: bytes=32 time<1ms TTL=128
4 Reply from 10.0.0.4: bytes=32 time<1ms TTL=128
5 Reply from 10.0.0.4: bytes=32 time<1ms TTL=128
```

```
 6
 7 Ping statistics for 10.0.0.4:
 8 Packets: Sent = 3, Received = 3, Lost = 0 (0% loss),
 9
10 Approximate round trip times in milliseconds:
11 Minimum = 0ms, Maximum = 0ms, Average = 0ms
```

Note

If you ping an instance from your customer gateway router, ensure that you are sourcing ping messages from an internal IP address, not a tunnel IP address. Some AMIs don't respond to ping messages from tunnel IP addresses.

1. (Optional) To test tunnel failover, you can temporarily disable one of the tunnels on your customer gateway, and repeat the above step. You cannot disable a tunnel on the AWS side of the VPN connection.

If your tunnels don't test successfully, see Troubleshooting Cisco IOS Customer Gateway Connectivity.

Example: Cisco IOS Device without Border Gateway Protocol

Topics

- A High-Level View of the Customer Gateway
- A Detailed View of the Customer Gateway and an Example Configuration
- How to Test the Customer Gateway Configuration

In this section we walk you through an example of the configuration information provided by your integration team if your customer gateway is a Cisco Integrated Services router running Cisco IOS software.

Two diagrams illustrate the example configuration. The first diagram shows the high-level layout of the customer gateway, and the second diagram shows details from the example configuration. You should use the real configuration information that you receive from your integration team, and apply it to your customer gateway.

A High-Level View of the Customer Gateway

The following diagram shows the general details of your customer gateway. Note that the VPN connection consists of two separate tunnels. Using redundant tunnels ensures continuous availability in the case that a device fails.

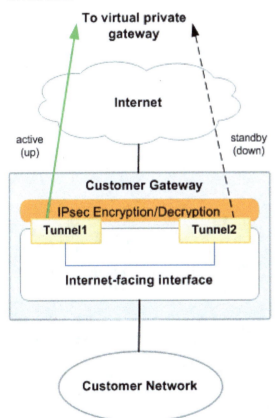

A Detailed View of the Customer Gateway and an Example Configuration

The diagram in this section illustrates an example Cisco IOS customer gateway (without BGP). Following the diagram, there is a corresponding example of the configuration information that your integration team should provide. The example configuration contains a set of information for each of the tunnels that you must configure.

In addition, the example configuration refers to this item that you must provide:

- *YOUR_UPLINK_ADDRESS*—The IP address for the Internet-routable external interface on the customer gateway. The address must be static, and may be behind a device performing network address translation (NAT). To ensure that NAT traversal (NAT-T) can function, you must adjust your firewall rules to unblock UDP port 4500.

The example configuration includes several example values to help you understand how configuration works. For example, we provide example values for the VPN connection ID (vpn-1a2b3c4d), virtual private gateway ID (vgw-12345678), the IP addresses (205.251.233.*, 169.254.255.*). You'll replace these example values with the actual values from the configuration information that you receive.

In addition, you must:

- Configure the outside interface.
- Configure the tunnel interface IDs (referred to as *Tunnel1* and *Tunnel2* in the example configuration).
- Ensure that the Crypto ISAKMP Policy Sequence number is unique.
- Ensure that the Crypto IPsec Transform Set and the Crypto ISAKMP Policy Sequence are harmonious with any other IPsec tunnels configured on the device.
- Ensure that the SLA monitoring number is unique.
- Configure all internal routing that moves traffic between the customer gateway and your local network.

In the following diagram and example configuration, you must replace the items in red italics with values that apply to your particular configuration.

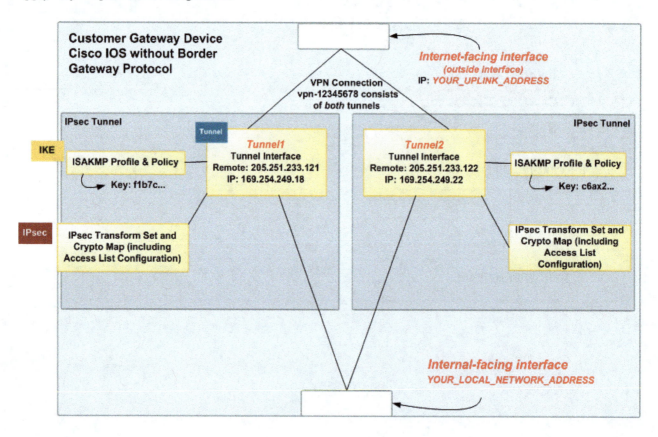

Warning

The following configuration information is an example of what you can expect your integration team to provide. Many of the values in the following example will be different from the actual configuration information that you receive. You must use the actual values and not the example values shown here, or your implementation will fail.

```
1  ! -------------------------------------------------------------------------
2  ! IPSec Tunnel #1
3  ! -------------------------------------------------------------------------
4  ! #1: Internet Key Exchange (IKE) Configuration
5  !
6  ! A policy is established for the supported ISAKMP encryption,
7  ! authentication, Diffie-Hellman, lifetime, and key parameters.
8  ! Please note, these sample configurations are for the minimum requirement of AES128, SHA1, and
      DH Group 2.
9  ! You will need to modify these sample configuration files to take advantage of AES256, SHA256,
      or other DH groups like 2, 14-18, 22, 23, and 24.
10 ! The address of the external interface for your customer gateway must be a static address.
11 ! Your customer gateway may reside behind a device performing network address translation (NAT).
12 ! To ensure that NAT traversal (NAT-T) can function, you must adjust your firewall rules to
      unblock UDP port 4500. If not behind NAT, we recommend disabling NAT-T.
13 !
14 ! Note that there are a global list of ISAKMP policies, each identified by
15 ! sequence number. This policy is defined as #200, which may conflict with
16 ! an existing policy using the same number. If so, we recommend changing
17 ! the sequence number to avoid conflicts.
18 !
19 crypto isakmp policy 200
20   encryption aes 128
21   authentication pre-share
22   group 2
23   lifetime 28800
24   hash sha
25 exit
26
27 ! The ISAKMP keyring stores the Pre Shared Key used to authenticate the
28 ! tunnel endpoints.
29 !
30 crypto keyring keyring-vpn-1a2b3c4d-0
31   local-address CUSTOMER_IP
32   pre-shared-key address 205.251.233.121 key PASSWORD
33 exit
34
35 ! An ISAKMP profile is used to associate the keyring with the particular
36 ! endpoint.
37 !
38 crypto isakmp profile isakmp-vpn-1a2b3c4d-0
39   local-address CUSTOMER_IP
40   match identity address 205.251.233.121
41   keyring keyring-vpn-1a2b3c4d-0
42 exit
43
44 ! #2: IPSec Configuration
45 !
46 ! The IPSec transform set defines the encryption, authentication, and IPSec
47 ! mode parameters.
```

```
48 !
49 ! Please note, you may use these additionally supported IPSec parameters for encryption like
       AES256 and other DH groups like 2, 5, 14-18, 22, 23, and 24.
50 !
51 crypto ipsec transform-set ipsec-prop-vpn-1a2b3c4d-0 esp-aes 128 esp-sha-hmac
52   mode tunnel
53 exit
54
55 ! The IPSec profile references the IPSec transform set and further defines
56 ! the Diffie-Hellman group and security association lifetime.
57 !
58 crypto ipsec profile ipsec-vpn-1a2b3c4d-0
59   set pfs group2
60   set security-association lifetime seconds 3600
61   set transform-set ipsec-prop-vpn-1a2b3c4d-0
62 exit
63
64 ! Additional parameters of the IPSec configuration are set here. Note that
65 ! these parameters are global and therefore impact other IPSec
66 ! associations.
67 ! This option instructs the router to clear the "Don't Fragment"
68 ! bit from packets that carry this bit and yet must be fragmented, enabling
69 ! them to be fragmented.
70 !
71 crypto ipsec df-bit clear
72
73 ! This option enables IPSec Dead Peer Detection, which causes periodic
74 ! messages to be sent to ensure a Security Association remains operational.
75 !
76 crypto isakmp keepalive 10 10 on-demand
77
78 ! This configures the gateway's window for accepting out of order
79 ! IPSec packets. A larger window can be helpful if too many packets
80 ! are dropped due to reordering while in transit between gateways.
81 !
82 crypto ipsec security-association replay window-size 128
83
84 ! This option instructs the router to fragment the unencrypted packets
85 ! (prior to encryption).
86 !
87 crypto ipsec fragmentation before-encryption
88
89
90 ! -------------------------------------------------------------------------------
91 ! #3: Tunnel Interface Configuration
92 !
93 ! A tunnel interface is configured to be the logical interface associated
94 ! with the tunnel. All traffic routed to the tunnel interface will be
95 ! encrypted and transmitted to the VPC. Similarly, traffic from the VPC
96 ! will be logically received on this interface.
97 !
98 ! Association with the IPSec security association is done through the
99 ! "tunnel protection" command.
100 !
```

```
101  ! The address of the interface is configured with the setup for your
102  ! Customer Gateway.  If the address changes, the Customer Gateway and VPN
103  ! Connection must be recreated with Amazon VPC.
104  !
105  interface Tunnel1
106     ip address 169.254.249.18 255.255.255.252
107     ip virtual-reassembly
108     tunnel source CUSTOMER_IP
109     tunnel destination 205.251.233.121
110     tunnel mode ipsec ipv4
111     tunnel protection ipsec profile ipsec-vpn-1a2b3c4d-0
112     ! This option causes the router to reduce the Maximum Segment Size of
113     ! TCP packets to prevent packet fragmentation.
114     ip tcp adjust-mss 1387
115     no shutdown
116  exit
117
118  ! -----------------------------------------------------------------------
119  ! #4 Static Route Configuration
120  !
121  ! Your Customer Gateway needs to set a static route for the prefix corresponding to your
122  ! VPC to send traffic over the tunnel interface.
123  ! An example for a VPC with the prefix 10.0.0.0/16 is provided below:
124  ! ip route 10.0.0.0 255.255.0.0 Tunnel1 track 100
125  !
126  ! SLA Monitor is used to provide a failover between the two tunnels. If the primary tunnel fails
          , the redundant tunnel will automatically be used
127  ! This sla is defined as #100, which may conflict with an existing sla using same number.
128  ! If so, we recommend changing the sequence number to avoid conflicts.
129  !
130  ip sla 100
131     icmp-echo 169.254.249.17 source-interface Tunnel1
132     timeout 1000
133     frequency 5
134  exit
135  ip sla schedule 100  life forever start-time now
136  track 100 ip sla 100 reachability
137  ! -----------------------------------------------------------------------
138  ! -----------------------------------------------------------------------
139  ! IPSec Tunnel #2
140  ! -----------------------------------------------------------------------
141  ! #1: Internet Key Exchange (IKE) Configuration
142  !
143  ! A policy is established for the supported ISAKMP encryption,
144  ! authentication, Diffie-Hellman, lifetime, and key parameters.
145  ! Please note, these sample configurations are for the minimum requirement of AES128, SHA1, and
          DH Group 2.
146  ! You will need to modify these sample configuration files to take advantage of AES256, SHA256,
          or other DH groups like 2, 14-18, 22, 23, and 24.
147  ! The address of the external interface for your customer gateway must be a static address.
148  ! Your customer gateway may reside behind a device performing network address translation (NAT).
149  ! To ensure that NAT traversal (NAT-T) can function, you must adjust your firewall rules to
          unblock UDP port 4500. If not behind NAT, we recommend disabling NAT-T.
150  !
```

```
151 ! Note that there are a global list of ISAKMP policies, each identified by
152 ! sequence number. This policy is defined as #201, which may conflict with
153 ! an existing policy using the same number. If so, we recommend changing
154 ! the sequence number to avoid conflicts.
155 !
156 crypto isakmp policy 201
157   encryption aes 128
158   authentication pre-share
159   group 2
160   lifetime 28800
161   hash sha
162 exit
163
164 ! The ISAKMP keyring stores the Pre Shared Key used to authenticate the
165 ! tunnel endpoints.
166 !
167 crypto keyring keyring-vpn-1a2b3c4d-1
168   local-address CUSTOMER_IP
169   pre-shared-key address 205.251.233.122 key PASSWORD
170 exit
171
172 ! An ISAKMP profile is used to associate the keyring with the particular
173 ! endpoint.
174 !
175 crypto isakmp profile isakmp-vpn-1a2b3c4d-1
176   local-address CUSTOMER_IP
177   match identity address 205.251.233.122
178   keyring keyring-vpn-1a2b3c4d-1
179 exit
180
181 ! #2: IPSec Configuration
182 !
183 ! The IPSec transform set defines the encryption, authentication, and IPSec
184 ! mode parameters.
185 ! Please note, you may use these additionally supported IPSec parameters for encryption like
        AES256 and other DH groups like 2, 5, 14-18, 22, 23, and 24.
186 !
187 crypto ipsec transform-set ipsec-prop-vpn-1a2b3c4d-1 esp-aes 128 esp-sha-hmac
188   mode tunnel
189 exit
190
191 ! The IPSec profile references the IPSec transform set and further defines
192 ! the Diffie-Hellman group and security association lifetime.
193 !
194 crypto ipsec profile ipsec-vpn-1a2b3c4d-1
195   set pfs group2
196   set security-association lifetime seconds 3600
197   set transform-set ipsec-prop-vpn-1a2b3c4d-1
198 exit
199
200 ! Additional parameters of the IPSec configuration are set here. Note that
201 ! these parameters are global and therefore impact other IPSec
202 ! associations.
203 ! This option instructs the router to clear the "Don't Fragment"
```

```
204  ! bit from packets that carry this bit and yet must be fragmented, enabling
205  ! them to be fragmented.
206  !
207  crypto ipsec df-bit clear
208
209  ! This option enables IPSec Dead Peer Detection, which causes periodic
210  ! messages to be sent to ensure a Security Association remains operational.
211  !
212  crypto isakmp keepalive 10 10 on-demand
213
214  ! This configures the gateway's window for accepting out of order
215  ! IPSec packets. A larger window can be helpful if too many packets
216  ! are dropped due to reordering while in transit between gateways.
217  !
218  crypto ipsec security-association replay window-size 128
219
220  ! This option instructs the router to fragment the unencrypted packets
221  ! (prior to encryption).
222  !
223  crypto ipsec fragmentation before-encryption
224
225
226  ! --------------------------------------------------------------------------
227  ! #3: Tunnel Interface Configuration
228  !
229  ! A tunnel interface is configured to be the logical interface associated
230  ! with the tunnel. All traffic routed to the tunnel interface will be
231  ! encrypted and transmitted to the VPC. Similarly, traffic from the VPC
232  ! will be logically received on this interface.
233  !
234  ! Association with the IPSec security association is done through the
235  ! "tunnel protection" command.
236  !
237  ! The address of the interface is configured with the setup for your
238  ! Customer Gateway.  If the address changes, the Customer Gateway and VPN
239  ! Connection must be recreated with Amazon VPC.
240  !
241  interface Tunnel2
242     ip address 169.254.249.22 255.255.255.252
243     ip virtual-reassembly
244     tunnel source CUSTOMER_IP
245     tunnel destination 205.251.233.122
246     tunnel mode ipsec ipv4
247     tunnel protection ipsec profile ipsec-vpn-1a2b3c4d-1
248     ! This option causes the router to reduce the Maximum Segment Size of
249     ! TCP packets to prevent packet fragmentation.
250     ip tcp adjust-mss 1387
251     no shutdown
252  exit
253
254  ! --------------------------------------------------------------------------
255  ! #4 Static Route Configuration
256  !
257  ! Your Customer Gateway needs to set a static route for the prefix corresponding to your
```

```
258 ! VPC to send traffic over the tunnel interface.
259 ! An example for a VPC with the prefix 10.0.0.0/16 is provided below:
260 ! ip route 10.0.0.0 255.255.0.0 Tunnel2 track 200
261 !
262 ! SLA Monitor is used to provide a failover between the two tunnels. If the primary tunnel fails
       , the redundant tunnel will automatically be used
263 ! This sla is defined as #200, which may conflict with an existing sla using same number.
264 ! If so, we recommend changing the sequence number to avoid conflicts.
265 !
266 ip sla 200
267    icmp-echo 169.254.249.21 source-interface Tunnel2
268    timeout 1000
269    frequency 5
270 exit
271 ip sla schedule 200  life forever start-time now
272 track 200 ip sla 200 reachability
273 ! -------------------------------------------------------------------------
```

How to Test the Customer Gateway Configuration

You can test the gateway configuration for each tunnel.

To test the customer gateway configuration for each tunnel

1. Ensure that the customer gateway has a static route to your VPC, as suggested in the configuration templates provided by AWS.

2. Ensure that a static route has been added to the VPN connection so that traffic can get back to your customer gateway. For example, if your local subnet prefix is 198.10.0.0/16, you need to add a static route with that CIDR range to your VPN connection. Make sure that both tunnels have a static route to your VPC.

Next you must test the connectivity for each tunnel by launching an instance into your VPC, and pinging the instance from your home network. Before you begin, make sure of the following:

- Use an AMI that responds to ping requests. We recommend that you use one of the Amazon Linux AMIs.
- Configure your instance's security group and network ACL to enable inbound ICMP traffic.
- Ensure that you have configured routing for your VPN connection - your subnet's route table must contain a route to the virtual private gateway. For more information, see Enable Route Propagation in Your Route Table in the *Amazon VPC User Guide*.

To test the end-to-end connectivity of each tunnel

1. Launch an instance of one of the Amazon Linux AMIs into your VPC. The Amazon Linux AMIs are listed in the launch wizard when you launch an instance from the AWS Management Console. For more information, see the Amazon VPC Getting Started Guide.

2. After the instance is running, get its private IP address (for example, 10.0.0.4). The console displays the address as part of the instance's details.

3. On a system in your home network, use the ping command with the instance's IP address. Make sure that the computer you ping from is behind the customer gateway. A successful response should be similar to the following.

```
1 ping 10.0.0.4
```

```
1 Pinging 10.0.0.4 with 32 bytes of data:
2
```

```
3 Reply from 10.0.0.4: bytes=32 time<1ms TTL=128
4 Reply from 10.0.0.4: bytes=32 time<1ms TTL=128
5 Reply from 10.0.0.4: bytes=32 time<1ms TTL=128
6
7 Ping statistics for 10.0.0.4:
8 Packets: Sent = 3, Received = 3, Lost = 0 (0% loss),
9
10 Approximate round trip times in milliseconds:
11 Minimum = 0ms, Maximum = 0ms, Average = 0ms
```

Note

If you ping an instance from your customer gateway router, ensure that you are sourcing ping messages from an internal IP address, not a tunnel IP address. Some AMIs don't respond to ping messages from tunnel IP addresses.

1. (Optional) To test tunnel failover, you can temporarily disable one of the tunnels on your customer gateway, and repeat the above step. You cannot disable a tunnel on the AWS side of the VPN connection.

If your tunnels don't test successfully, see Troubleshooting Cisco IOS Customer Gateway without Border Gateway Protocol Connectivity.

Example: Dell SonicWALL Device

This topic provides an example of how to configure your router if your customer gateway is a Dell SonicWALL router.

This section assumes that a VPN connection with static routing has been configured in the Amazon VPC console. For more information, see Adding a Virtual Private Gateway to Your VPC in the *Amazon VPC User Guide*.

Topics

- A High-Level View of the Customer Gateway
- Example Configuration File
- Configuring the SonicWALL Device Using the Management Interface
- How to Test the Customer Gateway Configuration

A High-Level View of the Customer Gateway

The following diagram shows the general details of your customer gateway. Note that the VPN connection consists of two separate tunnels: *Tunnel 1* and *Tunnel 2*. Using redundant tunnels ensures continuous availability in the case that a device fails.

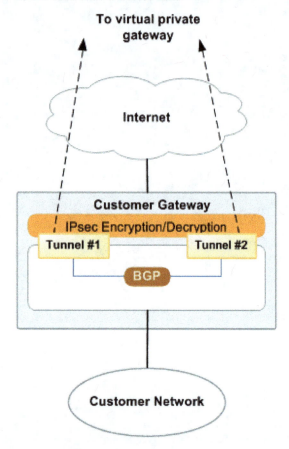

Example Configuration File

The configuration file that you download from the Amazon VPC console includes the values that you need in order to use the command line tools on OS 6.2 to configure each tunnel and the IKE and IPsec settings for your

SonicWALL device.

Important

The following configuration information uses example values — you must use the actual values and not the example values shown here, or your implementation will fail.

```
1  ! Amazon Web Services
2  ! Virtual Private Cloud
3  !
4  ! VPN Connection Configuration
5  ! ================================================================================
6  ! AWS utilizes unique identifiers to manipulate the configuration of
7  ! a VPN Connection. Each VPN Connection is assigned a VPN Connection Identifier
8  ! and is associated with two other identifiers, namely the
9  ! Customer Gateway Identifier and the Virtual Private Gateway Identifier.
10 !
11 ! Your VPN Connection ID                    : vpn-44a8938f
12 ! Your Virtual Private Gateway ID           : vgw-8db04f81
13 ! Your Customer Gateway ID                  : cgw-ff628496
14 !
15 ! This configuration consists of two tunnels. Both tunnels must be
16 ! configured on your Customer Gateway.
17 !
18 ! This configuration was tested on a SonicWALL TZ 600 running OS 6.2.5.1-26n
19 !
20 ! You may need to populate these values throughout the config based on your setup:
21 ! <vpc_subnet> - VPC address range
22 !
23 ! IPSec Tunnel !1
24 ! ================================================================================
25 ![\[Image NOT FOUND\]](http://docs.aws.amazon.com/AmazonVPC/latest/NetworkAdminGuide/images/IKE.
      png)
26 ! #1: Internet Key Exchange (IKE) Configuration
27 !
28 ! Please note, these sample configurations are for the minimum requirement of AES128, SHA1, and
      DH Group 2.
29 ! You can modify these sample configuration files to use AES128, SHA1, AES256, SHA256, or other
      DH groups like 2, 14-18, 22, 23, and 24.
30 ! The address of the external interface for your customer gateway must be a static address.
31 ! Your customer gateway may reside behind a device performing network address translation (NAT).
32 ! To ensure that NAT traversal (NAT-T) can function, you must adjust your firewall rules to
      unblock UDP port 4500. If not behind NAT, we recommend disabling NAT-T.
33 !
34 config
35 address-object ipv4 AWSVPC network 172.30.0.0/16
36 vpn policy tunnel-interface vpn-44a8938f-1
37 gateway primary 72.21.209.193
38 bound-to interface X1
39 auth-method shared-secret
40 shared-secret PRE-SHARED-KEY-IN-PLAIN-TEXT
41 ike-id local ip your_customer_gateway_IP_address
42 ike-id peer ip 72.21.209.193
43 end
44 !
45 ![\[Image NOT FOUND\]](http://docs.aws.amazon.com/AmazonVPC/latest/NetworkAdminGuide/images/
      IPsec.png)
```

```
46  ! #2: IPSec Configuration
47  !
48  ! The IPSec (Phase 2) proposal defines the protocol, authentication,
49  ! encryption, and lifetime parameters for our IPSec security association.
50  ! Please note, you may use these additionally supported IPSec parameters for encryption like
       AES256 and other DH groups like 2, 5, 14-18, 22, 23, and 24.
51  !
52  config
53  proposal ipsec lifetime 3600
54  proposal ipsec authentication sha1
55  proposal ipsec encryption aes128
56  proposal ipsec perfect-forward-secrecy dh-group 2
57  proposal ipsec protocol ESP
58  keep-alive
59  enable
60  commit
61  end
62  !
63  !
64  ! You can use other supported IPSec parameters for encryption such as AES256, and other DH
       groups such as 2, 5, 14-18, 22, 23, and 24.
65  ! IPSec Dead Peer Detection (DPD) will be enabled on the AWS Endpoint. We
66  ! recommend configuring DPD on your endpoint as follows:
67    - DPD Interval            : 120
68    - DPD Retries             : 3
69  ! To configure Dead Peer Detection for the SonicWall device, use the SonicOS management
       interface.
70  !
71  ![\[Image NOT FOUND\]](http://docs.aws.amazon.com/AmazonVPC/latest/NetworkAdminGuide/images/
       Tunnel.png)
72  ! #3: Tunnel Interface Configuration
73  !
74  ! The tunnel interface is configured with the internal IP address.
75  !
76  ! To establish connectivity between your internal network and the VPC, you
77  ! must have an interface facing your internal network in the "Trust" zone.
78  !
79  config
80  tunnel-interface vpn T1
81  ip-assignment VPN static
82  ip 169.254.44.242 netmask 255.255.255.252
83  !
84  !
85  ![\[Image NOT FOUND\]](http://docs.aws.amazon.com/AmazonVPC/latest/NetworkAdminGuide/images/BGP.
       png)
86  ! #4: Border Gateway Protocol (BGP) Configuration:
87  !
88  ! BGP is used within the tunnel to exchange prefixes between the
89  ! Virtual Private Gateway and your Customer Gateway. The Virtual Private Gateway
90  ! will announce the prefix corresponding to your VPC.
91  ! !
92  ! The local BGP Autonomous System Number (ASN) (65000)
93  ! is configured as part of your Customer Gateway. If the ASN must
94  ! be changed, the Customer Gateway and VPN Connection will need to be recreated with AWS.
```

```
 95 !
 96 routing
 97 bgp
 98 configure terminal
 99 router bgp YOUR_BGP_ASN
100 network <Local_subnet>/24
101 neighbor 169.254.44.242 remote-as 7224
102 neighbor 169.254.44.242 timers 10 30
103 neighbor 169.254.44.242 soft-reconfiguration inbound
104 end
105 write
106 exit
107 commit
108 end
109 !
110 ! IPSec Tunnel #2
111 ! -------------------------------------------------------------------------------
112 ![\[Image NOT FOUND\]](http://docs.aws.amazon.com/AmazonVPC/latest/NetworkAdminGuide/images/IKE.
        png)
113 ! #1: Internet Key Exchange (IKE) Configuration
114 !
115 ! Please note, these sample configurations are for the minimum requirement of AES128, SHA1, and
        DH Group 2.
116 ! You can modify these sample configuration files to use AES128, SHA1, AES256, SHA256, or other
        DH groups like 2, 14-18, 22, 23, and 24.
117 ! The address of the external interface for your customer gateway must be a static address.
118 ! Your customer gateway may reside behind a device performing network address translation (NAT).
119 ! To ensure that NAT traversal (NAT-T) can function, you must adjust your firewall rules to
        unblock UDP port 4500. If not behind NAT, we recommend disabling NAT-T.
120 !
121 config
122 address-object ipv4 AWSVPC network 172.30.0.0/16
123 vpn policy tunnel-interface vpn-44a8938f-1
124 gateway primary 72.21.209.225
125 bound-to interface X1
126 auth-method shared-secret
127 shared-secret PRE-SHARED-KEY-IN-PLAIN-TEXT
128 ike-id local ip your_customer_gateway_IP_address
129 ike-id peer ip 72.21.209.225
130 end
131 !
132 ![\[Image NOT FOUND\]](http://docs.aws.amazon.com/AmazonVPC/latest/NetworkAdminGuide/images/
        IPsec.png)
133 ! #2: IPSec Configuration
134 !
135 ! The IPSec (Phase 2) proposal defines the protocol, authentication,
136 ! encryption, and lifetime parameters for our IPSec security association.
137 ! Please note, you may use these additionally supported IPSec parameters for encryption like
        AES256 and other DH groups like 2, 5, 14-18, 22, 23, and 24.
138 !
139 config
140 proposal ipsec lifetime 3600
141 proposal ipsec authentication sha1
142 proposal ipsec encryption aes128
```

```
143 proposal ipsec perfect-forward-secrecy dh-group 2
144 proposal ipsec protocol ESP
145 keep-alive
146 enable
147 commit
148 end
149 !
150 !
151 ! You can use other supported IPSec parameters for encryption such as AES256, and other DH
        groups such as 2, 5, 14-18, 22, 23, and 24.
152 ! IPSec Dead Peer Detection (DPD) will be enabled on the AWS Endpoint. We
153 ! recommend configuring DPD on your endpoint as follows:
154   - DPD Interval              : 120
155   - DPD Retries               : 3
156 ! To configure Dead Peer Detection for the SonicWall device, use the SonicOS management
        interface.
157 !
158 ![\[Image NOT FOUND\]](http://docs.aws.amazon.com/AmazonVPC/latest/NetworkAdminGuide/images/
        Tunnel.png)
159 ! #3: Tunnel Interface Configuration
160 !
161 ! The tunnel interface is configured with the internal IP address.
162 !
163 ! To establish connectivity between your internal network and the VPC, you
164 ! must have an interface facing your internal network in the "Trust" zone.
165 !
166 config
167 tunnel-interface vpn T2
168 ip-assignment VPN static
169 ip 169.254.44.114 netmask 255.255.255.252
170 !
171 ![\[Image NOT FOUND\]](http://docs.aws.amazon.com/AmazonVPC/latest/NetworkAdminGuide/images/BGP.
        png)
172 ! #4: Border Gateway Protocol (BGP) Configuration:
173 !
174 ! BGP is used within the tunnel to exchange prefixes between the
175 ! Virtual Private Gateway and your Customer Gateway. The Virtual Private Gateway
176 ! will announce the prefix corresponding to your VPC.
177 !
178 ! The local BGP Autonomous System Number (ASN) (65000)
179 ! is configured as part of your Customer Gateway. If the ASN must
180 ! be changed, the Customer Gateway and VPN Connection will need to be recreated with AWS.
181 !
182 routing
183 bgp
184 configure terminal
185 router bgp YOUR_BGP_ASN
186 network <Local_subnet>/24
187 neighbor 169.254.44.114 remote-as 7224
188 neighbor 169.254.44.114 timers 10 30
189 neighbor 169.254.44.114 soft-reconfiguration inbound
190 end
191 write
192 exit
```

```
193 commit
194 end
```

Configuring the SonicWALL Device Using the Management Interface

You can also configure the SonicWALL device using the SonicOS management interface. For more information, see Configuring the SonicWALL Device Using the Management Interface.

You cannot configure BGP for the device using the management interface. Instead, use the command line instructions provided in the example configuration file above, under the section named **BGP**.

How to Test the Customer Gateway Configuration

You can test the gateway configuration for each tunnel.

To test the customer gateway configuration for each tunnel

1. On your customer gateway, determine whether the BGP status is `Active`.

   It takes approximately 30 seconds for a BGP peering to become active.

2. Ensure that the customer gateway is advertising a route to the virtual private gateway. The route may be the default route (`0.0.0.0/0`) or a more specific route you prefer.

When properly established, your BGP peering should be receiving one route from the virtual private gateway corresponding to the prefix that your VPC integration team specified for the VPC (for example, `10.0.0.0/24`). If the BGP peering is established, you are receiving a prefix, and you are advertising a prefix, your tunnel is configured correctly. Make sure that both tunnels are in this state.

Next you must test the connectivity for each tunnel by launching an instance into your VPC, and pinging the instance from your home network. Before you begin, make sure of the following:

- Use an AMI that responds to ping requests. We recommend that you use one of the Amazon Linux AMIs.
- Configure your instance's security group and network ACL to enable inbound ICMP traffic.
- Ensure that you have configured routing for your VPN connection: your subnet's route table must contain a route to the virtual private gateway. For more information, see Enable Route Propagation in Your Route Table in the *Amazon VPC User Guide*.

To test the end-to-end connectivity of each tunnel

1. Launch an instance of one of the Amazon Linux AMIs into your VPC. The Amazon Linux AMIs are listed in the launch wizard when you launch an instance from the Amazon EC2 Console. For more information, see the Amazon VPC Getting Started Guide.

2. After the instance is running, get its private IP address (for example, `10.0.0.4`). The console displays the address as part of the instance's details.

3. On a system in your home network, use the ping command with the instance's IP address. Make sure that the computer you ping from is behind the customer gateway. A successful response should be similar to the following.

```
1 ping 10.0.0.4
```

```
1 Pinging 10.0.0.4 with 32 bytes of data:
2
3 Reply from 10.0.0.4: bytes=32 time<1ms TTL=128
4 Reply from 10.0.0.4: bytes=32 time<1ms TTL=128
5 Reply from 10.0.0.4: bytes=32 time<1ms TTL=128
6
```

```
 7 Ping statistics for 10.0.0.4:
 8 Packets: Sent = 3, Received = 3, Lost = 0 (0% loss),
 9
10 Approximate round trip times in milliseconds:
11 Minimum = 0ms, Maximum = 0ms, Average = 0ms
```

Note

If you ping an instance from your customer gateway router, ensure that you are sourcing ping messages from an internal IP address, not a tunnel IP address. Some AMIs don't respond to ping messages from tunnel IP addresses.

1. (Optional) To test tunnel failover, you can temporarily disable one of the tunnels on your customer gateway, and repeat the above step. You cannot disable a tunnel on the AWS side of the VPN connection.

If your tunnels don't test successfully, see Troubleshooting Generic Device Customer Gateway Connectivity Using Border Gateway Protocol.

Example: Dell SonicWALL SonicOS Device Without Border Gateway Protocol

This topic provides an example of how to configure your router if your customer gateway is a Dell SonicWALL router running SonicOS 5.9 or 6.2.

This section assumes that a VPN connection with static routing has been configured in the Amazon VPC console. For more information, see Adding a Virtual Private Gateway to Your VPC in the *Amazon VPC User Guide*.

Topics

- A High-Level View of the Customer Gateway
- Example Configuration File
- Configuring the SonicWALL Device Using the Management Interface
- How to Test the Customer Gateway Configuration

A High-Level View of the Customer Gateway

The following diagram shows the general details of your customer gateway. Note that the VPN connection consists of two separate tunnels: *Tunnel 1* and *Tunnel 2*. Using redundant tunnels ensures continuous availability in the case that a device fails.

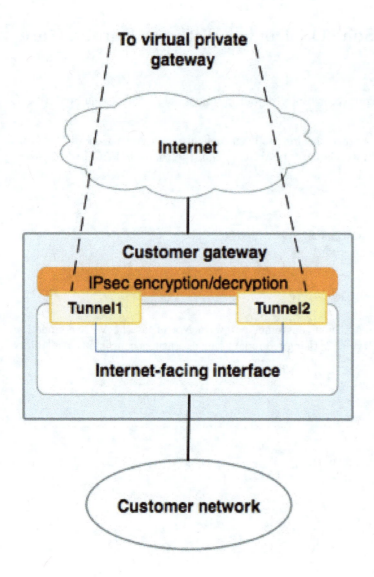

Example Configuration File

The configuration file that you download from the Amazon VPC console includes the values that you need in order to use the command line tools on OS 6.2 to configure each tunnel and the IKE and IPsec settings for your SonicWALL device.

Important

The following configuration information uses example values — you must use the actual values and not the example values shown here, or your implementation will fail.

```
1  ! Amazon Web Services
2  ! Virtual Private Cloud
3  !
4  ! VPN Connection Configuration
5  ! ================================================================================
6  ! AWS utilizes unique identifiers to manipulate the configuration of
7  ! a VPN Connection. Each VPN Connection is assigned a VPN Connection Identifier
8  ! and is associated with two other identifiers, namely the
9  ! Customer Gateway Identifier and the Virtual Private Gateway Identifier.
10 !
```

```
11 ! Your VPN Connection ID                      : vpn-44a8938f
12 ! Your Virtual Private Gateway ID             : vgw-8db04f81
13 ! Your Customer Gateway ID                    : cgw-ff628496
14 !
15 ! This configuration consists of two tunnels. Both tunnels must be
16 ! configured on your customer gateway.
17 !
18 ! This configuration was tested on a SonicWALL TZ 600 running OS 6.2.5.1-26n
19 !
20 ! You may need to populate these values throughout the config based on your setup:
21 ! <vpc_subnet> - VPC IP address range
22 ! ==============================================================================
23 ![\[Image NOT FOUND\]](http://docs.aws.amazon.com/AmazonVPC/latest/NetworkAdminGuide/images/IKE.
      png)
24 ! #1: Internet Key Exchange (IKE) Configuration
25 !
26 ! These sample configurations are for the minimum requirement of AES128, SHA1, and DH Group 2.
27 ! You can modify these sample configuration files to use AES128, SHA1, AES256, SHA256, or other
      DH groups like 2, 14-18, 22, 23, and 24.
28 ! The address of the external interface for your customer gateway must be a static address.
29 ! Your customer gateway may reside behind a device performing network address translation (NAT).
30 ! To ensure that NAT traversal (NAT-T) can function, you must adjust your firewall rules to
      unblock UDP port 4500. If not behind NAT, we recommend disabling NAT-T.
31 !
32 config
33 address-object ipv4 AWSVPC network 172.30.0.0/16
34 vpn policy tunnel-interface vpn-44a8938f-1
35 gateway primary 72.21.209.193
36 bound-to interface X1
37 auth-method shared-secret
38 shared-secret PRE-SHARED-KEY-IN-PLAIN-TEXT
39 ike-id local ip your_customer_gateway_IP_address
40 ike-id peer ip 72.21.209.193
41 end
42
43 ![\[Image NOT FOUND\]](http://docs.aws.amazon.com/AmazonVPC/latest/NetworkAdminGuide/images/
      IPsec.png)
44 ! #2: IPSec Configuration
45 !
46 ! The IPSec (Phase 2) proposal defines the protocol, authentication,
47 ! encryption, and lifetime parameters for our IPSec security association.
48 ! Please note, you may use these additionally supported IPSec parameters for encryption like
      AES256 and other DH groups like 2, 5, 14-18, 22, 23, and 24.
49 !
50 config
51 proposal ipsec lifetime 3600
52 proposal ipsec authentication sha1
53 proposal ipsec encryption aes128
54 proposal ipsec perfect-forward-secrecy dh-group 2
55 proposal ipsec protocol ESP
56 keep-alive
57 enable
58 commit
59 end
```

```
60  !
61  ! You can use other supported IPSec parameters for encryption such as AES256, and other DH
       groups such as 1,2, 5, 14-18, 22, 23, and 24.
62
63  ! IPSec Dead Peer Detection (DPD) will be enabled on the AWS Endpoint. We
64  ! recommend configuring DPD on your endpoint as follows:
65  !  - DPD Interval            : 120
66  !  - DPD Retries             : 3
67  ! To configure Dead Peer Detection for the SonicWall device, use the SonicOS management
       interface.
68  !
69  ![\[Image NOT FOUND\]](http://docs.aws.amazon.com/AmazonVPC/latest/NetworkAdminGuide/images/
       Tunnel.png)
70  ! #3: Tunnel Interface Configuration
71  !
72  ! The tunnel interface is configured with the internal IP address.
73  !
74  ! To establish connectivity between your internal network and the VPC, you
75  ! must have an interface facing your internal network in the "Trust" zone.
76  !
77  !
78  config
79  tunnel-interface vpn T1
80  ip-assignment VPN static
81  ip 169.254.255.6 netmask 255.255.255.252
82  exit
83  !
84  !
85  ! #4 Static Route Configuration
86  !
87  ! Create a firewall policy permitting traffic from your local subnet to the VPC subnet and vice
       versa
88  ! This example policy permits all traffic from the local subnet to the VPC through the tunnel
       interface.
89  !
90  !
91  policy interface T1 metric 1 source any destination name AWSVPC service any gateway
       169.254.255.5
92  !
93  IPSec Tunnel !2
94  ================================================================================
95  ![\[Image NOT FOUND\]](http://docs.aws.amazon.com/AmazonVPC/latest/NetworkAdminGuide/images/IKE.
       png)
96  ! #1: Internet Key Exchange (IKE) Configuration
97  !
98  ! These sample configurations are for the minimum requirement of AES128, SHA1, and DH Group 2.
99  ! You can modify these sample configuration files to use AES128, SHA1, AES256, SHA256, or other
       DH groups like 2, 14-18, 22, 23, and 24.
100 ! The address of the external interface for your customer gateway must be a static address.
101 ! Your customer gateway may reside behind a device performing network address translation (NAT).
102 ! To ensure that NAT traversal (NAT-T) can function, you must adjust your firewall rules to
       unblock UDP port 4500. If not behind NAT, we recommend disabling NAT-T.
103 !
104 config
```

```
105 address-object ipv4 AWSVPC network 172.30.0.0/16
106 vpn policy tunnel-interface vpn-44a8938f-2
107 gateway primary 72.21.209.225
108 bound-to interface X1
109 auth-method shared-secret
110 shared-secret PRE-SHARED-KEY-IN-PLAIN-TEXT
111 ike-id local ip your_customer_gateway_IP_address
112 ike-id peer ip 72.21.209.225
113 end
114 !
115 ![\[Image NOT FOUND\]](http://docs.aws.amazon.com/AmazonVPC/latest/NetworkAdminGuide/images/
        IPsec.png)
116 ! #2: IPSec Configuration
117 !
118 ! The IPSec (Phase 2) proposal defines the protocol, authentication,
119 ! encryption, and lifetime parameters for our IPSec security association.
120 ! Please note, you may use these additionally supported IPSec parameters for encryption like
        AES256 and other DH groups like 2, 5, 14-18, 22, 23, and 24.
121 !
122 config
123 proposal ipsec lifetime 3600
124 proposal ipsec authentication sha1
125 proposal ipsec encryption aes128
126 proposal ipsec perfect-forward-secrecy dh-group 2
127 proposal ipsec protocol ESP
128 keep-alive
129 enable
130 commit
131 end
132 !
133 ! You can use other supported IPSec parameters for encryption such as AES256, and other DH
        groups such as 1,2, 5, 14-18, 22, 23, and 24.
134 !
135 ! IPSec Dead Peer Detection (DPD) will be enabled on the AWS Endpoint. We
136 ! recommend configuring DPD on your endpoint as follows:
137 !   - DPD Interval            : 120
138 !   - DPD Retries             : 3
139 ! To configure Dead Peer Detection for the SonicWall device, use the SonicOS management
        interface.
140 !
141 ![\[Image NOT FOUND\]](http://docs.aws.amazon.com/AmazonVPC/latest/NetworkAdminGuide/images/
        Tunnel.png)
142 ! #3: Tunnel Interface Configuration
143 !
144 ! The tunnel interface is configured with the internal IP address.
145 !
146 ! To establish connectivity between your internal network and the VPC, you
147 ! must have an interface facing your internal network in the "Trust" zone.
148 !
149 !
150 config
151 tunnel-interface vpn T2
152 ip-assignment VPN static
153 ip 169.254.255.2 netmask 255.255.255.252
```

```
154 !
155 ! #4 Static Route Configuration
156 !
157 ! Create a firewall policy permitting traffic from your local subnet to the VPC subnet and vice
        versa
158 ! This example policy permits all traffic from the local subnet to the VPC through the tunnel
        interface.
159 !
160 !
161 policy interface T2 metric 1 source any destination name AWSVPC service any gateway
        169.254.255.1
```

Configuring the SonicWALL Device Using the Management Interface

The following procedure demonstrates how to configure the VPN tunnels on the SonicWALL device using the SonicOS management interface. You must replace the example values in the procedures with the values that are provided in the configuration file.

To configure the tunnels

1. Open the SonicWALL SonicOS management interface.

2. In the left pane, choose **VPN**, **Settings**. Under **VPN Policies**, choose **Add....**

3. In the VPN policy window on the **General ** tab, complete the following information:
   - **Policy Type**: Choose **Site to Site**.
   - **Authentication Method**: Choose **IKE using Preshared Secret**.
   - **Name**: Enter a name for the VPN policy. We recommend that you use the name of the VPN ID, as provided in the configuration file.
   - **IPsec Primary Gateway Name or Address**: Enter the IP address of the virtual private gateway (AWS endpoint) as provided in the configuration file; for example, 72.21.209.193.
   - **IPsec Secondary Gateway Name or Address**: Leave the default value.
   - **Shared Secret**: Enter the pre-shared key as provided in the configuration file, and enter it again in **Confirm Shared Secret**.
   - **Local IKE ID**: Enter the IPv4 address of the customer gateway (the SonicWALL device).
   - **Peer IKE ID**: Enter the IPv4 address of the virtual private gateway (AWS endpoint).

4. On the **Network** tab, complete the following information:
   - Under **Local Networks**, choose **Any address**. We recommend this option to prevent connectivity issues from your local network.
   - Under **Remote Networks**, choose **Choose a destination network from list**. Create an address object with the CIDR of your VPC in AWS.

5. On the **Proposals** tab, complete the following information.
   - Under **IKE (Phase 1) Proposal**, do the following:
     - **Exchange**: Choose **Main Mode**.
     - **DH Group**: Enter a value for the Diffie-Hellman group; for example, 2.
     - **Encryption**: Choose **AES-128** or **AES-256**.
     - **Authentication**: Choose **SHA1** or **SHA256**.
     - **Life Time**: Enter 28800.
   - Under **IKE (Phase 2) Proposal**, do the following:
     - **Protocol**: Choose **ESP**.
     - **Encryption**: Choose **AES-128** or **AES-256**.
     - **Authentication**: Choose **SHA1** or **SHA256**.
     - Select the **Enable Perfect Forward Secrecy** check box, and choose the Diffie-Hellman group.

- **Life Time**: Enter 3600. **Important**
  If you created your virtual private gateway before October 2015, you must specify Diffie-Hellman group 2, AES-128, and SHA1 for both phases.

6. On the **Advanced** tab, complete the following information:

   - Select **Enable Keep Alive**.
   - Select **Enable Phase2 Dead Peer Detection** and enter the following:
     - For **Dead Peer Detection Interval**, enter 60 (this is the minimum that the SonicWALL device accepts).
     - For **Failure Trigger Level**, enter 3.
   - For **VPN Policy bound to**, select **Interface X1**. This is the interface that's typically designated for public IP addresses.

7. Choose **OK**. On the **Settings** page, the **Enable** check box for the tunnel should be selected by default. A green dot indicates that the tunnel is up.

How to Test the Customer Gateway Configuration

You must first test the gateway configuration for each tunnel.

To test the customer gateway configuration for each tunnel

- On your customer gateway, verify that you have added a static route to the VPC CIDR IP space to use the tunnel interface.

Next, you must test the connectivity for each tunnel by launching an instance into your VPC and pinging the instance from your home network. Before you begin, make sure of the following:

- Use an AMI that responds to ping requests. We recommend that you use one of the Amazon Linux AMIs.
- Configure your instance's security group and network ACL to enable inbound ICMP traffic.
- Ensure that you have configured routing for your VPN connection; your subnet's route table must contain a route to the virtual private gateway. For more information, see Enable Route Propagation in Your Route Table in the *Amazon VPC User Guide*.

To test the end-to-end connectivity of each tunnel

1. Launch an instance of one of the Amazon Linux AMIs into your VPC. The Amazon Linux AMIs are available in the **Quick Start** menu when you use the Launch Instances wizard in the AWS Management Console. For more information, see the Amazon VPC Getting Started Guide.

2. After the instance is running, get its private IP address (for example, 10.0.0.4). The console displays the address as part of the instance's details.

3. On a system in your home network, use the ping command with the instance's IP address. Make sure that the computer you ping from is behind the customer gateway. A successful response should be similar to the following:

```
1 ping 10.0.0.4

1 Pinging 10.0.0.4 with 32 bytes of data:
2
3 Reply from 10.0.0.4: bytes=32 time<1ms TTL=128
4 Reply from 10.0.0.4: bytes=32 time<1ms TTL=128
5 Reply from 10.0.0.4: bytes=32 time<1ms TTL=128
6
7 Ping statistics for 10.0.0.4:
8 Packets: Sent = 3, Received = 3, Lost = 0 (0% loss),
9
10 Approximate round trip times in milliseconds:
```

11 Minimum = 0ms, Maximum = 0ms, Average = 0ms

Note

If you ping an instance from your customer gateway router, ensure that you are sourcing ping messages from an internal IP address, not a tunnel IP address. Some AMIs don't respond to ping messages from tunnel IP addresses.

If your tunnels don't test successfully, see Troubleshooting Generic Device Customer Gateway Connectivity Using Border Gateway Protocol.

Example: Fortinet Fortigate Device

Topics

- A High-Level View of the Customer Gateway
- A Detailed View of the Customer Gateway and an Example Configuration
- How to Test the Customer Gateway Configuration

The following topic provides example configuration information provided by your integration team if your customer gateway is a Fortinet Fortigate 40+ device.

Two diagrams illustrate the example configuration. The first diagram shows the high-level layout of the customer gateway, and the second diagram shows the details of the example configuration. You should use the real configuration information that you receive from your integration team and apply it to your customer gateway.

A High-Level View of the Customer Gateway

The following diagram shows the general details of your customer gateway. Note that the VPN connection consists of two separate tunnels. Using redundant tunnels ensures continuous availability in the case that a device fails.

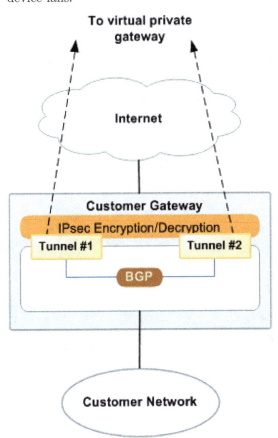

A Detailed View of the Customer Gateway and an Example Configuration

The diagram in this section illustrates an example Fortinet customer gateway. Following the diagram, there is a corresponding example of the configuration information your integration team should provide. The example

configuration contains a set of information for each of the tunnels that you must configure.

In addition, the example configuration refers to these items that you must provide:

- *YOUR_UPLINK_ADDRESS*—The IP address for the Internet-routable external interface on the customer gateway (which must be static, and may be behind a device performing network address translation (NAT).
- *YOUR_BGP_ASN*—The customer gateway's BGP ASN (we use 65000 by default)

The example configuration includes several example values to help you understand how configuration works. For example, we provide example values for the VPN connection ID (vpn-44a8938f), virtual private gateway ID (vgw-8db04f81), the IP addresses (72.21.209.*, 169.254.255.*), and the remote ASN (7224). You'll replace these example values with the actual values from the configuration information that you receive.

In the following diagram and example configuration, you must replace the items in red italics with values that apply to your particular configuration.

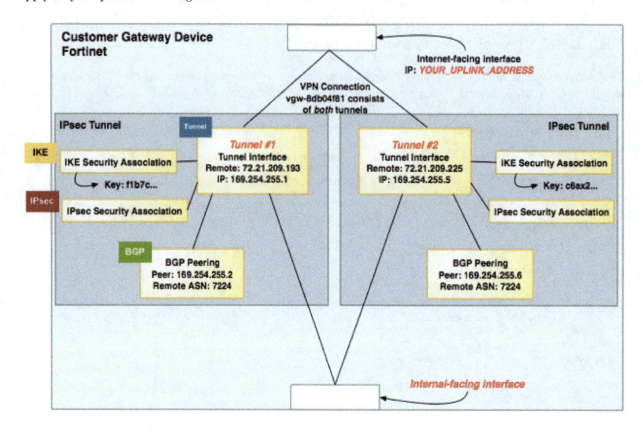

Warning

The following configuration information is an example of what you can expect your integration team to provide. Many of the values in the following example will be different from the actual configuration information that you receive. You must use the actual values and not the example values shown here, or your implementation will fail.

```
1  ! Amazon Web Services
2  ! Virtual Private Cloud
3
4  ! AWS utilizes unique identifiers to manipulate the configuration of
5  ! a VPN Connection. Each VPN Connection is assigned an identifier and is
6  ! associated with two other identifiers, namely the
7  ! Customer Gateway Identifier and Virtual Private Gateway Identifier.
8  !
9  ! Your VPN Connection ID          : vpn-44a8938f
10 ! Your Virtual Private Gateway ID           : vgw-8db04f81
```

```
11 ! Your Customer Gateway ID        : cgw-b4dc3961
12 !
13 !
14 ! This configuration consists of two tunnels. Both tunnels must be
15 ! configured on your Customer Gateway.
16 !
17 ! -------------------------------------------------------------------------
18 ! IPSec Tunnel #1
19 ! -------------------------------------------------------------------------
20
21 ![\[Image NOT FOUND\]](http://docs.aws.amazon.com/AmazonVPC/latest/NetworkAdminGuide/images/IKE.
      png)
22
23 ! #1: Internet Key Exchange (IKE) Configuration
24 !
25 ! A policy is established for the supported ISAKMP encryption,
26 ! authentication, Diffie-Hellman, lifetime, and key parameters.
27 ! Please note, these sample configurations are for the minimum requirement of AES128, SHA1, and
      DH Group 2.
28 ! You will need to modify these sample configuration files to take advantage of AES256, SHA256,
      or other DH groups like 2, 14-18, 22, 23, and 24.
29 !
30 ! The address of the external interface for your customer gateway must be a static address.
31 ! Your customer gateway may reside behind a device performing network address translation (NAT).
32 ! To ensure that NAT traversal (NAT-T) can function, you must adjust your firewall rules to
      unblock UDP port 4500. If not behind NAT, we recommend disabling NAT-T.
33 !
34 ! Configuration begins in root VDOM.
35 config vpn ipsec phase1-interface
36 edit vpn-44a8938f-0 ! Name must be shorter than 15 chars, best if shorter than 12
37   set interface "wan1"
38
39 ! The IPSec Dead Peer Detection causes periodic messages to be
40 ! sent to ensure a Security Association remains operational
41
42   set dpd enable
43   set local-gw YOUR_UPLINK_ADDRESS
44   set dhgrp 2
45   set proposal aes128-sha1
46   set keylife 28800
47   set remote-gw 72.21.209.193
48   set psksecret plain-text-password1
49   set dpd-retryinterval 10
50  next
51 end
52
53
54 ![\[Image NOT FOUND\]](http://docs.aws.amazon.com/AmazonVPC/latest/NetworkAdminGuide/images/
      IPsec.png)
55 ! #2: IPSec Configuration
56 !
57 ! The IPSec transform set defines the encryption, authentication, and IPSec
58 ! mode parameters.
59 !
```

```
60  ! Please note, you may use these additionally supported IPSec parameters for encryption like
        AES256 and other DH groups like 2, 5, 14-18, 22, 23, and 24.
61
62  config vpn ipsec phase2-interface
63   edit "vpn-44a8938f-0"
64     set phase1name "vpn-44a8938f-0"
65     set proposal aes128-sha1
66     set dhgrp 2
67     set keylifeseconds 3600
68   next
69
70
71  ![\[Image NOT FOUND\]](http://docs.aws.amazon.com/AmazonVPC/latest/NetworkAdminGuide/images/
        Tunnel.png)
72
73  ! -------------------------------------------------------------------------------
74  ! #3: Tunnel Interface Configuration
75  !
76  ! A tunnel interface is configured to be the logical interface associated
77  ! with the tunnel. All traffic routed to the tunnel interface will be
78  ! encrypted and transmitted to the VPC. Similarly, traffic from the VPC
79  ! will be logically received on this interface.
80  !
81  !
82  ! The address of the interface is configured with the setup for your
83  ! Customer Gateway.  If the address changes, the Customer Gateway and VPN
84  ! Connection must be recreated with Amazon VPC.
85  !
86
87
88  config system interface
89   edit "vpn-44a8938f-0"
90     set vdom "root"
91     set ip 169.254.255.2 255.255.255.255
92     set allowaccess ping
93     set type tunnel
94
95  !   This option causes the router to reduce the Maximum Segment Size of
96  !   TCP packets to prevent packet fragmentation.
97  !
98     set tcp-mss 1387
99     set remote-ip 169.254.255.1
100    set mtu 1427
101    set interface "wan1"
102  next
103
104
105 ![\[Image NOT FOUND\]](http://docs.aws.amazon.com/AmazonVPC/latest/NetworkAdminGuide/images/BGP.
        png)
106
107 ! -------------------------------------------------------------------------------
108
109 ! #4: Border Gateway Protocol (BGP) Configuration
110 !
```

```
111 ! BGP is used within the tunnel to exchange prefixes between the
112 ! Virtual Private Gateway and your Customer Gateway. The Virtual Private Gateway
113 ! will announce the prefix corresponding to your VPC.
114 !
115 !
116 !
117 ! The local BGP Autonomous System Number (ASN) (YOUR_BGP_ASN)
118 ! is configured as part of your Customer Gateway. If the ASN must
119 ! be changed, the Customer Gateway and VPN Connection will need to be recreated with AWS.
120 !
121
122 config router bgp
123  set as YOUR_BGP_ASN
124  config neighbor
125   edit 169.254.255.1
126    set remote-as 7224
127   end
128
129
130
131 ! Your Customer Gateway may announce a default route (0.0.0.0/0) to us.
132 ! This is done using prefix list and route-map in Fortigate.
133
134 config router bgp
135  config neighbor
136   edit 169.254.255.1
137    set capability-default-originate enable
138   end
139  end
140
141 config router prefix-list
142  edit "default_route"
143   config rule
144    edit 1
145     set prefix 0.0.0.0 0.0.0.0
146    next
147   end
148  set router-id YOUR_UPLINK_ADDRESS
149 end
150
151 config router route-map
152  edit "routemap1"
153   config rule
154    edit 1
155     set match-ip-address "default_route"
156    next
157   end
158  next
159 end
160
161
162
163 ! To advertise additional prefixes to Amazon VPC, add these prefixes to the 'network'
164 ! statement and identify the prefix you wish to advertise. Make sure the prefix is present
```

```
165 ! in the routing table of the device with a valid next-hop. If you want to advertise
166 ! 192.168.0.0/16 to Amazon, this can be done using the following:
167
168
169 config router bgp
170 config network
171  edit 1
172   set prefix 192.168.0.0 255.255.0.0
173  next
174 end
175 set router-id YOUR_UPLINK_ADDRESS
176 end
177
178 ! --------------------------------------------------------------------------------
179 ! #5 Firewall Policy Configuration
180 !
181 ! Create a firewall policy permitting traffic from your local subnet to the VPC subnet and vice
        versa
182 !
183 ! This example policy permits all traffic from the local subnet to the VPC
184 ! First, find the policies that exist
185
186 show firewall policy
187
188 ! Next, create a new firewall policy starting with the next available policy ID. If policies 1,
        2, 3, and 4 were shown, then in this example the policy created starts 5
189
190 config firewall policy
191 edit 5
192 set srcintf "vpn-44a8938f-0"
193 set dstintf internal
194  set srcaddr all
195  set dstaddr all
196 set action accept
197 set schedule always
198  set service ANY
199 next
200 end
201
202 config firewall policy
203 edit 5
204 set srcintf internal
205 set dstintf "vpn-44a8938f-0"
206  set srcaddr all
207  set dstaddr all
208 set action accept
209 set schedule always
210  set service ANY
211 next
212 end
213
214
215
216 ![\[Image NOT FOUND\]](http://docs.aws.amazon.com/AmazonVPC/latest/NetworkAdminGuide/images/IKE.
```

```
           png)
217
218  ! -------------------------------------------------------------------------
219  ! IPSec Tunnel #2
220  ! -------------------------------------------------------------------------
221  ! #1: Internet Key Exchange (IKE) Configuration
222  !
223  ! A policy is established for the supported ISAKMP encryption,
224  ! authentication, Diffie-Hellman, lifetime, and key parameters.
225  !
226  ! The address of the external interface for your customer gateway must be a static address.
227  ! Your customer gateway may reside behind a device performing network address translation (NAT).
228  ! To ensure that NAT traversal (NAT-T) can function, you must adjust your firewall rules to
           unblock UDP port 4500. If not behind NAT, we recommend disabling NAT-T.
229  !
230  ! Configuration begins in root VDOM.
231  config vpn ipsec phase1-interface
232  edit vpn-44a8938f-1 ! Name must be shorter than 15 chars, best if shorter than 12
233    set interface "wan1"
234
235  ! The IPSec Dead Peer Detection causes periodic messages to be
236  ! sent to ensure a Security Association remains operational
237
238    set dpd enable
239    set local-gw YOUR_UPLINK_ADDRESS
240    set dhgrp 2
241    set proposal aes128-sha1
242    set keylife 28800
243    set remote-gw 72.21.209.225
244    set psksecret plain-text-password2
245    set dpd-retryinterval 10
246  next
247  end
248
249  ![\[Image NOT FOUND\]](http://docs.aws.amazon.com/AmazonVPC/latest/NetworkAdminGuide/images/
        IPsec.png)
250
251  ! #2: IPSec Configuration
252  !
253  ! The IPSec transform set defines the encryption, authentication, and IPSec
254  ! mode parameters.
255  !
256  ! Please note, you may use these additionally supported IPSec parameters for encryption like
           AES256 and other DH groups like 2, 5, 14-18, 22, 23, and 24.
257
258  config vpn ipsec phase2-interface
259   edit "vpn-44a8938f-1"
260    set phase1name "vpn-44a8938f-1"
261    set proposal aes128-sha1
262    set dhgrp 2
263    set keylifeseconds 3600
264  next
265
266  ![\[Image NOT FOUND\]](http://docs.aws.amazon.com/AmazonVPC/latest/NetworkAdminGuide/images/
```

```
        Tunnel.png)
267
268 ! --------------------------------------------------------------------------------
269 ! #3: Tunnel Interface Configuration
270 !
271 ! A tunnel interface is configured to be the logical interface associated
272 ! with the tunnel. All traffic routed to the tunnel interface will be
273 ! encrypted and transmitted to the VPC. Similarly, traffic from the VPC
274 ! will be logically received on this interface.
275 !
276 !
277 ! The address of the interface is configured with the setup for your
278 ! Customer Gateway.  If the address changes, the Customer Gateway and VPN
279 ! Connection must be recreated with Amazon VPC.
280 !
281
282
283 config system interface
284   edit "vpn-44a8938f-1"
285     set vdom "root"
286     set ip 169.254.255.6 255.255.255.255
287     set allowaccess ping
288     set type tunnel
289
290 !  This option causes the router to reduce the Maximum Segment Size of
291 !  TCP packets to prevent packet fragmentation.
292 !
293     set tcp-mss 1387
294     set remote-ip 169.254.255.5
295     set mtu 1427
296     set interface "wan1"
297   next
298
299
300 ![\[Image NOT FOUND\]](http://docs.aws.amazon.com/AmazonVPC/latest/NetworkAdminGuide/images/BGP.
      png)
301
302 ! --------------------------------------------------------------------------------
303
304 ! #4: Border Gateway Protocol (BGP) Configuration
305 !
306 ! BGP is used within the tunnel to exchange prefixes between the
307 ! Virtual Private Gateway and your Customer Gateway. The Virtual Private Gateway
308 ! will announce the prefix corresponding to your VPC.
309 !
310 !
311 !
312 ! The local BGP Autonomous System Number (ASN) (YOUR_BGP_ASN)
313 ! is configured as part of your Customer Gateway. If the ASN must
314 ! be changed, the Customer Gateway and VPN Connection will need to be recreated with AWS.
315 !
316
317 config router bgp
318   set as YOUR_BGP_ASN
```

```
319  config neighbor
320    edit 169.254.255.5
321      set remote-as 7224
322    end
323
324
325
326  ! Your Customer Gateway may announce a default route (0.0.0.0/0) to us.
327  ! This is done using prefix list and route-map in Fortigate.
328
329  config router bgp
330   config neighbor
331    edit 169.254.255.5
332      set capability-default-originate enable
333     end
334   end
335
336  config router prefix-list
337   edit "default_route"
338    config rule
339      edit 1
340        set prefix 0.0.0.0 0.0.0.0
341      next
342     end
343    set router-id YOUR_UPLINK_ADDRESS
344  end
345
346  config router route-map
347   edit "routemap1"
348    config rule
349      edit 1
350        set match-ip-address "default_route"
351      next
352     end
353   next
354  end
355
356
357
358  ! To advertise additional prefixes to Amazon VPC, add these prefixes to the 'network'
359  ! statement and identify the prefix you wish to advertise. Make sure the prefix is present
360  ! in the routing table of the device with a valid next-hop. If you want to advertise
361  ! 192.168.0.0/16 to Amazon, this can be done using the following:
362
363
364  config router bgp
365   config network
366    edit 1
367      set prefix 192.168.0.0 255.255.0.0
368    next
369   end
370   set router-id YOUR_UPLINK_ADDRESS
371  end
372
```

```
373  !
374  ! -----------------------------------------------------------------------
375  ! #5 Firewall Policy Configuration
376  !
377  ! Create a firewall policy permitting traffic from your local subnet to the VPC subnet and vice
         versa
378  !
379  ! This example policy permits all traffic from the local subnet to the VPC
380  ! First, find the policies that exist
381
382  show firewall policy
383
384  ! Next, create a new firewall policy starting with the next available policy ID. If policies 1,
         2, 3, and 4 were shown, then in this example the policy created starts 5
385
386  config firewall policy
387  edit 5
388  set srcintf "vpn-44a8938f-1"
389  set dstintf internal
390   set srcaddr all
391   set dstaddr all
392  set action accept
393  set schedule always
394   set service ANY
395  next
396  end
397
398  config firewall policy
399  edit 5
400  set srcintf internal
401  set dstintf "vpn-44a8938f-1"
402   set srcaddr all
403   set dstaddr all
404  set action accept
405  set schedule always
406   set service ANY
407  next
408  end
409
410  ! -----------------------------------------------------------------------
```

How to Test the Customer Gateway Configuration

You can test the gateway configuration for each tunnel.

To test the customer gateway configuration for each tunnel

1. On your customer gateway, determine whether the BGP status is Active.

   It takes approximately 30 seconds for a BGP peering to become active.

2. Ensure that the customer gateway is advertising a route to the virtual private gateway. The route may be the default route (0.0.0.0/0) or a more specific route you prefer.

When properly established, your BGP peering should be receiving one route from the virtual private gateway corresponding to the prefix that your VPC integration team specified for the VPC (for example, 10.0.0.0/24).

If the BGP peering is established, you are receiving a prefix, and you are advertising a prefix, your tunnel is configured correctly. Make sure that both tunnels are in this state.

Next you must test the connectivity for each tunnel by launching an instance into your VPC, and pinging the instance from your home network. Before you begin, make sure of the following:

- Use an AMI that responds to ping requests. We recommend that you use one of the Amazon Linux AMIs.
- Configure your instance's security group and network ACL to enable inbound ICMP traffic.
- Ensure that you have configured routing for your VPN connection: your subnet's route table must contain a route to the virtual private gateway. For more information, see Enable Route Propagation in Your Route Table in the *Amazon VPC User Guide*.

To test the end-to-end connectivity of each tunnel

1. Launch an instance of one of the Amazon Linux AMIs into your VPC. The Amazon Linux AMIs are listed in the launch wizard when you launch an instance from the Amazon EC2 Console. For more information, see the Amazon VPC Getting Started Guide.

2. After the instance is running, get its private IP address (for example, 10.0.0.4). The console displays the address as part of the instance's details.

3. On a system in your home network, use the ping command with the instance's IP address. Make sure that the computer you ping from is behind the customer gateway. A successful response should be similar to the following.

```
1 ping 10.0.0.4
```

```
1 Pinging 10.0.0.4 with 32 bytes of data:
2
3 Reply from 10.0.0.4: bytes=32 time<1ms TTL=128
4 Reply from 10.0.0.4: bytes=32 time<1ms TTL=128
5 Reply from 10.0.0.4: bytes=32 time<1ms TTL=128
6
7 Ping statistics for 10.0.0.4:
8 Packets: Sent = 3, Received = 3, Lost = 0 (0% loss),
9
10 Approximate round trip times in milliseconds:
11 Minimum = 0ms, Maximum = 0ms, Average = 0ms
```

Note
If you ping an instance from your customer gateway router, ensure that you are sourcing ping messages from an internal IP address, not a tunnel IP address. Some AMIs don't respond to ping messages from tunnel IP addresses.

1. (Optional) To test tunnel failover, you can temporarily disable one of the tunnels on your customer gateway, and repeat the above step. You cannot disable a tunnel on the AWS side of the VPN connection.

Example: Juniper J-Series JunOS Device

Topics

- A High-Level View of the Customer Gateway
- A Detailed View of the Customer Gateway and an Example Configuration
- How to Test the Customer Gateway Configuration

In this section we walk you through an example of the configuration information provided by your integration team if your customer gateway is a Juniper J-Series router running JunOS 9.5 (or later) software.

Two diagrams illustrate the example configuration. The first diagram shows the high-level layout of the customer gateway, and the second diagram shows details from the example configuration. You should use the real configuration information that you receive from your integration team and apply it to your customer gateway.

A High-Level View of the Customer Gateway

The following diagram shows the general details of your customer gateway. Note that the VPN connection consists of two separate tunnels. Using redundant tunnels ensures continuous availability in the case that a device fails.

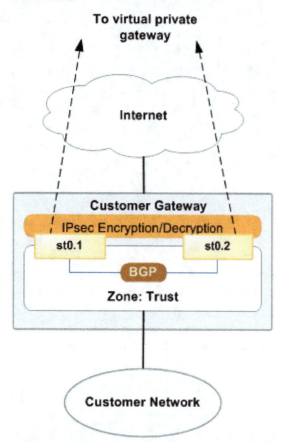

A Detailed View of the Customer Gateway and an Example Configuration

The diagram in this section illustrates an example Juniper JunOS customer gateway. Following the diagram, there is a corresponding example of the configuration information your integration team should provide. The example configuration contains a set of information for each of the tunnels that you must configure.

In addition, the example configuration refers to these items that you must provide:

- *YOUR_UPLINK_ADDRESS*—The IP address for the Internet-routable external interface on the customer gateway. The address must be static, and may be behind a device performing network address translation (NAT). To ensure that NAT traversal (NAT-T) can function, you must adjust your firewall rules to unblock UDP port 4500.
- *YOUR_BGP_ASN*—The customer gateway's BGP ASN (we use 65000 by default)

The example configuration includes several example values to help you understand how configuration works. For example, we provide example values for the VPN connection ID (vpn-44a8938f), virtual private gateway ID (vgw-8db04f81), the IP addresses (72.21.209.*, 169.254.255.*), and the remote ASN (7224). You'll replace these example values with the actual values from the configuration information that you receive.

In addition, you must:

- Configure the outside interface (referred to as *ge-0/0/0.0* in the example configuration).
- Configure the tunnel interface IDs (referred to as *st0.1* and *st0.2* in the example configuration).
- Configure all internal routing that moves traffic between the customer gateway and your local network.
- Identify the security zone for the uplink interface (the following configuration information uses the default "untrust" zone).
- Identify the security zone for the inside interface (the following configuration information uses the default "trust" zone).

In the following diagram and example configuration, you must replace the items in red italics with values that apply to your particular configuration.

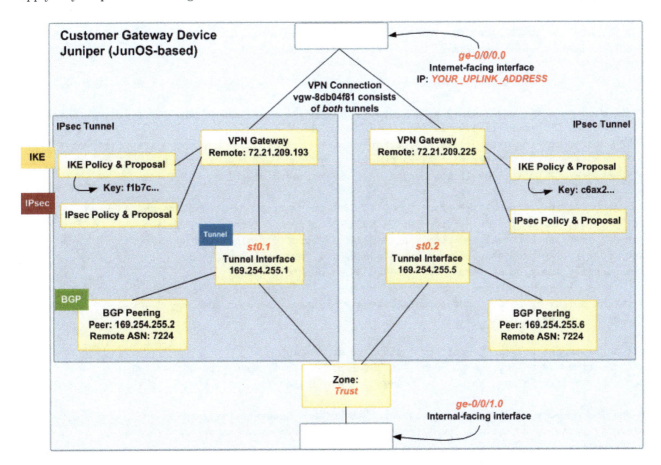

Warning

109

The following configuration information is an example of what you can expect your integration team to provide. Many of the values in the following example will be different from the actual configuration information that you receive. You must use the actual values and not the example values shown here, or your implementation will fail.

```
1  # Amazon Web Services
2  # Virtual Private Cloud
3  #
4  # AWS utilizes unique identifiers to manipulate the configuration of
5  # a VPN Connection. Each VPN Connection is assigned a VPN Connection
6  # Identifier and is associated with two other identifiers, namely the
7  # Customer Gateway Identifier and the Virtual Private Gateway Identifier.
8  #
9  # Your VPN Connection ID            : vpn-44a8938f
10 # Your Virtual Private Gateway ID : vgw-8db04f81
11 # Your Customer Gateway ID        : cgw-b4dc3961
12 #
13 # This configuration consists of two tunnels. Both tunnels must be
14 # configured on your Customer Gateway.
15 #
16 # --------------------------------------------------------------------
17 # IPsec Tunnel #1
18 # --------------------------------------------------------------------
19 ![\[Image NOT FOUND\]](http://docs.aws.amazon.com/AmazonVPC/latest/NetworkAdminGuide/images/IKE.
     png)
20 # #1: Internet Key Exchange (IKE) Configuration
21 #
22 # A proposal is established for the supported IKE encryption,
23 # authentication, Diffie-Hellman, and lifetime parameters.
24 #
25 # Please note, these sample configurations are for the minimum requirement of AES128, SHA1, and
     DH Group 2.
26 # You will need to modify these sample configuration files to take advantage of AES256, SHA256,
     or other DH groups like 2, 14-18, 22, 23, and 24.
27 # The address of the external interface for your customer gateway must be a static address.
28 # To ensure that NAT traversal (NAT-T) can function, you must adjust your firewall rules to
     unblock UDP port 4500. If not behind NAT, we recommend disabling NAT-T.
29 #
30 set security ike proposal ike-prop-vpn-44a8938f-1 authentication-method pre-shared-keys
31 set security ike proposal ike-prop-vpn-44a8938f-1 authentication-algorithm sha1
32 set security ike proposal ike-prop-vpn-44a8938f-1 encryption-algorithm aes-128-cbc
33 set security ike proposal ike-prop-vpn-44a8938f-1 lifetime-seconds 28800
34 set security ike proposal ike-prop-vpn-44a8938f-1 dh-group group2
35
36 # An IKE policy is established to associate a Pre Shared Key with the
37 # defined proposal.
38 #
39 set security ike policy ike-pol-vpn-44a8938f-1 mode main
40 set security ike policy ike-pol-vpn-44a8938f-1 proposals ike-prop-vpn-44a8938f-0
41 set security ike policy ike-pol-vpn-44a8938f-1 pre-shared-key ascii-text plain-text-password1
42
43 # The IKE gateway is defined to be the Virtual Private Gateway. The gateway
44 # configuration associates a local interface, remote IP address, and
45 # IKE policy.
46 #
47 # This example shows the outside of the tunnel as interface ge-0/0/0.0.
```

```
48 # This should be set to the interface that IP address YOUR_UPLINK_ADDRESS is
49 # associated with.
50 # This address is configured with the setup for your Customer Gateway.
51 #
52 # If the address changes, the Customer Gateway and VPN Connection must
53 # be recreated.
54 set security ike gateway gw-vpn-44a8938f-1 ike-policy ike-pol-vpn-44a8938f-0
55 set security ike gateway gw-vpn-44a8938f-1 external-interface ge-0/0/0.0
56 set security ike gateway gw-vpn-44a8938f-1 address 72.21.209.225
57
58 # Troubleshooting IKE connectivity can be aided by enabling IKE tracing.
59 # The configuration below will cause the router to log IKE messages to
60 # the 'kmd' log. Run 'show messages kmd' to retrieve these logs.
61 # set security ike traceoptions file kmd
62 # set security ike traceoptions file size 1024768
63 # set security ike traceoptions file files 10
64 # set security ike traceoptions flag all
65
66 ![\[Image NOT FOUND\]](http://docs.aws.amazon.com/AmazonVPC/latest/NetworkAdminGuide/images/
       IPsec.png)
67 # #2: IPsec Configuration
68 #
69 # The IPsec proposal defines the protocol, authentication, encryption, and
70 # lifetime parameters for our IPsec security association.
71 # Please note, you may use these additionally supported IPSec parameters for encryption like
       AES256 and other DH groups like 2, 5, 14-18, 22, 23, and 24.
72 #
73 set security ipsec proposal ipsec-prop-vpn-44a8938f-1 protocol esp
74 set security ipsec proposal ipsec-prop-vpn-44a8938f-1 authentication-algorithm hmac-sha1-96
75 set security ipsec proposal ipsec-prop-vpn-44a8938f-1 encryption-algorithm aes-128-cbc
76 set security ipsec proposal ipsec-prop-vpn-44a8938f-1 lifetime-seconds 3600
77
78 # The IPsec policy incorporates the Diffie-Hellman group and the IPsec
79 # proposal.
80 #
81 set security ipsec policy ipsec-pol-vpn-44a8938f-1 perfect-forward-secrecy keys group2
82 set security ipsec policy ipsec-pol-vpn-44a8938f-1 proposals ipsec-prop-vpn-44a8938f-0
83
84 # A security association is defined here. The IPsec Policy and IKE gateways
85 # are associated with a tunnel interface (st0.1).
86 # The tunnel interface ID is assumed; if other tunnels are defined on
87 # your router, you will need to specify a unique interface name
88 # (for example, st0.10).
89 #
90 set security ipsec vpn vpn-44a8938f-1 bind-interface st0.1
91 set security ipsec vpn vpn-44a8938f-1 ike gateway gw-vpn-44a8938f-0
92 set security ipsec vpn vpn-44a8938f-1 ike ipsec-policy ipsec-pol-vpn-44a8938f-0
93 set security ipsec vpn vpn-44a8938f-1 df-bit clear
94
95 # This option enables IPsec Dead Peer Detection, which causes periodic
96 # messages to be sent to ensure a Security Association remains operational.
97 #
98 set security ike gateway gw-vpn-44a8938f-1 dead-peer-detection
99
```

```
100 ![\[Image NOT FOUND\]](http://docs.aws.amazon.com/AmazonVPC/latest/NetworkAdminGuide/images/
        Tunnel.png)
101 # #3: Tunnel Interface Configuration
102 #
103
104 # The tunnel interface is configured with the internal IP address.
105 #
106 set interfaces st0.1 family inet address 169.254.255.2/30
107 set interfaces st0.1 family inet mtu 1436
108 set security zones security-zone trust interfaces st0.1
109
110 # The security zone protecting external interfaces of the router must be
111 # configured to allow IKE traffic inbound.
112 #
113 set security zones security-zone untrust host-inbound-traffic system-services ike
114
115 # The security zone protecting internal interfaces (including the logical
116 # tunnel interfaces) must be configured to allow BGP traffic inbound.
117 #
118 set security zones security-zone trust host-inbound-traffic protocols bgp
119
120 # This option causes the router to reduce the Maximum Segment Size of
121 # TCP packets to prevent packet fragmentation.
122 #
123 set security flow tcp-mss ipsec-vpn mss 1387
124
125 ![\[Image NOT FOUND\]](http://docs.aws.amazon.com/AmazonVPC/latest/NetworkAdminGuide/images/BGP.
        png)
126 # #4: Border Gateway Protocol (BGP) Configuration
127 #
128 # BGP is used within the tunnel to exchange prefixes between the
129 # Virtual Private Gateway and your Customer Gateway. The Virtual Private Gateway
130 # will announce the prefix corresponding to your VPC.
131 #
132 # Your Customer Gateway may announce a default route (0.0.0.0/0),
133 # which can be done with the EXPORT-DEFAULT policy.
134 #
135 # To advertise additional prefixes to Amazon VPC, add additional prefixes to the "default" term
136 # EXPORT-DEFAULT policy. Make sure the prefix is present in the routing table of the device with
137 # a valid next-hop.
138 #
139 # The BGP timers are adjusted to provide more rapid detection of outages.
140 #
141 # The local BGP Autonomous System Number (ASN) (YOUR_BGP_ASN) is configured
142 # as part of your Customer Gateway. If the ASN must be changed, the
143 # Customer Gateway and VPN Connection will need to be recreated with AWS.
144 #
145 # We establish a basic route policy to export a default route to the
146 # Virtual Private Gateway.
147 #
148 set policy-options policy-statement EXPORT-DEFAULT term default from route-filter 0.0.0.0/0
        exact
149 set policy-options policy-statement EXPORT-DEFAULT term default then accept
150 set policy-options policy-statement EXPORT-DEFAULT term reject then reject
```

```
151
152 set protocols bgp group ebgp type external
153
154 set protocols bgp group ebgp neighbor 169.254.255.1 export EXPORT-DEFAULT
155 set protocols bgp group ebgp neighbor 169.254.255.1 peer-as 7224
156 set protocols bgp group ebgp neighbor 169.254.255.1 hold-time 30
157 set protocols bgp group ebgp neighbor 169.254.255.1 local-as YOUR_BGP_ASN
158
159 # -------------------------------------------------------------------------
160 # IPsec Tunnel #2
161 # -------------------------------------------------------------------------
162 ![\[Image NOT FOUND\]](http://docs.aws.amazon.com/AmazonVPC/latest/NetworkAdminGuide/images/IKE.
       png)
163 # #1: Internet Key Exchange (IKE) Configuration
164 #
165 # A proposal is established for the supported IKE encryption,
166 # authentication, Diffie-Hellman, and lifetime parameters.
167 # Please note, these sample configurations are for the minimum requirement of AES128, SHA1, and
       DH Group 2.
168 # You will need to modify these sample configuration files to take advantage of AES256, SHA256,
       or other DH groups like 2, 14-18, 22, 23, and 24.
169 # The address of the external interface for your customer gateway must be a static address.
170 # To ensure that NAT traversal (NAT-T) can function, you must adjust your firewall rules to
       unblock UDP port 4500. If not behind NAT, we recommend disabling NAT-T.
171 #
172 set security ike proposal ike-prop-vpn-44a8938f-2 authentication-method pre-shared-keys
173 set security ike proposal ike-prop-vpn-44a8938f-2 authentication-algorithm sha1
174 set security ike proposal ike-prop-vpn-44a8938f-2 encryption-algorithm aes-128-cbc
175 set security ike proposal ike-prop-vpn-44a8938f-2 lifetime-seconds 28800
176 set security ike proposal ike-prop-vpn-44a8938f-2 dh-group group2
177
178 # An IKE policy is established to associate a Pre Shared Key with the
179 # defined proposal.
180 #
181 set security ike policy ike-pol-vpn-44a8938f-2 mode main
182 set security ike policy ike-pol-vpn-44a8938f-2 proposals ike-prop-vpn-44a8938f-2
183 set security ike policy ike-pol-vpn-44a8938f-2 pre-shared-key ascii-text plain-text-password2
184
185 # The IKE gateway is defined to be the Virtual Private Gateway. The gateway
186 # configuration associates a local interface, remote IP address, and
187 # IKE policy.
188 #
189 # This example shows the outside of the tunnel as interface ge-0/0/0.0.
190 # This should be set to the interface that IP address YOUR_UPLINK_ADDRESS is
191 # associated with.
192 # This address is configured with the setup for your Customer Gateway.
193 #
194 # If the address changes, the Customer Gateway and VPN Connection must be recreated.
195 #
196 set security ike gateway gw-vpn-44a8938f-2 ike-policy ike-pol-vpn-44a8938f-1
197 set security ike gateway gw-vpn-44a8938f-2 external-interface ge-0/0/0.0
198 set security ike gateway gw-vpn-44a8938f-2 address 72.21.209.193
199
200 # Troubleshooting IKE connectivity can be aided by enabling IKE tracing.
```

```
201  # The configuration below will cause the router to log IKE messages to
202  # the 'kmd' log. Run 'show messages kmd' to retrieve these logs.
203  # set security ike traceoptions file kmd
204  # set security ike traceoptions file size 1024768
205  # set security ike traceoptions file files 10
206  # set security ike traceoptions flag all
207
208  ![\[Image NOT FOUND\]](http://docs.aws.amazon.com/AmazonVPC/latest/NetworkAdminGuide/images/
         IPsec.png)
209  # #2: IPsec Configuration
210  #
211  # The IPsec proposal defines the protocol, authentication, encryption, and
212  # lifetime parameters for our IPsec security association.
213  # Please note, you may use these additionally supported IPSec parameters for encryption like
         AES256 and other DH groups like 2, 5, 14-18, 22, 23, and 24.
214  #
215  set security ipsec proposal ipsec-prop-vpn-44a8938f-2 protocol esp
216  set security ipsec proposal ipsec-prop-vpn-44a8938f-2 authentication-algorithm hmac-sha1-96
217  set security ipsec proposal ipsec-prop-vpn-44a8938f-2 encryption-algorithm aes-128-cbc
218  set security ipsec proposal ipsec-prop-vpn-44a8938f-2 lifetime-seconds 3600
219
220  # The IPsec policy incorporates the Diffie-Hellman group and the IPsec
221  # proposal.
222  #
223  set security ipsec policy ipsec-pol-vpn-44a8938f-2 perfect-forward-secrecy keys group2
224  set security ipsec policy ipsec-pol-vpn-44a8938f-2 proposals ipsec-prop-vpn-44a8938f-2
225
226  # A security association is defined here. The IPsec Policy and IKE gateways
227  # are associated with a tunnel interface (st0.2).
228  # The tunnel interface ID is assumed; if other tunnels are defined on
229  # your router, you will need to specify a unique interface name
230  # (for example, st0.20).
231  #
232  set security ipsec vpn vpn-44a8938f-2 bind-interface st0.2
233  set security ipsec vpn vpn-44a8938f-2 ike gateway gw-vpn-44a8938f-2
234  set security ipsec vpn vpn-44a8938f-2 ike ipsec-policy ipsec-pol-vpn-44a8938f-2
235  set security ipsec vpn vpn-44a8938f-2 df-bit clear
236
237  # This option enables IPsec Dead Peer Detection, which causes periodic
238  # messages to be sent to ensure a Security Association remains operational.
239  #
240  set security ike gateway gw-vpn-44a8938f-2 dead-peer-detection
241
242  ![\[Image NOT FOUND\]](http://docs.aws.amazon.com/AmazonVPC/latest/NetworkAdminGuide/images/
         Tunnel.png)
243  # #3: Tunnel Interface Configuration
244  #
245
246  # The tunnel interface is configured with the internal IP address.
247  #
248  set interfaces st0.2 family inet address 169.254.255.6/30
249  set interfaces st0.2 family inet mtu 1436
250  set security zones security-zone trust interfaces st0.2
251
```

```
252 # The security zone protecting external interfaces of the router must be
253 # configured to allow IKE traffic inbound.
254 #
255 set security zones security-zone untrust host-inbound-traffic system-services ike
256
257 # The security zone protecting internal interfaces (including the logical
258 # tunnel interfaces) must be configured to allow BGP traffic inbound.
259 #
260 set security zones security-zone trust host-inbound-traffic protocols bgp
261
262 # This option causes the router to reduce the Maximum Segment Size of
263 # TCP packets to prevent packet fragmentation.
264 #
265 set security flow tcp-mss ipsec-vpn mss 1387
266
267 ![\[Image NOT FOUND\]](http://docs.aws.amazon.com/AmazonVPC/latest/NetworkAdminGuide/images/BGP.
       png)
268 # #4: Border Gateway Protocol (BGP) Configuration
269 #
270 # BGP is used within the tunnel to exchange prefixes between the
271 # Virtual Private Gateway and your Customer Gateway. The Virtual Private Gateway
272 # will announce the prefix corresponding to your VPC.
273 #
274 # Your Customer Gateway may announce a default route (0.0.0.0/0),
275 # which can be done with the EXPORT-DEFAULT policy.
276 #
277 # To advertise additional prefixes to Amazon VPC, add additional prefixes to the "default" term
278 # EXPORT-DEFAULT policy. Make sure the prefix is present in the routing table of the device with
279 # a valid next-hop.
280 #
281 # The BGP timers are adjusted to provide more rapid detection of outages.
282 #
283 # The local BGP Autonomous System Number (ASN) (YOUR_BGP_ASN) is configured
284 # as part of your Customer Gateway. If the ASN must be changed, the
285 # Customer Gateway and VPN Connection will need to be recreated with AWS.
286 #
287 # We establish a basic route policy to export a default route to the
288 # Virtual Private Gateway.
289 #
290 set policy-options policy-statement EXPORT-DEFAULT term default from route-filter 0.0.0.0/0
       exact
291 set policy-options policy-statement EXPORT-DEFAULT term default then accept
292 set policy-options policy-statement EXPORT-DEFAULT term reject then reject
293
294 set protocols bgp group ebgp type external
295
296 set protocols bgp group ebgp neighbor 169.254.255.5 export EXPORT-DEFAULT
297 set protocols bgp group ebgp neighbor 169.254.255.5 peer-as 7224
298 set protocols bgp group ebgp neighbor 169.254.255.5 hold-time 30
299 set protocols bgp group ebgp neighbor 169.254.255.5 local-as YOUR_BGP_ASN
```

How to Test the Customer Gateway Configuration

You can test the gateway configuration for each tunnel.

To test the customer gateway configuration for each tunnel

1. On your customer gateway, determine whether the BGP status is `Active`.

   It takes approximately 30 seconds for a BGP peering to become active.

2. Ensure that the customer gateway is advertising a route to the virtual private gateway. The route may be the default route (`0.0.0.0/0`) or a more specific route you prefer.

When properly established, your BGP peering should be receiving one route from the virtual private gateway corresponding to the prefix that your VPC integration team specified for the VPC (for example, `10.0.0.0/24`). If the BGP peering is established, you are receiving a prefix, and you are advertising a prefix, your tunnel is configured correctly. Make sure that both tunnels are in this state.

Next you must test the connectivity for each tunnel by launching an instance into your VPC, and pinging the instance from your home network. Before you begin, make sure of the following:

- Use an AMI that responds to ping requests. We recommend that you use one of the Amazon Linux AMIs.
- Configure your instance's security group and network ACL to enable inbound ICMP traffic.
- Ensure that you have configured routing for your VPN connection: your subnet's route table must contain a route to the virtual private gateway. For more information, see Enable Route Propagation in Your Route Table in the *Amazon VPC User Guide*.

To test the end-to-end connectivity of each tunnel

1. Launch an instance of one of the Amazon Linux AMIs into your VPC. The Amazon Linux AMIs are listed in the launch wizard when you launch an instance from the Amazon EC2 Console. For more information, see the Amazon VPC Getting Started Guide.

2. After the instance is running, get its private IP address (for example, `10.0.0.4`). The console displays the address as part of the instance's details.

3. On a system in your home network, use the ping command with the instance's IP address. Make sure that the computer you ping from is behind the customer gateway. A successful response should be similar to the following.

```
1 ping 10.0.0.4
```

```
1 Pinging 10.0.0.4 with 32 bytes of data:
2
3 Reply from 10.0.0.4: bytes=32 time<1ms TTL=128
4 Reply from 10.0.0.4: bytes=32 time<1ms TTL=128
5 Reply from 10.0.0.4: bytes=32 time<1ms TTL=128
6
7 Ping statistics for 10.0.0.4:
8 Packets: Sent = 3, Received = 3, Lost = 0 (0% loss),
9
10 Approximate round trip times in milliseconds:
11 Minimum = 0ms, Maximum = 0ms, Average = 0ms
```

Note

If you ping an instance from your customer gateway router, ensure that you are sourcing ping messages from an internal IP address, not a tunnel IP address. Some AMIs don't respond to ping messages from tunnel IP addresses.

1. (Optional) To test tunnel failover, you can temporarily disable one of the tunnels on your customer gateway, and repeat the above step. You cannot disable a tunnel on the AWS side of the VPN connection.

If your tunnels don't test successfully, see Troubleshooting Juniper JunOS Customer Gateway Connectivity.

Example: Juniper SRX JunOS Device

Topics

- A High-Level View of the Customer Gateway
- A Detailed View of the Customer Gateway and an Example Configuration
- How to Test the Customer Gateway Configuration

In this section we walk you through an example of the configuration information provided by your integration team if your customer gateway is a Juniper SRX router running JunOS 11.0 (or later) software.

Two diagrams illustrate the example configuration. The first diagram shows the high-level layout of the customer gateway, and the second diagram shows details from the example configuration. You should use the real configuration information that you receive from your integration team and apply it to your customer gateway.

A High-Level View of the Customer Gateway

The following diagram shows the general details of your customer gateway. Note that the VPN connection consists of two separate tunnels. Using redundant tunnels ensures continuous availability in the case that a device fails.

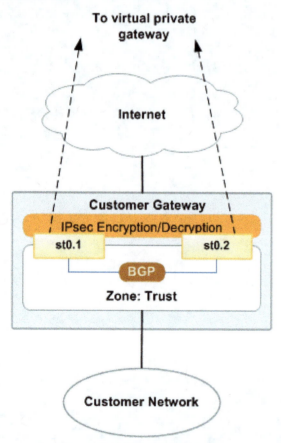

A Detailed View of the Customer Gateway and an Example Configuration

The diagram in this section illustrates an example Juniper JunOS 11.0+ customer gateway. Following the diagram, there is a corresponding example of the configuration information your integration team should provide.

The example configuration contains a set of information for each of the tunnels that you must configure.

In addition, the example configuration refers to these items that you must provide:

- *YOUR_UPLINK_ADDRESS*—The IP address for the Internet-routable external interface on the customer gateway. The address must be static, and may be behind a device performing network address translation (NAT). To ensure that NAT traversal (NAT-T) can function, you must adjust your firewall rules to unblock UDP port 4500.
- *YOUR_BGP_ASN*—The customer gateway's BGP ASN (we use 65000 by default)

The example configuration includes several example values to help you understand how configuration works. For example, we provide example values for the VPN connection ID (vpn-44a8938f), virtual private gateway ID (vgw-8db04f81), the IP addresses (72.21.209.*, 169.254.255.*), and the remote ASN (7224). You'll replace these example values with the actual values from the configuration information that you receive.

In addition, you must:

- Configure the outside interface (referred to as *ge-0/0/0.0* in the example configuration).
- Configure the tunnel interface IDs (referred to as *st0.1* and *st0.2* in the example configuration).
- Configure all internal routing that moves traffic between the customer gateway and your local network.
- Identify the security zone for the uplink interface (the following configuration information uses the default "untrust" zone).
- Identify the security zone for the inside interface (the following configuration information uses the default "trust" zone).

In the following diagram and example configuration, you must replace the items in red italics with values that apply to your particular configuration.

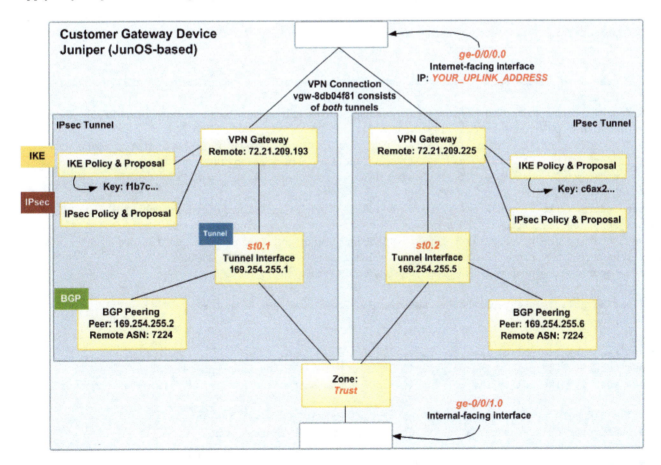

Warning

119

The following configuration information is an example of what you can expect your integration team to provide. Many of the values in the following example will be different from the actual configuration information that you receive. You must use the actual values and not the example values shown here, or your implementation will fail.

```
1  # Amazon Web Services
2  # Virtual Private Cloud
3  #
4  # AWS utilizes unique identifiers to manipulate the configuration of
5  # a VPN Connection. Each VPN Connection is assigned a VPN Connection
6  # Identifier and is associated with two other identifiers, namely the
7  # Customer Gateway Identifier and the Virtual Private Gateway Identifier.
8  #
9  # Your VPN Connection ID          : vpn-44a8938f
10 # Your Virtual Private Gateway ID : vgw-8db04f81
11 # Your Customer Gateway ID        : cgw-b4dc3961
12 #
13 # This configuration consists of two tunnels. Both tunnels must be
14 # configured on your Customer Gateway.
15 #
16 # --------------------------------------------------------------------
17 # IPsec Tunnel #1
18 # --------------------------------------------------------------------
19 ![\[Image NOT FOUND\]](http://docs.aws.amazon.com/AmazonVPC/latest/NetworkAdminGuide/images/IKE.
      png)
20 # #1: Internet Key Exchange (IKE) Configuration
21 #
22 # A proposal is established for the supported IKE encryption,
23 # authentication, Diffie-Hellman, and lifetime parameters.
24 #
25 # Please note, these sample configurations are for the minimum requirement of AES128, SHA1, and
      DH Group 2.
26 # You will need to modify these sample configuration files to take advantage of AES256, SHA256,
      or other DH groups like 2, 14-18, 22, 23, and 24.
27 # The address of the external interface for your customer gateway must be a static address.
28 # To ensure that NAT traversal (NAT-T) can function, you must adjust your firewall rules to
      unblock UDP port 4500. If not behind NAT, we recommend disabling NAT-T.
29 #
30 set security ike proposal ike-prop-vpn-44a8938f-1 authentication-method pre-shared-keys
31 set security ike proposal ike-prop-vpn-44a8938f-1 authentication-algorithm sha1
32 set security ike proposal ike-prop-vpn-44a8938f-1 encryption-algorithm aes-128-cbc
33 set security ike proposal ike-prop-vpn-44a8938f-1 lifetime-seconds 28800
34 set security ike proposal ike-prop-vpn-44a8938f-1 dh-group group2
35
36 # An IKE policy is established to associate a Pre Shared Key with the
37 # defined proposal.
38 #
39 set security ike policy ike-pol-vpn-44a8938f-1 mode main
40 set security ike policy ike-pol-vpn-44a8938f-1 proposals ike-prop-vpn-44a8938f-1
41 set security ike policy ike-pol-vpn-44a8938f-1 pre-shared-key ascii-text plain-text-password1
42
43 # The IKE gateway is defined to be the Virtual Private Gateway. The gateway
44 # configuration associates a local interface, remote IP address, and
45 # IKE policy.
46 #
47 # This example shows the outside of the tunnel as interface ge-0/0/0.0.
```

```
48 # This should be set to the interface that IP address YOUR_UPLINK_ADDRESS is
49 # associated with.
50 # This address is configured with the setup for your Customer Gateway.
51 #
52 # If the address changes, the Customer Gateway and VPN Connection must
53 # be recreated.
54 set security ike gateway gw-vpn-44a8938f-1 ike-policy ike-pol-vpn-44a8938f-1
55 set security ike gateway gw-vpn-44a8938f-1 external-interface ge-0/0/0.0
56 set security ike gateway gw-vpn-44a8938f-1 address 72.21.209.225
57 set security ike gateway gw-vpn-44a8938f-1 no-nat-traversal
58
59 # Troubleshooting IKE connectivity can be aided by enabling IKE tracing.
60 # The configuration below will cause the router to log IKE messages to
61 # the 'kmd' log. Run 'show messages kmd' to retrieve these logs.
62 # set security ike traceoptions file kmd
63 # set security ike traceoptions file size 1024768
64 # set security ike traceoptions file files 10
65 # set security ike traceoptions flag all
66
67 ![\[Image NOT FOUND\]](http://docs.aws.amazon.com/AmazonVPC/latest/NetworkAdminGuide/images/
      IPsec.png)
68 # #2: IPsec Configuration
69 #
70 # The IPsec proposal defines the protocol, authentication, encryption, and
71 # lifetime parameters for our IPsec security association.
72 # Please note, you may use these additionally supported IPSec parameters for encryption like
      AES256 and other DH groups like 2, 5, 14-18, 22, 23, and 24.
73 #
74 set security ipsec proposal ipsec-prop-vpn-44a8938f-1 protocol esp
75 set security ipsec proposal ipsec-prop-vpn-44a8938f-1 authentication-algorithm hmac-sha1-96
76 set security ipsec proposal ipsec-prop-vpn-44a8938f-1 encryption-algorithm aes-128-cbc
77 set security ipsec proposal ipsec-prop-vpn-44a8938f-1 lifetime-seconds 3600
78
79 # The IPsec policy incorporates the Diffie-Hellman group and the IPsec
80 # proposal.
81 #
82 set security ipsec policy ipsec-pol-vpn-44a8938f-1 perfect-forward-secrecy keys group2
83 set security ipsec policy ipsec-pol-vpn-44a8938f-1 proposals ipsec-prop-vpn-44a8938f-1
84
85 # A security association is defined here. The IPsec Policy and IKE gateways
86 # are associated with a tunnel interface (st0.1).
87 # The tunnel interface ID is assumed; if other tunnels are defined on
88 # your router, you will need to specify a unique interface name
89 # (for example, st0.10).
90 #
91 set security ipsec vpn vpn-44a8938f-1 bind-interface st0.1
92 set security ipsec vpn vpn-44a8938f-1 ike gateway gw-vpn-44a8938f-1
93 set security ipsec vpn vpn-44a8938f-1 ike ipsec-policy ipsec-pol-vpn-44a8938f-1
94 set security ipsec vpn vpn-44a8938f-1 df-bit clear
95
96 # This option enables IPsec Dead Peer Detection, which causes periodic
97 # messages to be sent to ensure a Security Association remains operational.
98 #
99 set security ike gateway gw-vpn-44a8938f-1 dead-peer-detection
```

```
100
101 ![\[Image NOT FOUND\]](http://docs.aws.amazon.com/AmazonVPC/latest/NetworkAdminGuide/images/
       Tunnel.png)
102 # #3: Tunnel Interface Configuration
103 #
104
105 # The tunnel interface is configured with the internal IP address.
106 #
107 set interfaces st0.1 family inet address 169.254.255.2/30
108 set interfaces st0.1 family inet mtu 1436
109 set security zones security-zone trust interfaces st0.1
110
111 # The security zone protecting external interfaces of the router must be
112 # configured to allow IKE traffic inbound.
113 #
114 set security zones security-zone untrust host-inbound-traffic system-services ike
115
116 # The security zone protecting internal interfaces (including the logical
117 # tunnel interfaces) must be configured to allow BGP traffic inbound.
118 #
119 set security zones security-zone trust host-inbound-traffic protocols bgp
120
121 # This option causes the router to reduce the Maximum Segment Size of
122 # TCP packets to prevent packet fragmentation.
123 #
124 set security flow tcp-mss ipsec-vpn mss 1387
125
126 ![\[Image NOT FOUND\]](http://docs.aws.amazon.com/AmazonVPC/latest/NetworkAdminGuide/images/BGP.
       png)
127 # #4: Border Gateway Protocol (BGP) Configuration
128 #
129 # BGP is used within the tunnel to exchange prefixes between the
130 # Virtual Private Gateway and your Customer Gateway. The Virtual Private Gateway
131 # will announce the prefix corresponding to your VPC.
132 #
133 # Your Customer Gateway may announce a default route (0.0.0.0/0),
134 # which can be done with the EXPORT-DEFAULT policy.
135 #
136 # To advertise additional prefixes to Amazon VPC, add additional prefixes to the "default" term
137 # EXPORT-DEFAULT policy. Make sure the prefix is present in the routing table of the device with
138 # a valid next-hop.
139 #
140 # The BGP timers are adjusted to provide more rapid detection of outages.
141 #
142 # The local BGP Autonomous System Number (ASN) (YOUR_BGP_ASN) is configured
143 # as part of your Customer Gateway. If the ASN must be changed, the
144 # Customer Gateway and VPN Connection will need to be recreated with AWS.
145 #
146 # We establish a basic route policy to export a default route to the
147 # Virtual Private Gateway.
148 #
149 set policy-options policy-statement EXPORT-DEFAULT term default from route-filter 0.0.0.0/0
       exact
150 set policy-options policy-statement EXPORT-DEFAULT term default then accept
```

```
151 set policy-options policy-statement EXPORT-DEFAULT term reject then reject
152
153 set protocols bgp group ebgp type external
154
155 set protocols bgp group ebgp neighbor 169.254.255.1 export EXPORT-DEFAULT
156 set protocols bgp group ebgp neighbor 169.254.255.1 peer-as 7224
157 set protocols bgp group ebgp neighbor 169.254.255.1 hold-time 30
158 set protocols bgp group ebgp neighbor 169.254.255.1 local-as YOUR_BGP_ASN
159
160 # --------------------------------------------------------------------------
161 # IPsec Tunnel #2
162 # --------------------------------------------------------------------------
163 ![\[Image NOT FOUND\]](http://docs.aws.amazon.com/AmazonVPC/latest/NetworkAdminGuide/images/IKE.
      png)
164 # #1: Internet Key Exchange (IKE) Configuration
165 #
166 # A proposal is established for the supported IKE encryption,
167 # authentication, Diffie-Hellman, and lifetime parameters.
168 # Please note, these sample configurations are for the minimum requirement of AES128, SHA1, and
      DH Group 2.
169 # You will need to modify these sample configuration files to take advantage of AES256, SHA256,
      or other DH groups like 2, 14-18, 22, 23, and 24.
170 # The address of the external interface for your customer gateway must be a static address.
171 # To ensure that NAT traversal (NAT-T) can function, you must adjust your firewall rules to
      unblock UDP port 4500. If not behind NAT, we recommend disabling NAT-T.
172 #
173 set security ike proposal ike-prop-vpn-44a8938f-2 authentication-method pre-shared-keys
174 set security ike proposal ike-prop-vpn-44a8938f-2 authentication-algorithm sha1
175 set security ike proposal ike-prop-vpn-44a8938f-2 encryption-algorithm aes-128-cbc
176 set security ike proposal ike-prop-vpn-44a8938f-2 lifetime-seconds 28800
177 set security ike proposal ike-prop-vpn-44a8938f-2 dh-group group2
178
179 # An IKE policy is established to associate a Pre Shared Key with the
180 # defined proposal.
181 #
182 set security ike policy ike-pol-vpn-44a8938f-2 mode main
183 set security ike policy ike-pol-vpn-44a8938f-2 proposals ike-prop-vpn-44a8938f-2
184 set security ike policy ike-pol-vpn-44a8938f-2 pre-shared-key ascii-text plain-text-password2
185
186 # The IKE gateway is defined to be the Virtual Private Gateway. The gateway
187 # configuration associates a local interface, remote IP address, and
188 # IKE policy.
189 #
190 # This example shows the outside of the tunnel as interface ge-0/0/0.0.
191 # This should be set to the interface that IP address YOUR_UPLINK_ADDRESS is
192 # associated with.
193 # This address is configured with the setup for your Customer Gateway.
194 #
195 # If the address changes, the Customer Gateway and VPN Connection must be recreated.
196 #
197 set security ike gateway gw-vpn-44a8938f-2 ike-policy ike-pol-vpn-44a8938f-2
198 set security ike gateway gw-vpn-44a8938f-2 external-interface ge-0/0/0.0
199 set security ike gateway gw-vpn-44a8938f-2 address 72.21.209.193
200 set security ike gateway gw-vpn-44a8938f-2 no-nat-traversal
```

```
201
202 # Troubleshooting IKE connectivity can be aided by enabling IKE tracing.
203 # The configuration below will cause the router to log IKE messages to
204 # the 'kmd' log. Run 'show messages kmd' to retrieve these logs.
205 # set security ike traceoptions file kmd
206 # set security ike traceoptions file size 1024768
207 # set security ike traceoptions file files 10
208 # set security ike traceoptions flag all
209
210 ![\[Image NOT FOUND\]](http://docs.aws.amazon.com/AmazonVPC/latest/NetworkAdminGuide/images/
       IPsec.png)
211 # #2: IPsec Configuration
212 #
213 # The IPsec proposal defines the protocol, authentication, encryption, and
214 # lifetime parameters for our IPsec security association.
215 # Please note, you may use these additionally supported IPSec parameters for encryption like
       AES256 and other DH groups like 2, 5, 14-18, 22, 23, and 24.
216 #
217 set security ipsec proposal ipsec-prop-vpn-44a8938f-2 protocol esp
218 set security ipsec proposal ipsec-prop-vpn-44a8938f-2 authentication-algorithm hmac-sha1-96
219 set security ipsec proposal ipsec-prop-vpn-44a8938f-2 encryption-algorithm aes-128-cbc
220 set security ipsec proposal ipsec-prop-vpn-44a8938f-2 lifetime-seconds 3600
221
222 # The IPsec policy incorporates the Diffie-Hellman group and the IPsec
223 # proposal.
224 #
225 set security ipsec policy ipsec-pol-vpn-44a8938f-2 perfect-forward-secrecy keys group2
226 set security ipsec policy ipsec-pol-vpn-44a8938f-2 proposals ipsec-prop-vpn-44a8938f-2
227
228 # A security association is defined here. The IPsec Policy and IKE gateways
229 # are associated with a tunnel interface (st0.2).
230 # The tunnel interface ID is assumed; if other tunnels are defined on
231 # your router, you will need to specify a unique interface name
232 # (for example, st0.20).
233 #
234 set security ipsec vpn vpn-44a8938f-2 bind-interface st0.2
235 set security ipsec vpn vpn-44a8938f-2 ike gateway gw-vpn-44a8938f-2
236 set security ipsec vpn vpn-44a8938f-2 ike ipsec-policy ipsec-pol-vpn-44a8938f-2
237 set security ipsec vpn vpn-44a8938f-2 df-bit clear
238
239 # This option enables IPsec Dead Peer Detection, which causes periodic
240 # messages to be sent to ensure a Security Association remains operational.
241 #
242 set security ike gateway gw-vpn-44a8938f-2 dead-peer-detection
243
244 ![\[Image NOT FOUND\]](http://docs.aws.amazon.com/AmazonVPC/latest/NetworkAdminGuide/images/
       Tunnel.png)
245 # #3: Tunnel Interface Configuration
246 #
247
248 # The tunnel interface is configured with the internal IP address.
249 #
250 set interfaces st0.2 family inet address 169.254.255.6/30
251 set interfaces st0.2 family inet mtu 1436
```

```
252 set security zones security-zone trust interfaces st0.2
253
254 # The security zone protecting external interfaces of the router must be
255 # configured to allow IKE traffic inbound.
256 #
257 set security zones security-zone untrust host-inbound-traffic system-services ike
258
259 # The security zone protecting internal interfaces (including the logical
260 # tunnel interfaces) must be configured to allow BGP traffic inbound.
261 #
262 set security zones security-zone trust host-inbound-traffic protocols bgp
263
264 # This option causes the router to reduce the Maximum Segment Size of
265 # TCP packets to prevent packet fragmentation.
266 #
267 set security flow tcp-mss ipsec-vpn mss 1387
268
269 ![\[Image NOT FOUND\]](http://docs.aws.amazon.com/AmazonVPC/latest/NetworkAdminGuide/images/BGP.
        png)
270 # #4: Border Gateway Protocol (BGP) Configuration
271 #
272 # BGP is used within the tunnel to exchange prefixes between the
273 # Virtual Private Gateway and your Customer Gateway. The Virtual Private Gateway
274 # will announce the prefix corresponding to your VPC.
275 #
276 # Your Customer Gateway may announce a default route (0.0.0.0/0),
277 # which can be done with the EXPORT-DEFAULT policy.
278 #
279 # To advertise additional prefixes to Amazon VPC, add additional prefixes to the "default" term
280 # EXPORT-DEFAULT policy. Make sure the prefix is present in the routing table of the device with
281 # a valid next-hop.
282 #
283 # The BGP timers are adjusted to provide more rapid detection of outages.
284 #
285 # The local BGP Autonomous System Number (ASN) (YOUR_BGP_ASN) is configured
286 # as part of your Customer Gateway. If the ASN must be changed, the
287 # Customer Gateway and VPN Connection will need to be recreated with AWS.
288 #
289 # We establish a basic route policy to export a default route to the
290 # Virtual Private Gateway.
291 #
292 set policy-options policy-statement EXPORT-DEFAULT term default from route-filter 0.0.0.0/0
        exact
293 set policy-options policy-statement EXPORT-DEFAULT term default then accept
294 set policy-options policy-statement EXPORT-DEFAULT term reject then reject
295
296 set protocols bgp group ebgp type external
297
298 set protocols bgp group ebgp neighbor 169.254.255.5 export EXPORT-DEFAULT
299 set protocols bgp group ebgp neighbor 169.254.255.5 peer-as 7224
300 set protocols bgp group ebgp neighbor 169.254.255.5 hold-time 30
301 set protocols bgp group ebgp neighbor 169.254.255.5 local-as YOUR_BGP_ASN
```

How to Test the Customer Gateway Configuration

You can test the gateway configuration for each tunnel.

To test the customer gateway configuration for each tunnel

1. On your customer gateway, determine whether the BGP status is `Active`.

   It takes approximately 30 seconds for a BGP peering to become active.

2. Ensure that the customer gateway is advertising a route to the virtual private gateway. The route may be the default route (`0.0.0.0/0`) or a more specific route you prefer.

When properly established, your BGP peering should be receiving one route from the virtual private gateway corresponding to the prefix that your VPC integration team specified for the VPC (for example, `10.0.0.0/24`). If the BGP peering is established, you are receiving a prefix, and you are advertising a prefix, your tunnel is configured correctly. Make sure that both tunnels are in this state.

Next you must test the connectivity for each tunnel by launching an instance into your VPC, and pinging the instance from your home network. Before you begin, make sure of the following:

- Use an AMI that responds to ping requests. We recommend that you use one of the Amazon Linux AMIs.
- Configure your instance's security group and network ACL to enable inbound ICMP traffic.
- Ensure that you have configured routing for your VPN connection: your subnet's route table must contain a route to the virtual private gateway. For more information, see Enable Route Propagation in Your Route Table in the *Amazon VPC User Guide*.

To test the end-to-end connectivity of each tunnel

1. Launch an instance of one of the Amazon Linux AMIs into your VPC. The Amazon Linux AMIs are listed in the launch wizard when you launch an instance from the Amazon EC2 Console. For more information, see the Amazon VPC Getting Started Guide.

2. After the instance is running, get its private IP address (for example, `10.0.0.4`). The console displays the address as part of the instance's details.

3. On a system in your home network, use the ping command with the instance's IP address. Make sure that the computer you ping from is behind the customer gateway. A successful response should be similar to the following.

```
1 ping 10.0.0.4
```

```
 1 Pinging 10.0.0.4 with 32 bytes of data:
 2
 3 Reply from 10.0.0.4: bytes=32 time<1ms TTL=128
 4 Reply from 10.0.0.4: bytes=32 time<1ms TTL=128
 5 Reply from 10.0.0.4: bytes=32 time<1ms TTL=128
 6
 7 Ping statistics for 10.0.0.4:
 8 Packets: Sent = 3, Received = 3, Lost = 0 (0% loss),
 9
10 Approximate round trip times in milliseconds:
11 Minimum = 0ms, Maximum = 0ms, Average = 0ms
```

Note
If you ping an instance from your customer gateway router, ensure that you are sourcing ping messages from an internal IP address, not a tunnel IP address. Some AMIs don't respond to ping messages from tunnel IP addresses.

1. (Optional) To test tunnel failover, you can temporarily disable one of the tunnels on your customer gateway, and repeat the above step. You cannot disable a tunnel on the AWS side of the VPN connection.

If your tunnels don't test successfully, see Troubleshooting Juniper JunOS Customer Gateway Connectivity.

Example: Juniper ScreenOS Device

Topics

- A High-Level View of the Customer Gateway
- A Detailed View of the Customer Gateway and an Example Configuration
- How to Test the Customer Gateway Configuration

In this section we walk you through an example of the configuration information provided by your integration team if your customer gateway is a Juniper SSG or Netscreen series device running Juniper ScreenOS software.

Two diagrams illustrate the example configuration. The first diagram shows the high-level layout of the customer gateway, and the second diagram shows details from the example configuration. You should use the real configuration information that you receive from your integration team and apply it to your customer gateway.

A High-Level View of the Customer Gateway

The following diagram shows the general details of your customer gateway. Note that the VPN connection consists of two separate tunnels. Using redundant tunnels ensures continuous availability in the case that a device fails.

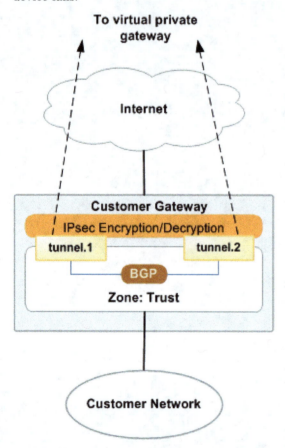

A Detailed View of the Customer Gateway and an Example Configuration

The diagram in this section illustrates an example Juniper ScreenOS customer gateway. Following the diagram, there is a corresponding example of the configuration information your integration team should provide. The

128

example configuration contains information for each of the tunnels that you must configure.

In addition, the example configuration refers to these items that you must provide:

- *YOUR_UPLINK_ADDRESS*—The IP address for the Internet-routable external interface on the customer gateway. The address must be static, and may be behind a device performing network address translation (NAT). To ensure that NAT traversal (NAT-T) can function, you must adjust your firewall rules to unblock UDP port 4500.
- *YOUR_BGP_ASN*—The customer gateway's BGP ASN (we use 65000 by default)

The example configuration includes several example values to help you understand how configuration works. For example, we provide example values for the VPN connection ID (vpn-44a8938f), virtual private gateway ID (vgw-8db04f81), the IP addresses (72.21.209.*, 169.254.255.*), and the remote ASN (7224). You'll replace these example values with the actual values from the configuration information that you receive.

In addition, you must:

- Configure the outside interface (referred to as *ethernet0/0* in the example configuration).
- Configure the tunnel interface IDs (referred to as *tunnel.1* and *tunnel.2* in the example configuration).
- Configure all internal routing that moves traffic between the customer gateway and your local network.

In the following diagram and example configuration, you must replace the items in red italics with values that apply to your particular configuration.

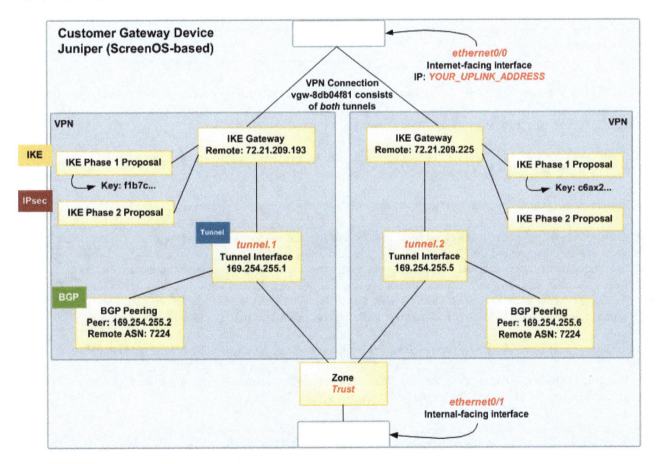

Warning

The following configuration information is an example of what you can expect your integration team to provide. Many of the values in the following example will be different from the configuration information that you receive. You must use the actual values and not the example values shown here, or your implementation will fail.

Important

The configuration below is appropriate for ScreenOS versions 6.2 and later. You can download a configuration that is specific to ScreenOS version 6.1. In the **Download Configuration** dialog box, select `Juniper Networks , Inc.` from the **Vendor** list, `SSG and ISG Series Routers` from the **Platform** list, and `ScreenOS 6.1` from the **Software** list.

```
1  # Amazon Web Services
2  # Virtual Private Cloud
3  #
4  # AWS utilizes unique identifiers to manipulate the configuration of a VPN
5  # Connection. Each VPN Connection is assigned a VPN Connection Identifier
6  # and is associated with two other identifiers, namely the Customer Gateway
7  # Identifier and the Virtual Private Gateway Identifier.
8  #
9  # Your VPN Connection ID          : vpn-44a8938f
10 # Your Virtual Private Gateway ID : vgw-8db04f81
11 # Your Customer Gateway ID        : cgw-b4dc3961
12 #
13 # This configuration consists of two tunnels. Both tunnels must be configured
14 # on your Customer Gateway.
15 #
16 # This configuration was tested on a Juniper SSG-5 running ScreenOS 6.3R2.
17 #
18 # -------------------------------------------------------------------------------
19 # IPsec Tunnel #1
20 # -------------------------------------------------------------------------------
21
22 ![\[Image NOT FOUND\]](http://docs.aws.amazon.com/AmazonVPC/latest/NetworkAdminGuide/images/IKE.
       png)
23 # #1: Internet Key Exchange (IKE) Configuration
24 #
25 # A proposal is established for the supported IKE encryption, authentication,
26 # Diffie-Hellman, and lifetime parameters.
27 #
28 # Please note, these sample configurations are for the minimum requirement of AES128, SHA1, and
       DH Group 2.
29 # You will need to modify these sample configuration files to take advantage of AES256, SHA256,
       or other DH groups like 2, 14-18, 22, 23, and 24.
30 # The address of the external interface for your customer gateway must be a static address.
31 # Your customer gateway may reside behind a device performing network address translation (NAT).
32 # To ensure that NAT traversal (NAT-T) can function, you must adjust your firewall rules to
       unblock UDP port 4500. If not behind NAT, we recommend disabling NAT-T.
33 #
34 set ike p1-proposal ike-prop-vpn-44a8938f-1 preshare group2 esp aes128 sha-1 second 28800
35
36 # The IKE gateway is defined to be the Virtual Private Gateway. The gateway configuration
37 # associates a local interface, remote IP address, and IKE policy.
38 #
39 # This example shows the outside of the tunnel as interface ethernet0/0. This
40 # should be set to the interface that IP address YOUR_UPLINK_ADDRESS is
41 # associated with.
42 # This address is configured with the setup for your Customer Gateway.
43 #
44 #If the address changes, the Customer Gateway and VPN Connection must be recreated.
45 #
46
```

```
47 set ike gateway gw-vpn-44a8938f-1 address 72.21.209.225 id 72.21.209.225 main outgoing-interface
       ethernet0/0 preshare "plain-text-password1" proposal ike-prop-vpn-44a8938f-1
48
49 # Troubleshooting IKE connectivity can be aided by enabling IKE debugging.
50 # To do so, run the following commands:
51 # clear dbuf          -- Clear debug buffer
52 # debug ike all       -- Enable IKE debugging
53 # get dbuf stream     -- View debug messages
54 # undebug all         -- Turn off debugging
55
56 ![\[Image NOT FOUND\]](http://docs.aws.amazon.com/AmazonVPC/latest/NetworkAdminGuide/images/
       IPsec.png)
57 # #2: IPsec Configuration
58 #
59 # The IPsec (Phase 2) proposal defines the protocol, authentication,
60 # encryption, and lifetime parameters for our IPsec security association.
61 # Please note, you may use these additionally supported IPSec parameters for encryption like
       AES256 and other DH groups like 2, 5, 14-18, 22, 23, and 24.
62 #
63
64 set ike p2-proposal ipsec-prop-vpn-44a8938f-1 group2 esp aes128 sha-1 second 3600
65 set ike gateway gw-vpn-44a8938f-1 dpd-liveness interval 10
66 set vpn IPSEC-vpn-44a8938f-1 gateway gw-vpn-44a8938f-1 replay tunnel proposal ipsec-prop-vpn-44
       a8938f-1
67
68 ![\[Image NOT FOUND\]](http://docs.aws.amazon.com/AmazonVPC/latest/NetworkAdminGuide/images/
       Tunnel.png)
69 # #3: Tunnel Interface Configuration
70 #
71 # The tunnel interface is configured with the internal IP address.
72 #
73 # To establish connectivity between your internal network and the VPC, you
74 # must have an interface facing your internal network in the "Trust" zone.
75 #
76
77 set interface tunnel.1 zone Trust
78 set interface tunnel.1 ip 169.254.255.2/30
79 set interface tunnel.1 mtu 1436
80 set vpn IPSEC-vpn-44a8938f-1 bind interface tunnel.1
81
82 # By default, the router will block asymmetric VPN traffic, which may occur
83 # with this VPN Connection. This occurs, for example, when routing policies
84 # cause traffic to sent from your router to VPC through one IPsec tunnel
85 # while traffic returns from VPC through the other.
86 #
87 # This command allows this traffic to be received by your device.
88
89 set zone Trust asymmetric-vpn
90
91
92 # This option causes the router to reduce the Maximum Segment Size of TCP
93 # packets to prevent packet fragmentation.
94 #
95
```

```
 96 set flow vpn-tcp-mss 1387
 97
 98 ![\[Image NOT FOUND\]](http://docs.aws.amazon.com/AmazonVPC/latest/NetworkAdminGuide/images/BGP.
       png)
 99 # #4: Border Gateway Protocol (BGP) Configuration
100 #
101 # BGP is used within the tunnel to exchange prefixes between the Virtual Private Gateway
102 # and your Customer Gateway. The Virtual Private Gateway will announce the prefix
103 # corresponding to your VPC.
104 #
105 # Your Customer Gateway may announce a default route (0.0.0.0/0).
106 #
107 # The BGP timers are adjusted to provide more rapid detection of outages.
108 #
109 # The local BGP Autonomous System Number (ASN) (YOUR_BGP_ASN) is configured
110 # as part of your Customer Gateway. If the ASN must be changed, the
111 # Customer Gateway and VPN Connection will need to be recreated with AWS.
112 #
113
114 set vrouter trust-vr
115 set max-ecmp-routes 2
116 set protocol bgp YOUR_BGP_ASN
117 set hold-time 30
118 set network 0.0.0.0/0
119 # To advertise additional prefixes to Amazon VPC, copy the 'network' statement and
120 # identify the prefix you wish to advertise (set ipv4 network X.X.X.X/X). Make sure the
121 # prefix is present in the routing table of the device with a valid next-hop.
122
123 set enable
124 set neighbor 169.254.255.1 remote-as 7224
125 set neighbor 169.254.255.1 enable
126 exit
127 exit
128 set interface tunnel.1 protocol bgp
129
130 # -------------------------------------------------------------------------
131 # IPsec Tunnel #2
132 # -------------------------------------------------------------------------
133
134 ![\[Image NOT FOUND\]](http://docs.aws.amazon.com/AmazonVPC/latest/NetworkAdminGuide/images/IKE.
       png)
135 # #1: Internet Key Exchange (IKE) Configuration
136 #
137 # A proposal is established for the supported IKE encryption, authentication,
138 # Diffie-Hellman, and lifetime parameters.
139 # Please note, these sample configurations are for the minimum requirement of AES128, SHA1, and
       DH Group 2.
140 # You will need to modify these sample configuration files to take advantage of AES256, SHA256,
       or other DH groups like 2, 14-18, 22, 23, and 24.
141 # The address of the external interface for your customer gateway must be a static address.
142 # Your customer gateway may reside behind a device performing network address translation (NAT).
143 # To ensure that NAT traversal (NAT-T) can function, you must adjust your firewall !rules to
       unblock UDP port 4500. If not behind NAT, we recommend disabling NAT-T.
144 #
```

```
145
146 set ike p1-proposal ike-prop-vpn-44a8938f-2 preshare group2 esp aes128 sha-1 second 28800
147
148 # The IKE gateway is defined to be the Virtual Private Gateway. The gateway configuration
149 # associates a local interface, remote IP address, and IKE policy.
150 #
151 # This example shows the outside of the tunnel as interface ethernet0/0. This
152 # should be set to the interface that IP address YOUR_UPLINK_ADDRESS is
153 # associated with.
154 #
155 # This address is configured with the setup for your Customer Gateway. If the
156 # address changes, the Customer Gateway and VPN Connection must be recreated.
157 #
158 set ike gateway gw-vpn-44a8938f-2 address 72.21.209.193 id 72.21.209.193 main outgoing-interface
        ethernet0/0 preshare "plain-text-password2" proposal ike-prop-vpn-44a8938f-2
159
160 # Troubleshooting IKE connectivity can be aided by enabling IKE debugging.
161 # To do so, run the following commands:
162 # clear dbuf          -- Clear debug buffer
163 # debug ike all       -- Enable IKE debugging
164 # get dbuf stream     -- View debug messages
165 # undebug all         -- Turn off debugging
166
167 ![\[Image NOT FOUND\]](http://docs.aws.amazon.com/AmazonVPC/latest/NetworkAdminGuide/images/
        IPsec.png)
168 # #2: IPsec Configuration
169 #
170 # The IPsec (Phase 2) proposal defines the protocol, authentication,
171 # encryption, and lifetime parameters for our IPsec security association.
172 # Please note, you may use these additionally supported IPSec parameters for encryption like
        AES256 and other DH groups like 2, 5, 14-18, 22, 23, and 24.
173 #
174
175 set ike p2-proposal ipsec-prop-vpn-44a8938f-2 group2 esp aes128 sha-1 second 3600
176 set ike gateway gw-vpn-44a8938f-2 dpd-liveness interval 10
177 set vpn IPSEC-vpn-44a8938f-2 gateway gw-vpn-44a8938f-2 replay tunnel proposal ipsec-prop-vpn-44
        a8938f-2
178
179 ![\[Image NOT FOUND\]](http://docs.aws.amazon.com/AmazonVPC/latest/NetworkAdminGuide/images/
        Tunnel.png)
180 # #3: Tunnel Interface Configuration
181 #
182 # The tunnel interface is configured with the internal IP address.
183 #
184 # To establish connectivity between your internal network and the VPC, you
185 # must have an interface facing your internal network in the "Trust" zone.
186
187 set interface tunnel.2 zone Trust
188 set interface tunnel.2 ip 169.254.255.6/30
189 set interface tunnel.2 mtu 1436
190 set vpn IPSEC-vpn-44a8938f-2 bind interface tunnel.2
191
192 # By default, the router will block asymmetric VPN traffic, which may occur
193 # with this VPN Connection. This occurs, for example, when routing policies
```

```
194 # cause traffic to sent from your router to VPC through one IPsec tunnel
195 # while traffic returns from VPC through the other.
196 #
197 # This command allows this traffic to be received by your device.
198
199 set zone Trust asymmetric-vpn
200
201 # This option causes the router to reduce the Maximum Segment Size of TCP
202 # packets to prevent packet fragmentation.
203
204 set flow vpn-tcp-mss 1387
205
206 ![\[Image NOT FOUND\]](http://docs.aws.amazon.com/AmazonVPC/latest/NetworkAdminGuide/images/BGP.
       png)
207 # #4: Border Gateway Protocol (BGP) Configuration
208 #
209 # BGP is used within the tunnel to exchange prefixes between the Virtual Private Gateway
210 # and your Customer Gateway. The Virtual Private Gateway will announce the prefix
211 # corresponding to your VPC.
212 #
213 # Your Customer Gateway may announce a default route (0.0.0.0/0).
214 #
215 # The BGP timers are adjusted to provide more rapid detection of outages.
216 #
217 # The local BGP Autonomous System Number (ASN) (YOUR_BGP_ASN) is configured
218 # as part of your Customer Gateway. If the ASN must be changed, the
219 # Customer Gateway and VPN Connection will need to be recreated with AWS.
220 #
221
222 set vrouter trust-vr
223 set max-ecmp-routes 2
224 set protocol bgp YOUR_BGP_ASN
225 set hold-time 30
226 set network 0.0.0.0/0
227 # To advertise additional prefixes to Amazon VPC, copy the 'network' statement and
228 # identify the prefix you wish to advertise (set ipv4 network X.X.X.X/X). Make sure the
229 # prefix is present in the routing table of the device with a valid next-hop.
230 set enable
231 set neighbor 169.254.255.5 remote-as 7224
232 set neighbor 169.254.255.5 enable
233 exit
234 exit
235 set interface tunnel.2 protocol bgp
```

How to Test the Customer Gateway Configuration

You can test the gateway configuration for each tunnel.

To test the customer gateway configuration for each tunnel

1. On your customer gateway, determine whether the BGP status is Active.

   It takes approximately 30 seconds for a BGP peering to become active.

2. Ensure that the customer gateway is advertising a route to the virtual private gateway. The route may be the default route (0.0.0.0/0) or a more specific route you prefer.

When properly established, your BGP peering should be receiving one route from the virtual private gateway corresponding to the prefix that your VPC integration team specified for the VPC (for example, 10.0.0.0/24). If the BGP peering is established, you are receiving a prefix, and you are advertising a prefix, your tunnel is configured correctly. Make sure that both tunnels are in this state.

Next you must test the connectivity for each tunnel by launching an instance into your VPC, and pinging the instance from your home network. Before you begin, make sure of the following:

- Use an AMI that responds to ping requests. We recommend that you use one of the Amazon Linux AMIs.
- Configure your instance's security group and network ACL to enable inbound ICMP traffic.
- Ensure that you have configured routing for your VPN connection: your subnet's route table must contain a route to the virtual private gateway. For more information, see Enable Route Propagation in Your Route Table in the *Amazon VPC User Guide*.

To test the end-to-end connectivity of each tunnel

1. Launch an instance of one of the Amazon Linux AMIs into your VPC. The Amazon Linux AMIs are listed in the launch wizard when you launch an instance from the Amazon EC2 Console. For more information, see the Amazon VPC Getting Started Guide.

2. After the instance is running, get its private IP address (for example, 10.0.0.4). The console displays the address as part of the instance's details.

3. On a system in your home network, use the ping command with the instance's IP address. Make sure that the computer you ping from is behind the customer gateway. A successful response should be similar to the following.

```
1 ping 10.0.0.4

1 Pinging 10.0.0.4 with 32 bytes of data:
2
3 Reply from 10.0.0.4: bytes=32 time<1ms TTL=128
4 Reply from 10.0.0.4: bytes=32 time<1ms TTL=128
5 Reply from 10.0.0.4: bytes=32 time<1ms TTL=128
6
7 Ping statistics for 10.0.0.4:
8 Packets: Sent = 3, Received = 3, Lost = 0 (0% loss),
9
10 Approximate round trip times in milliseconds:
11 Minimum = 0ms, Maximum = 0ms, Average = 0ms
```

Note
If you ping an instance from your customer gateway router, ensure that you are sourcing ping messages from an internal IP address, not a tunnel IP address. Some AMIs don't respond to ping messages from tunnel IP addresses.

1. (Optional) To test tunnel failover, you can temporarily disable one of the tunnels on your customer gateway, and repeat the above step. You cannot disable a tunnel on the AWS side of the VPN connection.

If your tunnels don't test successfully, see Troubleshooting Juniper ScreenOS Customer Gateway Connectivity.

135

Example: Netgate PfSense Device without Border Gateway Protocol

Topics

- A High-Level View of the Customer Gateway
- Example Configuration
- How to Test the Customer Gateway Configuration

This topic provides an example of how to configure your router if your customer gateway is a Netgate pfSense firewall running OS 2.2.5 or later.

This topic assumes that you've configured a VPN connection with static routing in the Amazon VPC console. For more information, see Adding a Hardware Virtual Private Gateway to Your VPC in the *Amazon VPC User Guide*.

A High-Level View of the Customer Gateway

The following diagram shows the general details of your customer gateway. Note that the VPN connection consists of two separate tunnels: *Tunnel 1* and *Tunnel 2*. Using redundant tunnels ensures continuous availability in the case that a device fails.

You should use the real configuration information that you receive from your integration team and apply it to your customer gateway.

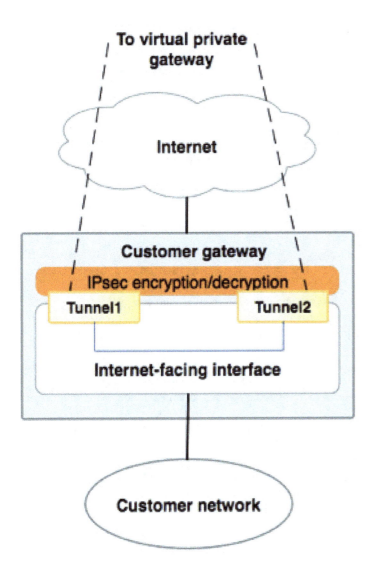

Example Configuration

The example configuration includes several example values to help you understand how configuration works. For example, we provide example values for the VPN connection ID (vpn-12345678), virtual private gateway ID (vgw-12345678), and placeholders for the AWS endpoints (AWS_ENDPOINT_1 and AWS_ENDPOINT_2).

In the following example configuration, you must replace the items in red italics with values that apply to your particular configuration.

Important
The following configuration information is an example of what you can expect an integration team to provide . Many of the values in the following example will be different from the actual configuration information that you receive. You must use the actual values and not the example values shown here, or your implementation will fail.

```
1 ! Amazon Web Services
2 ! Virtual Private Cloud
3
4 ! AWS utilizes unique identifiers to manipulate the configuration of
5 ! a VPN Connection. Each VPN Connection is assigned an identifier and is
6 ! associated with two other identifiers, namely the
```

```
 7 ! Customer Gateway Identifier and Virtual Private Gateway Identifier.
 8 !
 9 ! Your VPN Connection ID          : vpn-12345678
10 ! Your Virtual Private Gateway ID  : vgw-12345678
11 ! Your Customer Gateway ID         : cgw-12345678
12 !
13 !
14 ! This configuration consists of two tunnels. Both tunnels must be
15 ! configured on your Customer Gateway for redundancy.
16 !
17 ! -------------------------------------------------------------------------
18 ! IPSec Tunnel #1
19 ! -------------------------------------------------------------------------
20 ! #1: Internet Key Exchange (IKE) Configuration
21 !
22 ! A policy is established for the supported ISAKMP encryption, authentication, Diffie-Hellman,
     lifetime,
23 ! and key parameters.The IKE peer is configured with the supported IKE encryption,
     authentication, Diffie-Hellman, lifetime, and key
24 ! parameters.Please note, these sample configurations are for the minimum requirement of AES128,
     SHA1, and DH Group 2.
25 ! You will need to modify these sample configuration files to take advantage of AES256, SHA256,
     or other DH
26 ! groups like 2, 14-18, 22, 23, and 24. The address of the external interface for your customer
     gateway must be a static address.
27 ! Your customer gateway may reside behind a device performing network address translation (NAT).
     To
28 ! ensure that NAT traversal (NAT-T) can function, you must adjust your firewall
29 ! rules to unblock UDP port 4500. If not behind NAT, we recommend disabling NAT-T.
30 !
31 !
32 Go to VPN-->IPSec. Add a new Phase1 entry (click + button )
33
34 General information
35  a. Disabled : uncheck
36  b. Key Exchange version :V1
37  c. Internet Protocol : IPv4
38  d. Interface : WAN
39  e. Remote Gateway: AWS_ENPOINT_1
40  f. Description: Amazon-IKE-vpn-12345678-0
41
42 Phase 1 proposal (Authentication)
43  a. Authentication Method: Mutual PSK
44  b. Negotiation mode : Main
45  c. My identifier : My IP address
46  d. Peer identifier : Peer IP address
47  e. Pre-Shared Key: plain-text-password1
48
49 Phase 1 proposal (Algorithms)
50  a. Encryption algorithm : aes128
51  b. Hash algorithm :  sha1
52  c. DH key group :  2
53  d. Lifetime : 28800 seconds
54
```

55 Advanced Options
56 a. Disable Rekey : uncheck
57 b. Responder Only : uncheck
58 c. NAT Traversal : Auto
59 d. Deed Peer Detection : Enable DPD
60   Delay between requesting peer acknowledgement : 10 seconds
61   Number of consecutive failures allowed before disconnect : 3 retries
62
63
64
65 ! #2: IPSec Configuration
66 !
67 ! The IPSec transform set defines the encryption, authentication, and IPSec
68 ! mode parameters.
69 ! Please note, you may use these additionally supported IPSec parameters for encryption like
       AES256 and other DH groups like 2, 5, 14-18, 22, 23, and 24.
70
71 Expand the VPN configuration clicking in "+" and then create a new Phase2 entry as follows:
72
73 a. Disabled :uncheck
74 b. Mode : Tunnel
75 c. Local Network : Type: LAN subnet
76   Address : ! Enter your local network CIDR in the Address tab
77 d. Remote Network : Type : Network
78   Address : ! Enter your remote network CIDR in the Address tab
79 e. Description : Amazon-IPSec-vpn-12345678-0
80
81 Phase 2 proposal (SA/Key Exchange)
82 a. Protocol : ESP
83 b. Encryption algorigthms :aes128
84   c. Hash algorithms : sha1
85   d. PFS key group :   2
86 e. Lifetime : 3600 seconds
87
88 Advanced Options
89
90 Automatically ping host : ! Provide the IP address of an EC2 instance in VPC that will respond
       to ICMP.
91
92
93 ! --
94
95
96 ! --
97 ! IPSec Tunnel #2
98 ! --
99 ! #1: Internet Key Exchange (IKE) Configuration
100 !
101 ! A policy is established for the supported ISAKMP encryption, authentication, Diffie-Hellman,
       lifetime,
102 ! and key parameters.The IKE peer is configured with the supported IKE encryption,
       authentication, Diffie-Hellman, lifetime, and key
103 ! parameters.Please note, these sample configurations are for the minimum requirement of AES128,
       SHA1, and DH Group 2.

104 ! You will need to modify these sample configuration files to take advantage of AES256, SHA256,
     or other DH
105 ! groups like 2, 14-18, 22, 23, and 24. The address of the external interface for your customer
     gateway must be a static address.
106 ! Your customer gateway may reside behind a device performing network address translation (NAT).
     To
107 ! ensure that NAT traversal (NAT-T) can function, you must adjust your firewall
108 ! rules to unblock UDP port 4500. If not behind NAT, we recommend disabling NAT-T.
109 !
110 !
111 Go to VPN-->IPSec. Add a new Phase1 entry (click + button)
112
113 General information
114 a. Disabled : uncheck
115 b. Key Exchange version :V1
116 c. Internet Protocol : IPv4
117 d. Interface : WAN
118 e. Remote Gateway: AWS_ENPOINT_2
119 f. Description: Amazon-IKE-vpn-12345678-1
120
121 Phase 1 proposal (Authentication)
122 a. Authentication Method: Mutual PSK
123 b. Negotiation mode : Main
124 c. My identifier : My IP address
125 d. Peer identifier : Peer IP address
126 e. Pre-Shared Key: plain-text-password2
127
128 Phase 1 proposal (Algorithms)
129 a. Encryption algorithm : aes128
130 b. Hash algorithm : sha1
131 c. DH key group : 2
132 d. Lifetime : 28800 seconds
133
134 Advanced Options
135 a. Disable Rekey : uncheck
136 b. Responder Only : uncheck
137 c. NAT Traversal : Auto
138 d. Deed Peer Detection : Enable DPD
139   Delay between requesting peer acknowledgement : 10 seconds
140   Number of consecutive failures allowed before disconnect : 3 retries
141
142
143
144 ! #2: IPSec Configuration
145 !
146 ! The IPSec transform set defines the encryption, authentication, and IPSec
147 ! mode parameters.
148 ! Please note, you may use these additionally supported IPSec parameters for encryption like
     AES256 and other DH groups like 2, 5, 14-18, 22, 23, and 24.
149
150 Expand the VPN configuration clicking in "+" and then create a new Phase2 entry as follows:
151
152 a. Disabled :uncheck
153 b. Mode : Tunnel

```
154  c. Local Network : Type: LAN subnet
155     Address :  ! Enter your local network CIDR in the Address tab
156  d. Remote Network : Type : Network
157     Address :  ! Enter your remote network CIDR in the Address tab
158  e. Description : Amazon-IPSec-vpn-12345678-1
159
160  Phase 2 proposal (SA/Key Exchange)
161  a. Protocol : ESP
162  b. Encryption algorigthms :aes128
163   c. Hash algorithms : sha1
164   d. PFS key group :    2
165  e. Lifetime : 3600 seconds
166
167  Advanced Options
168
169  Automatically ping host : ! Provide the IP address of an EC2 instance in VPC that will respond
         to ICMP.
```

How to Test the Customer Gateway Configuration

You must first test the gateway configuration for each tunnel.

To test the customer gateway configuration for each tunnel

- In the Amazon VPC console, ensure that a static route has been added to the VPN connection so that traffic can get back to your customer gateway. For example, if your local subnet prefix is 198.10.0.0/16, you must add a static route with that CIDR range to your VPN connection. Make sure that both tunnels have a static route to your VPC.

Next you must test the connectivity for each tunnel by launching an instance into your VPC, and pinging the instance from your home network. Before you begin, make sure of the following:

- Use an AMI that responds to ping requests. We recommend that you use one of the Amazon Linux AMIs.
- Configure your instance's security group and network ACL to enable inbound ICMP traffic.
- Ensure that you have configured routing for your VPN connection - your subnet's route table must contain a route to the virtual private gateway. For more information, see Enable Route Propagation in Your Route Table in the *Amazon VPC User Guide*.

To test the end-to-end connectivity of each tunnel

1. Launch an instance from one of the Amazon Linux AMIs into your VPC. The Amazon Linux AMIs are available in the Quick Start menu when you use the Launch Instances Wizard in the Amazon EC2 console. For more information, see Launching an Instancein the *Amazon EC2 User Guide for Linux Instances*.

2. After the instance is running, get its private IP address (for example, 10.0.0.4). The console displays the address as part of the instance's details.

3. On a system in your home network, use the ping command with the instance's IP address. Make sure that the computer you ping from is behind the customer gateway. A successful response should be similar to the following.

```
1 ping 10.0.0.4
```

```
1 Pinging 10.0.0.4 with 32 bytes of data:
2
3 Reply from 10.0.0.4: bytes=32 time<1ms TTL=128
4 Reply from 10.0.0.4: bytes=32 time<1ms TTL=128
5 Reply from 10.0.0.4: bytes=32 time<1ms TTL=128
```

```
 6
 7 Ping statistics for 10.0.0.4:
 8 Packets: Sent = 3, Received = 3, Lost = 0 (0% loss),
 9
10 Approximate round trip times in milliseconds:
11 Minimum = 0ms, Maximum = 0ms, Average = 0ms
```

Note

If you ping an instance from your customer gateway router, ensure that you are sourcing ping messages from an internal IP address, not a tunnel IP address. Some AMIs don't respond to ping messages from tunnel IP addresses.

1. (Optional) To test tunnel failover, you can temporarily disable one of the tunnels on your customer gateway, and repeat the above step. You cannot disable a tunnel on the AWS side of the VPN connection.

Example: Palo Alto Networks Device

Topics

- A High-Level View of the Customer Gateway
- A Detailed View of the Customer Gateway and an Example Configuration
- How to Test the Customer Gateway Configuration

The following topic provides example configuration information provided by your integration team if your customer gateway is a Palo Alto Networks PANOS 4.1.2+ device.

Two diagrams illustrate the example configuration. The first diagram shows the high-level layout of the customer gateway, and the second diagram shows the details of the example configuration. You should use the real configuration information that you receive from your integration team and apply it to your customer gateway.

A High-Level View of the Customer Gateway

The following diagram shows the general details of your customer gateway. Note that the VPN connection consists of two separate tunnels. Using redundant tunnels ensures continuous availability in the case that a device fails.

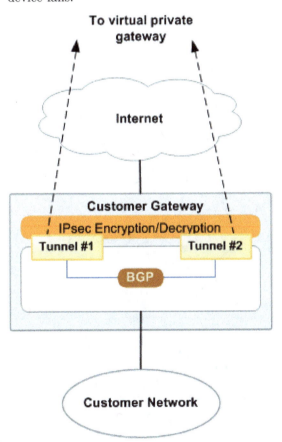

A Detailed View of the Customer Gateway and an Example Configuration

The diagram in this section illustrates an example Palo Alto customer gateway. Following the diagram, there is a corresponding example of the configuration information your integration team should provide. The example

configuration contains a set of information for each of the tunnels that you must configure.

In addition, the example configuration refers to these items that you must provide:

- *YOUR_UPLINK_ADDRESS*—The IP address for the Internet-routable external interface on the customer gateway (which must be static, and may be behind a device performing network address translation (NAT); however, NAT traversal (NAT-T) is not supported).
- *YOUR_BGP_ASN*—The customer gateway's BGP ASN (we use 65000 by default)

The example configuration includes several example values to help you understand how configuration works. For example, we provide example values for the VPN connection ID (vpn-44a8938f), virtual private gateway ID (vgw-8db04f81), the IP addresses (72.21.209.*, 169.254.255.*), and the remote ASN (7224). You'll replace these example values with the actual values from the configuration information that you receive.

In the following diagram and example configuration, you must replace the items in red italics with values that apply to your particular configuration.

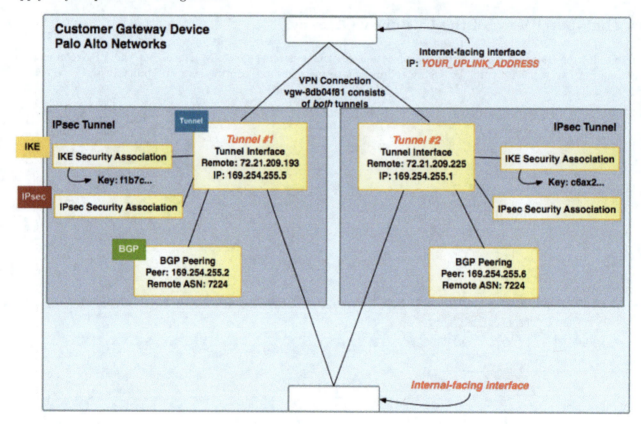

Warning

The following configuration information is an example of what you can expect your integration team to provide. Many of the values in the following example will be different from the actual configuration information that you receive. You must use the actual values and not the example values shown here, or your implementation will fail.

```
1 ! Amazon Web Services
2 ! Virtual Private Cloud
3
4 ! AWS utilizes unique identifiers to manipulate the configuration of
5 ! a VPN Connection. Each VPN Connection is assigned an identifier and is
6 ! associated with two other identifiers, namely the
7 ! Customer Gateway Identifier and Virtual Private Gateway Identifier.
8 !
9 ! Your VPN Connection ID          : vpn-44a8938f
```

```
10 ! Your Virtual Private Gateway ID  : vgw-8db04f81
11 ! Your Customer Gateway ID         : cgw-b4dc3961
12 !
13 !
14 ! This configuration consists of two tunnels. Both tunnels must be
15 ! configured on your Customer Gateway.
16 !
17 ! -----------------------------------------------------------------------
18 ! IPSec Tunnel #1
19 ! -----------------------------------------------------------------------
20
21 ![\[Image NOT FOUND\]](http://docs.aws.amazon.com/AmazonVPC/latest/NetworkAdminGuide/images/IKE.
      png)
22
23 ! #1: Internet Key Exchange (IKE) Configuration
24 !
25 ! A policy is established for the supported ISAKMP encryption,
26 ! authentication, Diffie-Hellman, lifetime, and key parameters.
27 ! Please note, these sample configurations are for the minimum requirement of AES128, SHA1, and
      DH Group 2.
28 ! You will need to modify these sample configuration files to take advantage of AES256, SHA256,
      or other DH groups like 2, 14-18, 22, 23, and 24.
29 ! The address of the external interface for your customer gateway must be a static address.
30 ! Your customer gateway may reside behind a device performing network address translation (NAT).
31 ! To ensure that NAT traversal (NAT-T) can function, you must adjust your firewall rules to
      unblock UDP port 4500. If not behind NAT, we recommend disabling NAT-T.
32 !
33
34  configure
35  edit network ike crypto-profiles ike-crypto-profiles ike-crypto-vpn-44a8938f-0
36    set dh-group group2
37    set hash sha1
38    set lifetime seconds  28800
39    set encryption aes128
40    top
41
42  edit network ike gateway ike-vpn-44a8938f-0
43    set protocol ikev1 dpd interval 10 retry 3 enable yes
44    set protocol ikev1 ike-crypto-profile ike-crypto-vpn-44a8938f-0 exchange-mode main
45    set authentication pre-shared-key key plain-text-password1
46    set local-address ip YOUR_UPLINK_ADDRESS
47    set local-address interface ethernet1/1
48    set peer-address ip 72.21.209.193
49  top
50
51
52 ![\[Image NOT FOUND\]](http://docs.aws.amazon.com/AmazonVPC/latest/NetworkAdminGuide/images/
      IPsec.png)
53 ! #2: IPSec Configuration
54 !
55 ! The IPSec transform set defines the encryption, authentication, and IPSec
56 ! mode parameters.
57 !
58 ! Please note, you may use these additionally supported IPSec parameters for encryption like
```

```
          AES256 and other DH groups like 2, 5, 14-18, 22, 23, and 24.
59
60  edit network ike crypto-profiles ipsec-crypto-profiles ipsec-vpn-44a8938f-0
61    set esp authentication sha1
62    set esp encryption aes128
63    set dh-group group2 lifetime seconds 3600
64  top
65
66
67
68  ![\[Image NOT FOUND\]](http://docs.aws.amazon.com/AmazonVPC/latest/NetworkAdminGuide/images/
        Tunnel.png)
69
70  ! --------------------------------------------------------------------------------
71  ! #3: Tunnel Interface Configuration
72  !
73  ! A tunnel interface is configured to be the logical interface associated
74  ! with the tunnel. All traffic routed to the tunnel interface will be
75  ! encrypted and transmitted to the VPC. Similarly, traffic from the VPC
76  ! will be logically received on this interface.
77  !
78  ! Association with the IPSec security association is done through the
79  ! "tunnel protection" command.
80  !
81  ! The address of the interface is configured with the setup for your
82  ! Customer Gateway.  If the address changes, the Customer Gateway and VPN
83  ! Connection must be recreated with Amazon VPC.
84  !
85
86
87  edit network interface tunnel
88    set ip 169.254.255.5/30
89    set units tunnel.1
90    set mtu 1427
91  top
92
93  edit network tunnel ipsec ipsec-tunnel-1
94    set auto-key ike-gateway ike-vpn-44a8938f-0
95    set auto-key ipsec-crypto-profile ipsec-vpn-44a8938f-0
96    set tunnel-interface tunnel.1
97    set anti-replay yes
98
99
100
101 ![\[Image NOT FOUND\]](http://docs.aws.amazon.com/AmazonVPC/latest/NetworkAdminGuide/images/BGP.
        png)
102
103 ! --------------------------------------------------------------------------------
104
105 ! #4: Border Gateway Protocol (BGP) Configuration
106 !
107 ! BGP is used within the tunnel to exchange prefixes between the
108 ! Virtual Private Gateway and your Customer Gateway. The Virtual Private Gateway
109 ! will announce the prefix corresponding to your VPC.
```

```
110  !
111  !
112  !
113  ! The local BGP Autonomous System Number (ASN) (YOUR_BGP_ASN)
114  ! is configured as part of your Customer Gateway. If the ASN must
115  ! be changed, the Customer Gateway and VPN Connection will need to be recreated with AWS.
116  !
117
118
119  edit network virtual-router default protocol bgp
120    set enable yes
121    set router-id YOUR_UPLINK_ADDRESS
122    set local-as YOUR_BGP_ASN
123     edit peer-group AmazonBGP
124      edit peer amazon-tunnel-44a8938f-0
125       set connection-options keep-alive-interval 10
126       set connection-options hold-time 30
127       set enable yes
128       set local-address ip 169.254.255.5/30
129       set local-address interface tunnel.1
130       set peer-as 7224
131       set peer-address ip 169.254.255.2
132       top
133
134
135
136  ! Your Customer Gateway may announce a default route (0.0.0.0/0) to us.
137
138  edit network virtual-router default protocol bgp policy
139    set export rules vr-export action allow
140    set match address-prefix 0.0.0.0/0 exact yes
141    set used-by AmazonBGP enable yes
142  top
143
144
145  ! To advertise additional prefixes to Amazon VPC, add these prefixes to the 'address-prefix'
146  ! statement and identify the prefix you wish to advertise. Make sure the prefix is present
147  ! in the routing table of the device with a valid next-hop. If you want to advertise
148  ! 192.168.0.0/16 to Amazon, this can be done using the following.
149
150  edit network virtual-router default protocol bgp policy
151    set export rules vr-export action allow
152    set match address-prefix 192.168.0.0/16 exact yes
153    set used-by AmazonBGP enable yes
154  top
155
156
157  !
158
159
160
161
162  ![\[Image NOT FOUND\]](http://docs.aws.amazon.com/AmazonVPC/latest/NetworkAdminGuide/images/IKE.
      png)
```

```
163  ! --------------------------------------------------------------------
164  ! IPSec Tunnel #2
165  ! --------------------------------------------------------------------
166  ! #1: Internet Key Exchange (IKE) Configuration
167  !
168  ! A policy is established for the supported ISAKMP encryption,
169  ! authentication, Diffie-Hellman, lifetime, and key parameters.
170  ! Please note, these sample configurations are for the minimum requirement of AES128, SHA1, and
        DH Group 2.
171  ! You will need to modify these sample configuration files to take advantage of AES256, SHA256,
        or other DH groups like 2, 14-18, 22, 23, and 24.
172  ! The address of the external interface for your customer gateway must be a static address.
173  ! Your customer gateway may reside behind a device performing network address translation (NAT).
174  ! To ensure that NAT traversal (NAT-T) can function, you must adjust your firewall !rules to
        unblock UDP port 4500. If not behind NAT, we recommend disabling NAT-T.
175  !
176
177   configure
178   edit network ike crypto-profiles ike-crypto-profiles ike-crypto-vpn-44a8938f-1
179     set dh-group group2
180     set hash sha1
181     set lifetime seconds  28800
182     set encryption aes128
183     top
184
185   edit network ike gateway ike-vpn-44a8938f-1
186     set protocol ikev1 dpd interval 10 retry 3 enable yes
187     set protocol ikev1 ike-crypto-profile ike-crypto-vpn-35a6445c-1 exchange-mode main
188     set authentication pre-shared-key key plain-text-password2
189     set local-address ip YOUR_UPLINK_ADDRESS
190     set local-address interface ethernet1/1
191     set peer-address ip 72.21.209.225
192   top
193
194
195
196
197  ![\[Image NOT FOUND\]](http://docs.aws.amazon.com/AmazonVPC/latest/NetworkAdminGuide/images/
        IPsec.png)
198
199  ! #2: IPSec Configuration
200  !
201  ! The IPSec transform set defines the encryption, authentication, and IPSec
202  ! mode parameters.
203  !
204  ! Please note, you may use these additionally supported IPSec parameters for encryption like
        AES256 and other DH groups like 2, 5, 14-18, 22, 23, and 24.
205
206   edit network ike crypto-profiles ipsec-crypto-profiles ipsec-vpn-44a8938f-1
207     set esp authentication sha1
208     set esp encryption aes128
209     set dh-group group2 lifetime seconds 3600
210   top
211
```

```
212
213
214  ![\[Image NOT FOUND\]](http://docs.aws.amazon.com/AmazonVPC/latest/NetworkAdminGuide/images/
     Tunnel.png)
215
216  ! ---------------------------------------------------------------------------
217  ! #3: Tunnel Interface Configuration
218  !
219  ! A tunnel interface is configured to be the logical interface associated
220  ! with the tunnel. All traffic routed to the tunnel interface will be
221  ! encrypted and transmitted to the VPC. Similarly, traffic from the VPC
222  ! will be logically received on this interface.
223  !
224  ! Association with the IPSec security association is done through the
225  ! "tunnel protection" command.
226  !
227  ! The address of the interface is configured with the setup for your
228  ! Customer Gateway.  If the address changes, the Customer Gateway and VPN
229  ! Connection must be recreated with Amazon VPC.
230  !
231
232
233  edit network interface tunnel
234    set ip 169.254.255.1/30
235    set units tunnel.2
236    set mtu 1427
237  top
238
239  edit network tunnel ipsec ipsec-tunnel-2
240    set auto-key ike-gateway ike-vpn-44a8938f-1
241    set auto-key ipsec-crypto-profile ipsec-vpn-44a8938f-1
242    set tunnel-interface tunnel.2
243    set anti-replay yes
244
245
246
247
248  ![\[Image NOT FOUND\]](http://docs.aws.amazon.com/AmazonVPC/latest/NetworkAdminGuide/images/BGP.
     png)
249
250  ! #4: Border Gateway Protocol (BGP) Configuration
251  !
252  ! BGP is used within the tunnel to exchange prefixes between the
253  ! Virtual Private Gateway and your Customer Gateway. The Virtual Private Gateway
254  ! will announce the prefix corresponding to your VPC.
255  !
256  !
257  !
258  ! The local BGP Autonomous System Number (ASN) (YOUR_BGP_ASN)
259  ! is configured as part of your Customer Gateway. If the ASN must
260  ! be changed, the Customer Gateway and VPN Connection will need to be recreated with AWS.
261  !
262
263
```

```
264  edit network virtual-router default protocol bgp
265    set enable yes
266    set router-id YOUR_UPLINK_ADDRESS
267    set local-as YOUR_BGP_ASN
268     edit peer-group AmazonBGP
269      edit peer amazon-tunnel-44a8938f-1
270       set connection-options keep-alive-interval 10
271       set connection-options hold-time 30
272       set enable yes
273       set local-address ip 169.254.255.1/30
274       set local-address interface tunnel.2
275       set peer-as 7224
276       set peer-address ip 169.254.255.6.113
277       top
278
279
280
281  ! Your Customer Gateway may announce a default route (0.0.0.0/0) to us.
282
283   edit network virtual-router default protocol bgp policy
284     set export rules vr-export action allow
285     set match address-prefix 0.0.0.0/0 exact yes
286     set used-by AmazonBGP enable yes
287  top
288
289
290  ! To advertise additional prefixes to Amazon VPC, add these prefixes to the 'address-prefix'
291  ! statement and identify the prefix you wish to advertise. Make sure the prefix is present
292  ! in the routing table of the device with a valid next-hop. If you want to advertise
293  ! 192.168.0.0/16 to Amazon, this can be done using the following.
294
295   edit network virtual-router default protocol bgp policy
296     set export rules vr-export action allow
297     set match address-prefix 192.168.0.0/16 exact yes
298     set used-by AmazonBGP enable yes
299  top
300
301
302  !
```

How to Test the Customer Gateway Configuration

You can test the gateway configuration for each tunnel.

To test the customer gateway configuration for each tunnel

1. On your customer gateway, determine whether the BGP status is `Active`.

   It takes approximately 30 seconds for a BGP peering to become active.

2. Ensure that the customer gateway is advertising a route to the virtual private gateway. The route may be the default route (0.0.0.0/0) or a more specific route you prefer.

When properly established, your BGP peering should be receiving one route from the virtual private gateway corresponding to the prefix that your VPC integration team specified for the VPC (for example, `10.0.0.0/24`).

If the BGP peering is established, you are receiving a prefix, and you are advertising a prefix, your tunnel is configured correctly. Make sure that both tunnels are in this state.

Next you must test the connectivity for each tunnel by launching an instance into your VPC, and pinging the instance from your home network. Before you begin, make sure of the following:

- Use an AMI that responds to ping requests. We recommend that you use one of the Amazon Linux AMIs.
- Configure your instance's security group and network ACL to enable inbound ICMP traffic.
- Ensure that you have configured routing for your VPN connection: your subnet's route table must contain a route to the virtual private gateway. For more information, see Enable Route Propagation in Your Route Table in the *Amazon VPC User Guide*.

To test the end-to-end connectivity of each tunnel

1. Launch an instance of one of the Amazon Linux AMIs into your VPC. The Amazon Linux AMIs are listed in the launch wizard when you launch an instance from the Amazon EC2 Console. For more information, see the Amazon VPC Getting Started Guide.

2. After the instance is running, get its private IP address (for example, 10.0.0.4). The console displays the address as part of the instance's details.

3. On a system in your home network, use the ping command with the instance's IP address. Make sure that the computer you ping from is behind the customer gateway. A successful response should be similar to the following.

```
1 ping 10.0.0.4
```

```
1 Pinging 10.0.0.4 with 32 bytes of data:
2
3 Reply from 10.0.0.4: bytes=32 time<1ms TTL=128
4 Reply from 10.0.0.4: bytes=32 time<1ms TTL=128
5 Reply from 10.0.0.4: bytes=32 time<1ms TTL=128
6
7 Ping statistics for 10.0.0.4:
8 Packets: Sent = 3, Received = 3, Lost = 0 (0% loss),
9
10 Approximate round trip times in milliseconds:
11 Minimum = 0ms, Maximum = 0ms, Average = 0ms
```

Note
If you ping an instance from your customer gateway router, ensure that you are sourcing ping messages from an internal IP address, not a tunnel IP address. Some AMIs don't respond to ping messages from tunnel IP addresses.

1. (Optional) To test tunnel failover, you can temporarily disable one of the tunnels on your customer gateway, and repeat the above step. You cannot disable a tunnel on the AWS side of the VPN connection.

Example: Yamaha Device

Topics

- A High-Level View of the Customer Gateway
- A Detailed View of the Customer Gateway and an Example Configuration
- How to Test the Customer Gateway Configuration

In this section we walk you through an example of the configuration information provided by your integration team if your customer gateway is a Yamaha RT107e, RTX1200, RTX1210, RTX1500, RTX3000, or SRT100 router.

Two diagrams illustrate the example configuration. The first diagram shows the high-level layout of the customer gateway, and the second diagram shows the details of the example configuration. You should use the real configuration information that you receive from your integration team and apply it to your customer gateway.

A High-Level View of the Customer Gateway

The following diagram shows the general details of your customer gateway. Note that the VPN connection consists of two separate tunnels. Using redundant tunnels ensures continuous availability in the case that a device fails.

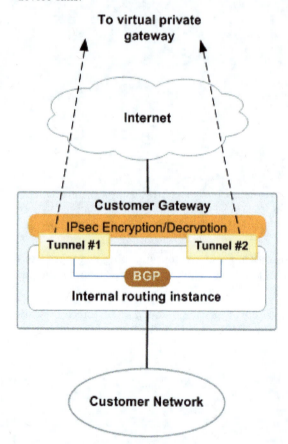

A Detailed View of the Customer Gateway and an Example Configuration

The diagram in this section illustrates an example Yamaha customer gateway. Following the diagram, there is a corresponding example of the configuration information your integration team should provide. The example configuration contains a set of information for each of the tunnels that you must configure.

In addition, the example configuration refers to these items that you must provide:

- *YOUR_UPLINK_ADDRESS*—The IP address for the Internet-routable external interface on the customer gateway. The address must be static, and may be behind a device performing network address translation (NAT). To ensure that NAT traversal (NAT-T) can function, you must adjust your firewall rules to unblock UDP port 4500.
- *YOUR_LOCAL_NETWORK_ADDRESS*—The IP address that is assigned to the LAN interface connected to your local network (most likely a private address such as 192.168.0.1)
- *YOUR_BGP_ASN*—The customer gateway's BGP ASN (we use 65000 by default)

The example configuration includes several example values to help you understand how configuration works. For example, we provide example values for the VPN connection ID (vpn-44a8938f), virtual private gateway ID (vgw-8db04f81), the IP addresses (72.21.209.*, 169.254.255.*), and the remote ASN (7224). You'll replace these example values with the actual values from the configuration information that you receive.

In addition, you must also:

- Configure the outside interface (referred to as *LAN3* in the example configuration).
- Configure the tunnel interface IDs (referred to as *Tunnel #1* and *Tunnel #2* in the example configuration).
- Configure all internal routing that moves traffic between the customer gateway and your local network.

In the following diagram and example configuration, you must replace the items in red italics with values that apply to your particular configuration.

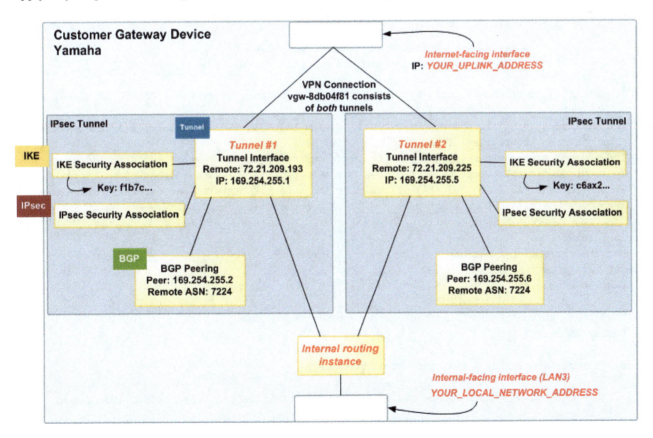

Warning

153

The following configuration information is an example of what you can expect your integration team to provide. Many of the values in the following example will be different from the actual configuration information that you receive. You must use the actual values and not the example values shown here, or your implementation will fail.

```
1  # Amazon Web Services
2  # Virtual Private Cloud
3
4  # AWS utilizes unique identifiers to manage the configuration of
5  # a VPN Connection. Each VPN Connection is assigned an identifier and is
6  # associated with two other identifiers, namely the
7  # Customer Gateway Identifier and Virtual Private Gateway Identifier.
8  #
9  # Your VPN Connection ID              : vpn-44a8938f
10 # Your Virtual Private Gateway ID     : vgw-8db04f81
11 # Your Customer Gateway ID            : cgw-b4dc3961
12 #
13 #
14 # This configuration consists of two tunnels. Both tunnels must be
15 # configured on your Customer Gateway.
16 #
17 # -------------------------------------------------------------------
18 # IPsec Tunnel #1
19 # -------------------------------------------------------------------
20
21 ![\[Image NOT FOUND\]](http://docs.aws.amazon.com/AmazonVPC/latest/NetworkAdminGuide/images/IKE.
     png)
22
23 # #1: Internet Key Exchange (IKE) Configuration
24 #
25 # A policy is established for the supported ISAKMP encryption,
26 # authentication, Diffie-Hellman, lifetime, and key parameters.
27 #
28 # Please note, these sample configurations are for the minimum requirement of AES128, SHA1, and
     DH Group 2.
29 # You will need to modify these sample configuration files to take advantage of AES256, SHA256,
     or other DH groups like 2, 14-18, 22, 23, and 24.
30 # The address of the external interface for your customer gateway must be a static address.
31 # Your customer gateway may reside behind a device performing network address translation (NAT).
32 # To ensure that NAT traversal (NAT-T) can function, you must adjust your firewall !rules to
     unblock UDP port 4500. If not behind NAT, we recommend disabling NAT-T.
33 #
34 tunnel select 1
35 ipsec ike encryption 1 aes-cbc
36 ipsec ike group 1 modp1024
37 ipsec ike hash 1 sha
38
39 # This line stores the Pre Shared Key used to authenticate the
40 # tunnel endpoints.
41 #
42 ipsec ike pre-shared-key 1 text plain-text-password1
43
44 ![\[Image NOT FOUND\]](http://docs.aws.amazon.com/AmazonVPC/latest/NetworkAdminGuide/images/
     IPsec.png)
45
46 # #2: IPsec Configuration
```

```
47
48  # The IPsec policy defines the encryption, authentication, and IPsec
49  # mode parameters.
50  # Please note, you may use these additionally supported IPSec parameters for encryption like
        AES256 and other DH groups like 2, 5, 14-18, 22, 23, and 24.
51  #
52  # Note that there are a global list of IPSec policies, each identified by
53  # sequence number. This policy is defined as #201, which may conflict with
54  # an existing policy using the same number. If so, we recommend changing
55  # the sequence number to avoid conflicts.
56  #
57
58  ipsec tunnel 201
59  ipsec sa policy 201 1 esp aes-cbc  sha-hmac
60
61  # The IPsec profile references the IPsec policy and further defines
62  # the Diffie-Hellman group and security association lifetime.
63
64  ipsec ike duration ipsec-sa 1 3600
65  ipsec ike pfs 1 on
66
67  # Additional parameters of the IPsec configuration are set here. Note that
68  # these parameters are global and therefore impact other IPsec
69  # associations.
70  # This option instructs the router to clear the "Don't Fragment"
71  # bit from packets that carry this bit and yet must be fragmented, enabling
72  # them to be fragmented.
73  #
74  ipsec tunnel outer df-bit clear
75
76  # This option enables IPsec Dead Peer Detection, which causes periodic
77  # messages to be sent to ensure a Security Association remains operational.
78
79  ipsec ike keepalive use 1 on dpd 10 3
80
81  ![\[Image NOT FOUND\]](http://docs.aws.amazon.com/AmazonVPC/latest/NetworkAdminGuide/images/
        Tunnel.png)
82
83  # --------------------------------------------------------------------------------
84  # #3: Tunnel Interface Configuration
85  #
86  # A tunnel interface is configured to be the logical interface associated
87  # with the tunnel. All traffic routed to the tunnel interface will be
88  # encrypted and transmitted to the VPC. Similarly, traffic from the VPC
89  # will be logically received on this interface.
90  #
91  #
92  # The address of the interface is configured with the setup for your
93  # Customer Gateway.  If the address changes, the Customer Gateway and VPN
94  # Connection must be recreated with Amazon VPC.
95  #
96  ipsec ike local address 1 YOUR_LOCAL_NETWORK_ADDRESS
97  ipsec ike remote address 1 72.21.209.225
98  ip tunnel address 169.254.255.2/30
```

```
 99 ip tunnel remote address 169.254.255.1
100
101 # This option causes the router to reduce the Maximum Segment Size of
102 # TCP packets to prevent packet fragmentation
103
104 ip tunnel tcp mss limit 1387
105 tunnel enable 1
106 tunnel select none
107 ipsec auto refresh on
108
109 ![\[Image NOT FOUND\]](http://docs.aws.amazon.com/AmazonVPC/latest/NetworkAdminGuide/images/BGP.
        png)
110
111 # ------------------------------------------------------------------------------
112 # #4: Border Gateway Protocol (BGP) Configuration
113 #
114 # BGP is used within the tunnel to exchange prefixes between the
115 # Virtual Private Gateway and your Customer Gateway. The Virtual Private Gateway
116 # will announce the prefix corresponding to your VPC.
117 #
118 # Your Customer Gateway may announce a default route (0.0.0.0/0),
119 # which can be done with the 'network' and 'default-originate' statements.
120 #
121 # The BGP timers are adjusted to provide more rapid detection of outages.
122 #
123 # The local BGP Autonomous System Number (ASN) (YOUR_BGP_ASN) is configured
124 # as part of your Customer Gateway. If the ASN must be changed, the
125 # Customer Gateway and VPN Connection will need to be recreated with AWS.
126 #
127 bgp use on
128 bgp autonomous-system YOUR_BGP_ASN
129 bgp neighbor 1 7224 169.254.255.1 hold-time=30 local-address=169.254.255.2
130
131 # To advertise additional prefixes to Amazon VPC, copy the 'network' statement and
132 # identify the prefix you wish to advertise. Make sure the
133 # prefix is present in the routing table of the device with a valid next-hop.
134 # For example, the following two lines will advertise 192.168.0.0/16 and 10.0.0.0/16 to Amazon
        VPC
135 #
136 # bgp import filter 1 equal 10.0.0.0/16
137 # bgp import filter 1 equal 192.168.0.0/16
138 #
139
140 bgp import filter 1 equal 0.0.0.0/0
141 bgp import 7224 static filter 1
142
143 ![\[Image NOT FOUND\]](http://docs.aws.amazon.com/AmazonVPC/latest/NetworkAdminGuide/images/IKE.
        png)
144
145 # ------------------------------------------------------------------------------
146 # IPsec Tunnel #2
147 # ------------------------------------------------------------------------------
148
149
```

```
150 # #1: Internet Key Exchange (IKE) Configuration
151 #
152 # A policy is established for the supported ISAKMP encryption,
153 # authentication, Diffie-Hellman, lifetime, and key parameters.
154 #
155 # Please note, these sample configurations are for the minimum requirement of AES128, SHA1, and
        DH Group 2.
156 # You will need to modify these sample configuration files to take advantage of AES256, SHA256,
        or other DH groups like 2, 14-18, 22, 23, and 24.
157 # The address of the external interface for your customer gateway must be a static address.
158 # Your customer gateway may reside behind a device performing network address translation (NAT).
159 # To ensure that NAT traversal (NAT-T) can function, you must adjust your firewall rules to
        unblock UDP port 4500. If not behind NAT, we recommend disabling NAT-T.
160 #
161 tunnel select 2
162 ipsec ike encryption 2 aes-cbc
163 ipsec ike group 2 modp1024
164 ipsec ike hash 2 sha
165
166 # This line stores the Pre Shared Key used to authenticate the
167 # tunnel endpoints.
168 #
169 ipsec ike pre-shared-key 2 text plain-text-password2
170
171 ![\[Image NOT FOUND\]](http://docs.aws.amazon.com/AmazonVPC/latest/NetworkAdminGuide/images/
        IPsec.png)
172
173 # #2: IPsec Configuration
174
175 # The IPsec policy defines the encryption, authentication, and IPsec
176 # mode parameters.
177 # Please note, you may use these additionally supported IPSec parameters for encryption like
        AES256 and other DH groups like 2, 5, 14-18, 22, 23, and 24.
178 #
179 # Note that there are a global list of IPsec policies, each identified by
180 # sequence number. This policy is defined as #202, which may conflict with
181 # an existing policy using the same number. If so, we recommend changing
182 # the sequence number to avoid conflicts.
183 #
184
185 ipsec tunnel 202
186 ipsec sa policy 202 2 esp aes-cbc  sha-hmac
187
188 # The IPsec profile references the IPsec policy and further defines
189 # the Diffie-Hellman group and security association lifetime.
190
191 ipsec ike duration ipsec-sa 2 3600
192 ipsec ike pfs 2 on
193
194 # Additional parameters of the IPsec configuration are set here. Note that
195 # these parameters are global and therefore impact other IPsec
196 # associations.
197 # This option instructs the router to clear the "Don't Fragment"
198 # bit from packets that carry this bit and yet must be fragmented, enabling
```

```
199  # them to be fragmented.
200  #
201  ipsec tunnel outer df-bit clear
202
203  # This option enables IPsec Dead Peer Detection, which causes periodic
204  # messages to be sent to ensure a Security Association remains operational.
205
206  ipsec ike keepalive use 2 on dpd 10 3
207
208  ![\[Image NOT FOUND\]](http://docs.aws.amazon.com/AmazonVPC/latest/NetworkAdminGuide/images/
        Tunnel.png)
209
210  # ------------------------------------------------------------------------------
211  # #3: Tunnel Interface Configuration
212  #
213  # A tunnel interface is configured to be the logical interface associated
214  # with the tunnel. All traffic routed to the tunnel interface will be
215  # encrypted and transmitted to the VPC. Similarly, traffic from the VPC
216  # will be logically received on this interface.
217  #
218  # Association with the IPsec security association is done through the
219  # "tunnel protection" command.
220  #
221  # The address of the interface is configured with the setup for your
222  # Customer Gateway.  If the address changes, the Customer Gateway and VPN
223  # Connection must be recreated with Amazon VPC.
224  #
225  ipsec ike local address 2 YOUR_LOCAL_NETWORK_ADDRESS
226  ipsec ike remote address 2 72.21.209.193
227  ip tunnel address 169.254.255.6/30
228  ip tunnel remote address 169.254.255.5
229
230  # This option causes the router to reduce the Maximum Segment Size of
231  # TCP packets to prevent packet fragmentation
232
233  ip tunnel tcp mss limit 1387
234  tunnel enable 2
235  tunnel select none
236  ipsec auto refresh on
237
238  ![\[Image NOT FOUND\]](http://docs.aws.amazon.com/AmazonVPC/latest/NetworkAdminGuide/images/BGP.
        png)
239
240  # ------------------------------------------------------------------------------
241  # #4: Border Gateway Protocol (BGP) Configuration
242  #
243  # BGP is used within the tunnel to exchange prefixes between the
244  # Virtual Private Gateway and your Customer Gateway. The Virtual Private Gateway
245  # will announce the prefix corresponding to your VPC.
246  #
247  # Your Customer Gateway may announce a default route (0.0.0.0/0),
248  # which can be done with the 'network' and 'default-originate' statements.
249  #
250  #
```

```
251  # The BGP timers are adjusted to provide more rapid detection of outages.
252  #
253  # The local BGP Autonomous System Number (ASN) (YOUR_BGP_ASN) is configured
254  # as part of your Customer Gateway. If the ASN must be changed, the
255  # Customer Gateway and VPN Connection will need to be recreated with AWS.
256  #
257  bgp use on
258  bgp autonomous-system YOUR_BGP_ASN
259  bgp neighbor 2 7224 169.254.255.5 hold-time=30 local-address=169.254.255.6
260
261  # To advertise additional prefixes to Amazon VPC, copy the 'network' statement and
262  # identify the prefix you wish to advertise. Make sure the
263  # prefix is present in the routing table of the device with a valid next-hop.
264  # For example, the following two lines will advertise 192.168.0.0/16 and 10.0.0.0/16 to Amazon
         VPC
265  #
266  # bgp import filter 1 equal 10.0.0.0/16
267  # bgp import filter 1 equal 192.168.0.0/16
268  #
269
270  bgp import filter 1 equal 0.0.0.0/0
271  bgp import 7224 static filter 1
272
273  bgp configure refresh
```

How to Test the Customer Gateway Configuration

You can test the gateway configuration for each tunnel.

To test the customer gateway configuration for each tunnel

1. On your customer gateway, determine whether the BGP status is `Active`.

   It takes approximately 30 seconds for a BGP peering to become active.

2. Ensure that the customer gateway is advertising a route to the virtual private gateway. The route may be the default route (`0.0.0.0/0`) or a more specific route you prefer.

When properly established, your BGP peering should be receiving one route from the virtual private gateway corresponding to the prefix that your VPC integration team specified for the VPC (for example, `10.0.0.0/24`). If the BGP peering is established, you are receiving a prefix, and you are advertising a prefix, your tunnel is configured correctly. Make sure that both tunnels are in this state.

Next you must test the connectivity for each tunnel by launching an instance into your VPC, and pinging the instance from your home network. Before you begin, make sure of the following:

- Use an AMI that responds to ping requests. We recommend that you use one of the Amazon Linux AMIs.
- Configure your instance's security group and network ACL to enable inbound ICMP traffic.
- Ensure that you have configured routing for your VPN connection: your subnet's route table must contain a route to the virtual private gateway. For more information, see Enable Route Propagation in Your Route Table in the *Amazon VPC User Guide*.

To test the end-to-end connectivity of each tunnel

1. Launch an instance of one of the Amazon Linux AMIs into your VPC. The Amazon Linux AMIs are listed in the launch wizard when you launch an instance from the Amazon EC2 Console. For more information, see the Amazon VPC Getting Started Guide.

2. After the instance is running, get its private IP address (for example, 10.0.0.4). The console displays the address as part of the instance's details.

3. On a system in your home network, use the ping command with the instance's IP address. Make sure that the computer you ping from is behind the customer gateway. A successful response should be similar to the following.

```
1 ping 10.0.0.4
```

```
1 Pinging 10.0.0.4 with 32 bytes of data:
2
3 Reply from 10.0.0.4: bytes=32 time<1ms TTL=128
4 Reply from 10.0.0.4: bytes=32 time<1ms TTL=128
5 Reply from 10.0.0.4: bytes=32 time<1ms TTL=128
6
7 Ping statistics for 10.0.0.4:
8 Packets: Sent = 3, Received = 3, Lost = 0 (0% loss),
9
10 Approximate round trip times in milliseconds:
11 Minimum = 0ms, Maximum = 0ms, Average = 0ms
```

Note

If you ping an instance from your customer gateway router, ensure that you are sourcing ping messages from an internal IP address, not a tunnel IP address. Some AMIs don't respond to ping messages from tunnel IP addresses.

1. (Optional) To test tunnel failover, you can temporarily disable one of the tunnels on your customer gateway, and repeat the above step. You cannot disable a tunnel on the AWS side of the VPN connection.

If your tunnels don't test successfully, see Troubleshooting Yamaha Customer Gateway Connectivity.

Example: Generic Customer Gateway Using Border Gateway Protocol

Topics

- A High-Level View of the Customer Gateway
- A Detailed View of the Customer Gateway and an Example Configuration
- How to Test the Customer Gateway Configuration

If your customer gateway isn't one of the types discussed earlier in this guide, your integration team will provide you with generic information that you can use to configure your customer gateway. This section contains an example of that information.

Two diagrams illustrate the example configuration. The first diagram shows the high-level layout of the customer gateway, and the second diagram shows details from the example configuration. You should use the real configuration information that you receive from your integration team and apply it to your customer gateway.

A High-Level View of the Customer Gateway

The following diagram shows the general details of your customer gateway. Note that the VPN connection consists of two separate tunnels. Using redundant tunnels ensures continuous availability in the case that a device fails.

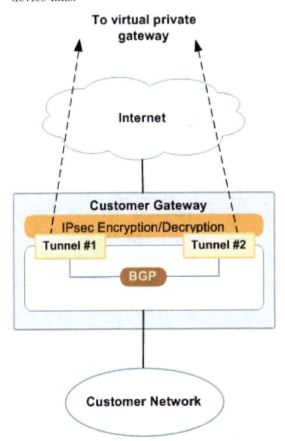

A Detailed View of the Customer Gateway and an Example Configuration

The diagram in this section illustrates an example generic customer gateway. Following the diagram, there is a corresponding example of the configuration information your integration team should provide. The example configuration contains a set of information for each of the tunnels that you must configure.

In addition, the example configuration refers to these items that you must provide:

- *YOUR_UPLINK_ADDRESS*—The IP address for the Internet-routable external interface on the customer gateway. The address must be static, and may be behind a device performing network address translation (NAT). To ensure that NAT traversal (NAT-T) can function, you must adjust your firewall rules to unblock UDP port 4500.
- *YOUR_BGP_ASN*—The customer gateway's BGP ASN (we use 65000 by default)

The example configuration includes several example values to help you understand how configuration works. For example, we provide example values for the VPN connection ID (vpn-44a8938f), virtual private gateway ID (vgw-8db04f81), the IP addresses (72.21.209.*, 169.254.255.*), and the remote ASN (7224). You'll replace these example values with the actual values from the configuration information that you receive.

In the following diagram and example configuration, you must replace the items in red italics with values that apply to your particular configuration.

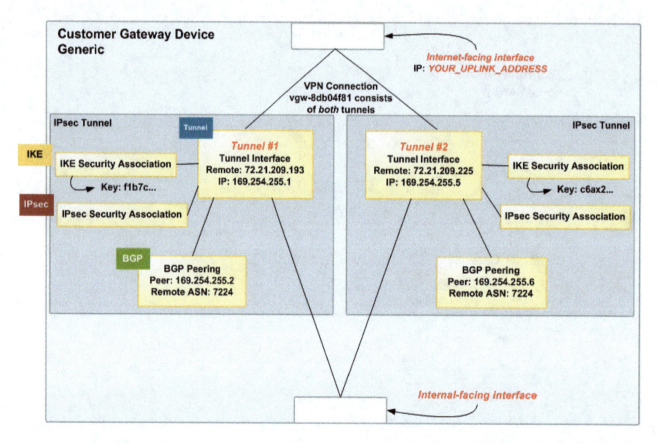

1 Amazon Web Services
2 Virtual Private Cloud
3
4 VPN Connection Configuration
5 ==
6 AWS utilizes unique identifiers to manipulate the configuration of
7 a VPN Connection. Each VPN Connection is assigned a VPN identifier
8 and is associated with two other identifiers, namely the

9 Customer Gateway Identifier and the Virtual Private Gateway Identifier.

10

11 Your VPN Connection ID   : vpn-44a8938f

12 Your Virtual Private Gateway ID : vgw-8db04f81

13 Your Customer Gateway ID   : cgw-b4dc3961

14

15 A VPN Connection consists of a pair of IPsec tunnel security associations (SAs).

16 It is important that both tunnel security associations be configured.

17

18

19 IPsec Tunnel #1

20 ==

21 ![\[Image NOT FOUND\]](http://docs.aws.amazon.com/AmazonVPC/latest/NetworkAdminGuide/images/IKE.png)

22 #1: Internet Key Exchange Configuration

23

24 Configure the IKE SA as follows:

25 Please note, these sample configurations are for the minimum requirement of AES128, SHA1, and DH Group 2.

26 You will need to modify these sample configuration files to take advantage of AES256, SHA256, or other DH groups like 2, 14-18, 22, 23, and 24.

27 The address of the external interface for your customer gateway must be a static address.

28 Your customer gateway may reside behind a device performing network address translation (NAT).

29 To ensure that NAT traversal (NAT-T) can function, you must adjust your firewall rules to unblock UDP port 4500. If not behind NAT, we recommend disabling NAT-T.

30 - IKE version   : IKEv1

31 - Authentication Method   : Pre-Shared Key

32 - Pre-Shared Key   : plain-text-password1

33 - Authentication Algorithm : sha1

34 - Encryption Algorithm   : aes-128-cbc

35 - Lifetime   : 28800 seconds

36 - Phase 1 Negotiation Mode : main

37 - Diffie-Hellman   : Group 2

38

39 ![\[Image NOT FOUND\]](http://docs.aws.amazon.com/AmazonVPC/latest/NetworkAdminGuide/images/IPsec.png)

40 #2: IPsec Configuration

41

42 Configure the IPsec SA as follows:

43 Please note, you may use these additionally supported IPSec parameters for encryption like AES256 and other DH groups like 2, 5, 14-18, 22, 23, and 24.

44 - Protocol   : esp

45 - Authentication Algorithm : hmac-sha1-96

46 - Encryption Algorithm   : aes-128-cbc

47 - Lifetime   : 3600 seconds

48 - Mode   : tunnel

49 - Perfect Forward Secrecy : Diffie-Hellman Group 2

50

51 IPsec Dead Peer Detection (DPD) will be enabled on the AWS Endpoint. We

52 recommend configuring DPD on your endpoint as follows:

53 - DPD Interval   : 10

54 - DPD Retries   : 3

55

56 IPsec ESP (Encapsulating Security Payload) inserts additional

57 headers to transmit packets. These headers require additional space,
58 which reduces the amount of space available to transmit application data.
59 To limit the impact of this behavior, we recommend the following
60 configuration on your Customer Gateway:
61 - TCP MSS Adjustment   : 1387 bytes
62 - Clear Don't Fragment Bit : enabled
63 - Fragmentation   : Before encryption
64
65 ![\[Image NOT FOUND\]](http://docs.aws.amazon.com/AmazonVPC/latest/NetworkAdminGuide/images/
     Tunnel.png)
66 #3: Tunnel Interface Configuration
67
68 Your Customer Gateway must be configured with a tunnel interface that is
69 associated with the IPsec tunnel. All traffic transmitted to the tunnel
70 interface is encrypted and transmitted to the Virtual Private Gateway.
71
72 The Customer Gateway and Virtual Private Gateway each have two addresses that relate
73 to this IPsec tunnel. Each contains an outside address, upon which encrypted
74 traffic is exchanged. Each also contain an inside address associated with
75 the tunnel interface.
76
77 The Customer Gateway outside IP address was provided when the Customer Gateway
78 was created. Changing the IP address requires the creation of a new
79 Customer Gateway.
80
81 The Customer Gateway inside IP address should be configured on your tunnel
82 interface.
83
84 Outside IP Addresses:
85 - Customer Gateway: : YOUR_UPLINK_ADDRESS
86 - Virtual Private Gateway   : 72.21.209.193
87
88 Inside IP Addresses
89 - Customer Gateway   : 169.254.255.2/30
90 - Virtual Private Gateway   : 169.254.255.1/30
91
92 Configure your tunnel to fragment at the optimal size:
93 - Tunnel interface MTU   : 1436 bytes
94
95 ![\[Image NOT FOUND\]](http://docs.aws.amazon.com/AmazonVPC/latest/NetworkAdminGuide/images/BGP.
     png)
96 #4: Border Gateway Protocol (BGP) Configuration:
97
98 The Border Gateway Protocol (BGPv4) is used within the tunnel, between the inside
99 IP addresses, to exchange routes from the VPC to your home network. Each
100 BGP router has an Autonomous System Number (ASN). Your ASN was provided
101 to AWS when the Customer Gateway was created.
102
103 BGP Configuration Options:
104 - Customer Gateway ASN   : YOUR_BGP_ASN
105 - Virtual Private Gateway ASN : 7224
106 - Neighbor IP Address   : 169.254.255.1
107 - Neighbor Hold Time   : 30
108

109 Configure BGP to announce routes to the Virtual Private Gateway. The gateway
110 will announce prefixes to your customer gateway based upon the prefix you
111 assigned to the VPC at creation time.

112

113 IPsec Tunnel #2

114 ==

115 ![\[Image NOT FOUND\]](http://docs.aws.amazon.com/AmazonVPC/latest/NetworkAdminGuide/images/IKE.png)

116 #1: Internet Key Exchange Configuration

117

118 Configure the IKE SA as follows:

119 Please note, these sample configurations are for the minimum requirement of AES128, SHA1, and DH Group 2.

120 You will need to modify these sample configuration files to take advantage of AES256, SHA256, or other DH groups like 2, 14-18, 22, 23, and 24.

121 The address of the external interface for your customer gateway must be a static address.

122 Your customer gateway may reside behind a device performing network address translation (NAT).

123 To ensure that NAT traversal (NAT-T) can function, you must adjust your firewall rules to unblock UDP port 4500. If not behind NAT, we recommend disabling NAT-T.

124 - IKE version   : IKEv1
125 - Authentication Method : Pre-Shared Key
126 - Pre-Shared Key   : plain-text-password2
127 - Authentication Algorithm : sha1
128 - Encryption Algorithm   : aes-128-cbc
129 - Lifetime   : 28800 seconds
130 - Phase 1 Negotiation Mode : main
131 - Diffie-Hellman   : Group 2

132

133 ![\[Image NOT FOUND\]](http://docs.aws.amazon.com/AmazonVPC/latest/NetworkAdminGuide/images/IPsec.png)

134 #2: IPsec Configuration

135

136 Configure the IPsec SA as follows:

137 Please note, you may use these additionally supported IPSec parameters for encryption like AES256 and other DH groups like 2, 5, 14-18, 22, 23, and 24.

138 - Protocol   : esp
139 - Authentication Algorithm : hmac-sha1-96
140 - Encryption Algorithm   : aes-128-cbc
141 - Lifetime   : 3600 seconds
142 - Mode   : tunnel
143 - Perfect Forward Secrecy : Diffie-Hellman Group 2

144

145 IPsec Dead Peer Detection (DPD) will be enabled on the AWS Endpoint. We
146 recommend configuring DPD on your endpoint as follows:

147 - DPD Interval   : 10
148 - DPD Retries   : 3

149

150 IPsec ESP (Encapsulating Security Payload) inserts additional
151 headers to transmit packets. These headers require additional space,
152 which reduces the amount of space available to transmit application data.
153 To limit the impact of this behavior, we recommend the following
154 configuration on your Customer Gateway:

155 - TCP MSS Adjustment   : 1387 bytes
156 - Clear Don't Fragment Bit : enabled

157 - Fragmentation   : Before encryption
158
159 ![\[Image NOT FOUND\]](http://docs.aws.amazon.com/AmazonVPC/latest/NetworkAdminGuide/images/
    Tunnel.png)
160 #3: Tunnel Interface Configuration
161
162 Your Customer Gateway must be configured with a tunnel interface that is
163 associated with the IPsec tunnel. All traffic transmitted to the tunnel
164 interface is encrypted and transmitted to the Virtual Private Gateway.
165
166 The Customer Gateway and Virtual Private Gateway each have two addresses that relate
167 to this IPsec tunnel. Each contains an outside address, upon which encrypted
168 traffic is exchanged. Each also contain an inside address associated with
169 the tunnel interface.
170
171 The Customer Gateway outside IP address was provided when the Customer Gateway
172 was created. Changing the IP address requires the creation of a new
173 Customer Gateway.
174
175 The Customer Gateway inside IP address should be configured on your tunnel
176 interface.
177
178 Outside IP Addresses:
179 - Customer Gateway: : YOUR_UPLINK_ADDRESS
180 - Virtual Private Gateway   : 72.21.209.193
181
182 Inside IP Addresses
183 - Customer Gateway   : 169.254.255.6/30
184 - Virtual Private Gateway   : 169.254.255.5/30
185
186 Configure your tunnel to fragment at the optimal size:
187 - Tunnel interface MTU   : 1436 bytes
188
189 ![\[Image NOT FOUND\]](http://docs.aws.amazon.com/AmazonVPC/latest/NetworkAdminGuide/images/BGP.
    png) "
190 #4: Border Gateway Protocol (BGP) Configuration:
191
192 The Border Gateway Protocol (BGPv4) is used within the tunnel, between the inside
193 IP addresses, to exchange routes from the VPC to your home network. Each
194 BGP router has an Autonomous System Number (ASN). Your ASN was provided
195 to AWS when the Customer Gateway was created.
196
197 BGP Configuration Options:
198 - Customer Gateway ASN   : YOUR_BGP_ASN
199 - Virtual Private Gateway ASN : 7224
200 - Neighbor IP Address   : 169.254.255.5
201 - Neighbor Hold Time   : 30
202
203 Configure BGP to announce routes to the Virtual Private Gateway. The gateway
204 will announce prefixes to your customer gateway based upon the prefix you
205 assigned to the VPC at creation time.

How to Test the Customer Gateway Configuration

You can test the gateway configuration for each tunnel.

To test the customer gateway configuration for each tunnel

1. On your customer gateway, determine whether the BGP status is `Active`.

   It takes approximately 30 seconds for a BGP peering to become active.

2. Ensure that the customer gateway is advertising a route to the virtual private gateway. The route may be the default route (`0.0.0.0/0`) or a more specific route you prefer.

When properly established, your BGP peering should be receiving one route from the virtual private gateway corresponding to the prefix that your VPC integration team specified for the VPC (for example, `10.0.0.0/24`). If the BGP peering is established, you are receiving a prefix, and you are advertising a prefix, your tunnel is configured correctly. Make sure that both tunnels are in this state.

Next you must test the connectivity for each tunnel by launching an instance into your VPC, and pinging the instance from your home network. Before you begin, make sure of the following:

- Use an AMI that responds to ping requests. We recommend that you use one of the Amazon Linux AMIs.
- Configure your instance's security group and network ACL to enable inbound ICMP traffic.
- Ensure that you have configured routing for your VPN connection: your subnet's route table must contain a route to the virtual private gateway. For more information, see Enable Route Propagation in Your Route Table in the *Amazon VPC User Guide*.

To test the end-to-end connectivity of each tunnel

1. Launch an instance of one of the Amazon Linux AMIs into your VPC. The Amazon Linux AMIs are listed in the launch wizard when you launch an instance from the Amazon EC2 Console. For more information, see the Amazon VPC Getting Started Guide.

2. After the instance is running, get its private IP address (for example, `10.0.0.4`). The console displays the address as part of the instance's details.

3. On a system in your home network, use the ping command with the instance's IP address. Make sure that the computer you ping from is behind the customer gateway. A successful response should be similar to the following.

```
1 ping 10.0.0.4
```

```
1 Pinging 10.0.0.4 with 32 bytes of data:
2
3 Reply from 10.0.0.4: bytes=32 time<1ms TTL=128
4 Reply from 10.0.0.4: bytes=32 time<1ms TTL=128
5 Reply from 10.0.0.4: bytes=32 time<1ms TTL=128
6
7 Ping statistics for 10.0.0.4:
8 Packets: Sent = 3, Received = 3, Lost = 0 (0% loss),
9
10 Approximate round trip times in milliseconds:
11 Minimum = 0ms, Maximum = 0ms, Average = 0ms
```

Note
If you ping an instance from your customer gateway router, ensure that you are sourcing ping messages from an internal IP address, not a tunnel IP address. Some AMIs don't respond to ping messages from tunnel IP addresses.

1. (Optional) To test tunnel failover, you can temporarily disable one of the tunnels on your customer gateway, and repeat the above step. You cannot disable a tunnel on the AWS side of the VPN connection.

If your tunnels don't test successfully, see Troubleshooting Generic Device Customer Gateway Connectivity Using Border Gateway Protocol.

Example: Generic Customer Gateway without Border Gateway Protocol

Topics

- A High-Level View of the Customer Gateway
- A Detailed View of the Customer Gateway and an Example Configuration
- How to Test the Customer Gateway Configuration

If your customer gateway isn't one of the types discussed earlier in this guide, your integration team will provide you with generic information that you can use to configure your customer gateway. This section contains an example of that information.

Two diagrams illustrate the example configuration. The first diagram shows the high-level layout of the customer gateway, and the second diagram shows details from the example configuration. You should use the real configuration information that you receive from your integration team and apply it to your customer gateway.

A High-Level View of the Customer Gateway

The following diagram shows the general details of your customer gateway. Note that the VPN connection consists of two separate tunnels: *Tunnel 1* and *Tunnel 2*. Using redundant tunnels ensures continuous availability in the case that a device fails.

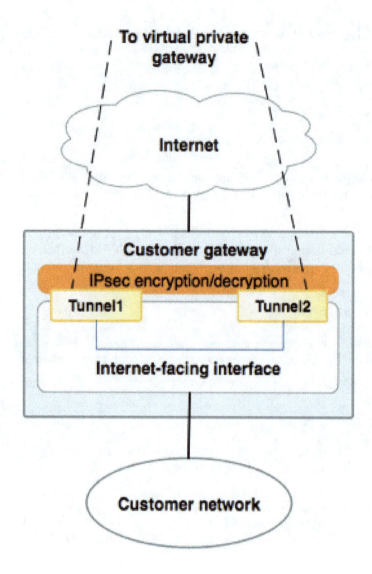

A Detailed View of the Customer Gateway and an Example Configuration

The diagram in this section illustrates an example generic customer gateway (without BGP). Following the diagram, there is a corresponding example of the configuration information your integration team should provide. The example configuration contains a set of information for each of the tunnels that you must configure.

The diagram in this section illustrates a generic customer gateway that uses static routing for its VPN connection (meaning that it does not support dynamic routing, or Border Gateway Protocol (BGP). Following the diagram, there is a corresponding example of the configuration information your integration team should give you. The example configuration contains a set of information for each of the two tunnels you must configure.

In addition, the example configuration refers to one item that you must provide:

- *YOUR_UPLINK_ADDRESS*—The IP address for the Internet-routable external interface on the customer gateway. The address must be static, and may be behind a device performing network address translation (NAT). To ensure that NAT traversal (NAT-T) can function, you must adjust your firewall rules to unblock UDP port 4500.

The example configuration includes several example values to help you understand how configuration works. For example, we provide example values for the VPN connection ID (vpn-44a8938f), virtual private gateway ID

170

(vgw-8db04f81), and the VGW IP addresses (72.21.209.*, 169.254.255.*). You'll replace these example values with the actual values from the configuration information that you receive.

In the following diagram and example configuration, you must replace the items in red italics with values that apply to your particular configuration.

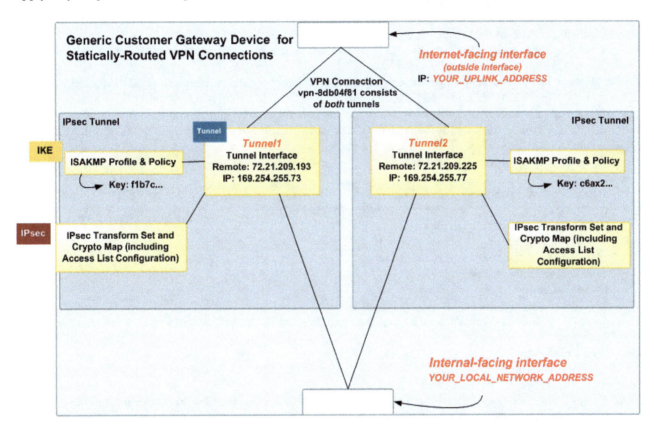

Important

The following configuration information is an example of what you can expect an integration team to provide . Many of the values in the following example will be different from the actual configuration information that you receive. You must use the actual values and not the example values shown here, or your implementation will fail.

```
1  Amazon Web Services
2  Virtual Private Cloud
3
4  VPN Connection Configuration
5  ================================================================================
6  AWS utilizes unique identifiers to manipulate the configuration of
7  a VPN Connection. Each VPN Connection is assigned a VPN Connection Identifier
8  and is associated with two other identifiers, namely the
9  Customer Gateway Identifier and the Virtual Private Gateway Identifier.
10
11 Your VPN Connection ID                 : vpn-44a8938f
12 Your Virtual Private Gateway ID        : vgw-8db04f81
13 Your Customer Gateway ID               : cgw-ff628496
14
15 A VPN Connection consists of a pair of IPSec tunnel security associations (SAs).
16 It is important that both tunnel security associations be configured.
17
18
```

```
19 IPSec Tunnel #1
20 ================================================================================
21 ![\[Image NOT FOUND\]](http://docs.aws.amazon.com/AmazonVPC/latest/NetworkAdminGuide/images/IKE.
      png)
22 #1: Internet Key Exchange Configuration
23
24 Configure the IKE SA as follows
25 Please note, these sample configurations are for the minimum requirement of AES128, SHA1, and DH
      Group 2.
26 You will need to modify these sample configuration files to take advantage of AES256, SHA256, or
      other DH groups like 2, 14-18, 22, 23, and 24.
27 The address of the external interface for your customer gateway must be a static address.
28 Your customer gateway may reside behind a device performing network address translation (NAT).
29 To ensure that NAT traversal (NAT-T) can function, you must adjust your firewall rules to
      unblock UDP port 4500. If not behind NAT, we recommend disabling NAT-T.
30   - IKE version             : IKEv1
31   - Authentication Method   : Pre-Shared Key
32   - Pre-Shared Key          : PRE-SHARED-KEY-IN-PLAIN-TEXT
33   - Authentication Algorithm : sha1
34   - Encryption Algorithm    : aes-128-cbc
35   - Lifetime                : 28800 seconds
36   - Phase 1 Negotiation Mode : main
37   - Diffie-Hellman          : Group 2
38
39 ![\[Image NOT FOUND\]](http://docs.aws.amazon.com/AmazonVPC/latest/NetworkAdminGuide/images/
      IPsec.png)
40 #2: IPSec Configuration
41
42 Configure the IPSec SA as follows:
43 Please note, you may use these additionally supported IPSec parameters for encryption like
      AES256 and other DH groups like 2, 5, 14-18, 22, 23, and 24.
44   - Protocol                : esp
45   - Authentication Algorithm : hmac-sha1-96
46   - Encryption Algorithm    : aes-128-cbc
47   - Lifetime                : 3600 seconds
48   - Mode                    : tunnel
49   - Perfect Forward Secrecy : Diffie-Hellman Group 2
50
51 IPSec Dead Peer Detection (DPD) will be enabled on the AWS Endpoint. We
52 recommend configuring DPD on your endpoint as follows:
53   - DPD Interval            : 10
54   - DPD Retries             : 3
55
56 IPSec ESP (Encapsulating Security Payload) inserts additional
57 headers to transmit packets. These headers require additional space,
58 which reduces the amount of space available to transmit application data.
59 To limit the impact of this behavior, we recommend the following
60 configuration on your Customer Gateway:
61   - TCP MSS Adjustment      : 1387 bytes
62   - Clear Don't Fragment Bit : enabled
63   - Fragmentation           : Before encryption
64
65 ![\[Image NOT FOUND\]](http://docs.aws.amazon.com/AmazonVPC/latest/NetworkAdminGuide/images/
      Tunnel.png)
```

66 #3: Tunnel Interface Configuration

67

68 Your Customer Gateway must be configured with a tunnel interface that is
69 associated with the IPSec tunnel. All traffic transmitted to the tunnel
70 interface is encrypted and transmitted to the Virtual Private Gateway.

71

72 The Customer Gateway and Virtual Private Gateway each have two addresses that relate
73 to this IPSec tunnel. Each contains an outside address, upon which encrypted
74 traffic is exchanged. Each also contain an inside address associated with
75 the tunnel interface.

76

77 The Customer Gateway outside IP address was provided when the Customer Gateway
78 was created. Changing the IP address requires the creation of a new
79 Customer Gateway.

80

81 The Customer Gateway inside IP address should be configured on your tunnel
82 interface.

83

84 Outside IP Addresses:
85 - Customer Gateway   : YOUR_UPLINK_ADDRESS
86 - Virtual Private Gateway   : 72.21.209.193

87

88 Inside IP Addresses
89 - Customer Gateway   : 169.254.255.74/30
90 - Virtual Private Gateway   : 169.254.255.73/30

91

92 Configure your tunnel to fragment at the optimal size:
93 - Tunnel interface MTU   : 1436 bytes

94

95 #4: Static Routing Configuration:

96

97 To route traffic between your internal network and your VPC,
98 you will need a static route added to your router.

99

100 Static Route Configuration Options:

101

102 - Next hop   : 169.254.255.73

103

104 You should add static routes towards your internal network on the VGW.
105 The VGW will then send traffic towards your internal network over
106 the tunnels.

107

108

109

110 IPSec Tunnel #2
111 ==
112 ![\[Image NOT FOUND\]](http://docs.aws.amazon.com/AmazonVPC/latest/NetworkAdminGuide/images/IKE.
     png)
113 #1: Internet Key Exchange Configuration

114

115 Configure the IKE SA as follows:
116 Please note, these sample configurations are for the minimum requirement of AES128, SHA1, and DH
     Group 2.
117 You will need to modify these sample configuration files to take advantage of AES256, SHA256, or

other DH groups like 2, 14-18, 22, 23, and 24.
118 The address of the external interface for your customer gateway must be a static address.
119 Your customer gateway may reside behind a device performing network address translation (NAT).
120 To ensure that NAT traversal (NAT-T) can function, you must adjust your firewall rules to
   unblock UDP port 4500. If not behind NAT, we recommend disabling NAT-T.
121   - IKE version   : IKEv1
122   - Authentication Method   : Pre-Shared Key
123   - Pre-Shared Key   : PRE-SHARED-KEY-IN-PLAIN-TEXT
124   - Authentication Algorithm : sha1
125   - Encryption Algorithm   : aes-128-cbc
126   - Lifetime   : 28800 seconds
127   - Phase 1 Negotiation Mode : main
128   - Diffie-Hellman   : Group 2
129
130 ![\[Image NOT FOUND\]](http://docs.aws.amazon.com/AmazonVPC/latest/NetworkAdminGuide/images/
   IPsec.png)
131 #2: IPSec Configuration
132
133 Configure the IPSec SA as follows:
134 Please note, you may use these additionally supported IPSec parameters for encryption like
   AES256 and other DH groups like 2, 5, 14-18, 22, 23, and 24.
135   - Protocol   : esp
136   - Authentication Algorithm : hmac-sha1-96
137   - Encryption Algorithm   : aes-128-cbc
138   - Lifetime   : 3600 seconds
139   - Mode   : tunnel
140   - Perfect Forward Secrecy : Diffie-Hellman Group 2
141
142 IPSec Dead Peer Detection (DPD) will be enabled on the AWS Endpoint. We
143 recommend configuring DPD on your endpoint as follows:
144   - DPD Interval   : 10
145   - DPD Retries   : 3
146
147 IPSec ESP (Encapsulating Security Payload) inserts additional
148 headers to transmit packets. These headers require additional space,
149 which reduces the amount of space available to transmit application data.
150 To limit the impact of this behavior, we recommend the following
151 configuration on your Customer Gateway:
152   - TCP MSS Adjustment   : 1387 bytes
153   - Clear Don't Fragment Bit : enabled
154   - Fragmentation   : Before encryption
155
156 ![\[Image NOT FOUND\]](http://docs.aws.amazon.com/AmazonVPC/latest/NetworkAdminGuide/images/
   Tunnel.png)
157 #3: Tunnel Interface Configuration
158
159 Your Customer Gateway must be configured with a tunnel interface that is
160 associated with the IPSec tunnel. All traffic transmitted to the tunnel
161 interface is encrypted and transmitted to the Virtual Private Gateway.
162
163 The Customer Gateway and Virtual Private Gateway each have two addresses that relate
164 to this IPSec tunnel. Each contains an outside address, upon which encrypted
165 traffic is exchanged. Each also contain an inside address associated with
166 the tunnel interface.

```
167
168 The Customer Gateway outside IP address was provided when the Customer Gateway
169 was created. Changing the IP address requires the creation of a new
170 Customer Gateway.
171
172 The Customer Gateway inside IP address should be configured on your tunnel
173 interface.
174
175 Outside IP Addresses:
176   - Customer Gateway                    : YOUR_UPLINK_ADDRESS
177   - Virtual Private Gateway             : 72.21.209.225
178
179 Inside IP Addresses
180   - Customer Gateway                    : 169.254.255.78/30
181   - Virtual Private Gateway             : 169.254.255.77/30
182
183 Configure your tunnel to fragment at the optimal size:
184   - Tunnel interface MTU     : 1436 bytes
185
186 #4: Static Routing Configuration:
187
188 To route traffic between your internal network and your VPC,
189 you will need a static route added to your router.
190
191 Static Route Configuration Options:
192
193   - Next hop        : 169.254.255.77
194
195 You should add static routes towards your internal network on the VGW.
196 The VGW will then send traffic towards your internal network over
197 the tunnels.
```

How to Test the Customer Gateway Configuration

You must first test the gateway configuration for each tunnel.

To test the customer gateway configuration for each tunnel

- On your customer gateway, verify that you have added a static route to the VPC CIDR IP space to use the tunnel interface.

Next you must test the connectivity for each tunnel by launching an instance into your VPC, and pinging the instance from your home network. Before you begin, make sure of the following:

- Use an AMI that responds to ping requests. We recommend that you use one of the Amazon Linux AMIs.
- Configure your instance's security group and network ACL to enable inbound ICMP traffic.
- Ensure that you have configured routing for your VPN connection - your subnet's route table must contain a route to the virtual private gateway. For more information, see Enable Route Propagation in Your Route Table in the *Amazon VPC User Guide*.

To test the end-to-end connectivity of each tunnel

1. Launch an instance of one of the Amazon Linux AMIs into your VPC. The Amazon Linux AMIs are available in the Quick Start menu when you use the Launch Instances Wizard in the AWS Management Console. For more information, see the Amazon VPC Getting Started Guide.

2. After the instance is running, get its private IP address (for example, 10.0.0.4). The console displays the address as part of the instance's details.

3. On a system in your home network, use the ping command with the instance's IP address. Make sure that the computer you ping from is behind the customer gateway. A successful response should be similar to the following.

```
1 PROMPT> ping 10.0.0.4
2 Pinging 10.0.0.4 with 32 bytes of data:
3
4 Reply from 10.0.0.4: bytes=32 time<1ms TTL=128
5 Reply from 10.0.0.4: bytes=32 time<1ms TTL=128
6 Reply from 10.0.0.4: bytes=32 time<1ms TTL=128
7
8 Ping statistics for 10.0.0.4:
9 Packets: Sent = 3, Received = 3, Lost = 0 (0% loss),
10
11 Approximate round trip times in milliseconds:
12 Minimum = 0ms, Maximum = 0ms, Average = 0ms
```

Note

If you ping an instance from your customer gateway router, ensure that you are sourcing ping messages from an internal IP address, not a tunnel IP address. Some AMIs don't respond to ping messages from tunnel IP addresses.

If your tunnels don't test successfully, see Troubleshooting Generic Device Customer Gateway Connectivity Using Border Gateway Protocol.

Troubleshooting

The following topics contain troubleshooting information that you can use if your tunnels aren't in the correct state when you test your customer gateway.

Topics

- Troubleshooting Cisco ASA Customer Gateway Connectivity
- Troubleshooting Cisco IOS Customer Gateway Connectivity
- Troubleshooting Cisco IOS Customer Gateway without Border Gateway Protocol Connectivity
- Troubleshooting Juniper JunOS Customer Gateway Connectivity
- Troubleshooting Juniper ScreenOS Customer Gateway Connectivity
- Troubleshooting Yamaha Customer Gateway Connectivity
- Troubleshooting Generic Device Customer Gateway Connectivity Using Border Gateway Protocol
- Troubleshooting Generic Device Customer Gateway without Border Gateway Protocol Connectivity

Troubleshooting Cisco ASA Customer Gateway Connectivity

When you troubleshoot the connectivity of a Cisco customer gateway, you need to consider three things: IKE, IPsec, and routing. You can troubleshoot these areas in any order, but we recommend that you start with IKE (at the bottom of the network stack) and move up.

Important
Some Cisco ASAs only support Active/Standby mode. When you use these Cisco ASAs, you can have only one active tunnel at a time. The other standby tunnel becomes active only if the first tunnel becomes unavailable. The standby tunnel may produce the following error in your log files, which can be ignored: `Rejecting IPSec tunnel: no matching crypto map entry for remote proxy 0.0.0.0/0.0.0.0/0/0 local proxy 0.0.0.0/0.0.0.0/0/0 on interface outside`

IKE

Use the following command. The response shows a customer gateway with IKE configured correctly.

```
1 ciscoasa# show crypto isakmp sa

1    Active SA: 2
2    Rekey SA: 0 (A tunnel will report 1 Active and 1 Rekey SA during rekey)
3 Total IKE SA: 2
4
5 1   IKE Peer: AWS_ENDPOINT_1
6     Type   : L2L          Role    : initiator
7     Rekey  : no           State   : MM_ACTIVE
```

You should see one or more lines containing an *src* of the remote gateway specified in the tunnels. The *state* should be MM_ACTIVE and *status* should be ACTIVE. The absence of an entry, or any entry in another state, indicates that IKE is not configured properly.

For further troubleshooting, run the following commands to enable log messages that provide diagnostic information.

```
1 router# term mon
2 router# debug crypto isakmp
```

To disable debugging, use the following command.

```
1 router# no debug crypto isakmp
```

IPsec

Use the following command. The response shows a customer gateway with IPsec configured correctly.

```
1 ciscoasa# show crypto ipsec sa

1 interface: outside
2     Crypto map tag: VPN_crypto_map_name, seq num: 2, local addr: 172.25.50.101
3
4     access-list integ-ppe-loopback extended permit ip any vpc_subnet subnet_mask
5     local ident (addr/mask/prot/port): (0.0.0.0/0.0.0.0/0/0)
6     remote ident (addr/mask/prot/port): (vpc_subnet/subnet_mask/0/0)
7     current_peer: integ-ppe1
8
```

```
 9   #pkts encaps: 0, #pkts encrypt: 0, #pkts digest: 0
10   #pkts decaps: 0, #pkts decrypt: 0, #pkts verify: 0
11   #pkts compressed: 0, #pkts decompressed: 0
12   #pkts not compressed: 0, #pkts comp failed: 0, #pkts decomp failed: 0
13   #pre-frag successes: 0, #pre-frag failures: 0, #fragments created: 0
14   #PMTUs sent: 0, #PMTUs rcvd: 0, #decapsulated frgs needing reassembly: 0
15   #send errors: 0, #recv errors: 0
16
17   local crypto endpt.: 172.25.50.101, remote crypto endpt.: AWS_ENDPOINT_1
18
19   path mtu 1500, ipsec overhead 74, media mtu 1500
20   current outbound spi: 6D9F8D3B
21   current inbound spi : 48B456A6
22
23  inbound esp sas:
24   spi: 0x48B456A6 (1219778214)
25     transform: esp-aes esp-sha-hmac no compression
26     in use settings ={L2L, Tunnel, PFS Group 2, }
27     slot: 0, conn_id: 4710400, crypto-map: VPN_cry_map_1
28     sa timing: remaining key lifetime (kB/sec): (4374000/3593)
29     IV size: 16 bytes
30     replay detection support: Y
31     Anti replay bitmap:
32      0x00000000 0x00000001
33  outbound esp sas:
34   spi: 0x6D9F8D3B (1839172923)
35     transform: esp-aes esp-sha-hmac no compression
36     in use settings ={L2L, Tunnel, PFS Group 2, }
37     slot: 0, conn_id: 4710400, crypto-map: VPN_cry_map_1
38     sa timing: remaining key lifetime (kB/sec): (4374000/3593)
39     IV size: 16 bytes
40     replay detection support: Y
41     Anti replay bitmap:
42      0x00000000 0x00000001
```

For each tunnel interface, you should see both an inbound esp sas and outbound esp sas. This assumes that an SA is listed (for example, spi: 0x48B456A6), and IPsec is configured correctly.

In Cisco ASA, the IPsec will only come up after "interesting traffic" is sent. To always keep the IPsec active, we recommend configuring SLA monitor. SLA monitor will continue to send interesting traffic, keeping the IPsec active.

You can also use the following ping command to force your IPsec to start negotiation and go up.

```
1 ping ec2_instance_ip_address
```

```
 1 Pinging ec2_instance_ip_address with 32 bytes of data:
 2
 3 Reply from ec2_instance_ip_address: bytes=32 time<1ms TTL=128
 4 Reply from ec2_instance_ip_address: bytes=32 time<1ms TTL=128
 5 Reply from ec2_instance_ip_address: bytes=32 time<1ms TTL=128
 6
 7 Ping statistics for 10.0.0.4:
 8 Packets: Sent = 3, Received = 3, Lost = 0 (0% loss),
 9
10 Approximate round trip times in milliseconds:
11 Minimum = 0ms, Maximum = 0ms, Average = 0ms
```

For further troubleshooting, use the following command to enable debugging.

```
1 router# debug crypto ipsec
```

To disable debugging, use the following command.

```
1 router# no debug crypto ipsec
```

Routing

Ping the other end of the tunnel. If this is working, then your IPsec should be up and running fine. If this is not working, check your access lists, and refer the previous IPsec section.

If you are not able to reach your instances, check the following:

1. Verify that the access-list is configured to allow traffic that is associated with the crypto map.

   You can do this using the following command:

   ```
   1 ciscoasa# show run crypto
   ```

   ```
   1 crypto ipsec transform-set transform-amzn esp-aes esp-sha-hmac
   2 crypto map VPN_crypto_map_name 1 match address access-list-name
   3 crypto map VPN_crypto_map_name 1 set pfs
   4 crypto map VPN_crypto_map_name 1 set peer AWS_ENDPOINT_1 AWS_ENDPOINT_2
   5 crypto map VPN_crypto_map_name 1 set transform-set transform-amzn
   6 crypto map VPN_crypto_map_name 1 set security-association lifetime seconds 3600
   ```

2. Next, check the access list as follows.

   ```
   1 ciscoasa# show run access-list access-list-name
   ```

   ```
   1 access-list access-list-name extended permit ip any vpc_subnet subnet_mask
   ```

   For example:

   ```
   1 access-list access-list-name extended permit ip any 10.0.0.0 255.255.0.0
   ```

3. Verify that this access list is correct. The example access list in the previous step allows all internal traffic to the VPC subnet 10.0.0.0/16.

4. Run a traceroute from the Cisco ASA device, to see if it reaches the Amazon routers (for example, *AWS_ENDPOINT_1/AWS_ENDPOINT_2*).

   If this reaches the Amazon router, then check the static routes you added in the Amazon console, and also the security groups for the particular instances.

5. For further troubleshooting, review the configuration.

Troubleshooting Cisco IOS Customer Gateway Connectivity

When you troubleshoot the connectivity of a Cisco customer gateway you need to consider four things: IKE, IPsec, tunnel, and BGP. You can troubleshoot these areas any order, but we recommend that you start with IKE (at the bottom of the network stack) and move up.

IKE

Use the following command. The response shows a customer gateway with IKE configured correctly.

```
1 router# show crypto isakmp sa
```

```
1 IPv4 Crypto ISAKMP SA
2 dst              src              state        conn-id slot status
3 192.168.37.160   72.21.209.193    QM_IDLE         2001   0 ACTIVE
4 192.168.37.160   72.21.209.225    QM_IDLE         2002   0 ACTIVE
```

You should see one or more lines containing a *src* of the Remote Gateway specified in the tunnels. The *state* should be QM_IDLE and *status* should be ACTIVE. The absence of an entry, or any entry in another indicate that IKE is not configured properly.

For further troubleshooting, run the following commands to enable log messages that provide diagnostic information.

```
1 router# term mon
2 router# debug crypto isakmp
```

To disable debugging, use the following command.

```
1 router# no debug crypto isakmp
```

IPsec

Use the following command. The response shows a customer gateway with IPsec configured correctly.

```
1 router# show crypto ipsec sa
```

```
1  interface: Tunnel1
2     Crypto map tag: Tunnel1-head-0, local addr 192.168.37.160
3
4     protected vrf: (none)
5     local  ident (addr/mask/prot/port): (0.0.0.0/0.0.0.0/0/0)
6     remote ident (addr/mask/prot/port): (0.0.0.0/0.0.0.0/0/0)
7     current_peer 72.21.209.225 port 500
8      PERMIT, flags={origin_is_acl,}
9      #pkts encaps: 149, #pkts encrypt: 149, #pkts digest: 149
10     #pkts decaps: 146, #pkts decrypt: 146, #pkts verify: 146
11     #pkts compressed: 0, #pkts decompressed: 0
12     #pkts not compressed: 0, #pkts compr. failed: 0
13     #pkts not decompressed: 0, #pkts decompress failed: 0
14     #send errors 0, #recv errors 0
15
16     local crypto endpt.: 174.78.144.73, remote crypto endpt.: 72.21.209.225
17     path mtu 1500, ip mtu 1500, ip mtu idb FastEthernet0
```

```
18      current outbound spi: 0xB8357C22(3090512930)
19
20      inbound esp sas:
21       spi: 0x6ADB173(112046451)
22        transform: esp-aes esp-sha-hmac ,
23        in use settings ={Tunnel, }
24        conn id: 1, flow_id: Motorola SEC 2.0:1, crypto map: Tunnel1-head-0
25        sa timing: remaining key lifetime (k/sec): (4467148/3189)
26        IV size: 16 bytes
27        replay detection support: Y  replay window size: 128
28        Status: ACTIVE
29
30      inbound ah sas:
31
32      inbound pcp sas:
33
34      outbound esp sas:
35       spi: 0xB8357C22(3090512930)
36        transform: esp-aes esp-sha-hmac ,
37        in use settings ={Tunnel, }
38        conn id: 2, flow_id: Motorola SEC 2.0:2, crypto map: Tunnel1-head-0
39        sa timing: remaining key lifetime (k/sec): (4467148/3189)
40        IV size: 16 bytes
41        replay detection support: Y  replay window size: 128
42        Status: ACTIVE
43
44      outbound ah sas:
45
46      outbound pcp sas:
47
48  interface: Tunnel2
49      Crypto map tag: Tunnel2-head-0, local addr 174.78.144.73
50
51      protected vrf: (none)
52      local  ident (addr/mask/prot/port): (0.0.0.0/0.0.0.0/0/0)
53      remote ident (addr/mask/prot/port): (0.0.0.0/0.0.0.0/0/0)
54      current_peer 72.21.209.193 port 500
55       PERMIT, flags={origin_is_acl,}
56      #pkts encaps: 26, #pkts encrypt: 26, #pkts digest: 26
57      #pkts decaps: 24, #pkts decrypt: 24, #pkts verify: 24
58      #pkts compressed: 0, #pkts decompressed: 0
59      #pkts not compressed: 0, #pkts compr. failed: 0
60      #pkts not decompressed: 0, #pkts decompress failed: 0
61      #send errors 0, #recv errors 0
62
63      local crypto endpt.: 174.78.144.73, remote crypto endpt.: 72.21.209.193
64      path mtu 1500, ip mtu 1500, ip mtu idb FastEthernet0
65      current outbound spi: 0xF59A3FF6(4120526838)
66
67      inbound esp sas:
68       spi: 0xB6720137(3060924727)
69        transform: esp-aes esp-sha-hmac ,
70        in use settings ={Tunnel, }
71        conn id: 3, flow_id: Motorola SEC 2.0:3, crypto map: Tunnel2-head-0
```

```
72    sa timing: remaining key lifetime (k/sec): (4387273/3492)
73    IV size: 16 bytes
74    replay detection support: Y  replay window size: 128
75    Status: ACTIVE
76
77  inbound ah sas:
78
79  inbound pcp sas:
80
81  outbound esp sas:
82   spi: 0xF59A3FF6(4120526838)
83    transform: esp-aes esp-sha-hmac ,
84    in use settings ={Tunnel, }
85    conn id: 4, flow_id: Motorola SEC 2.0:4, crypto map: Tunnel2-head-0
86    sa timing: remaining key lifetime (k/sec): (4387273/3492)
87    IV size: 16 bytes
88    replay detection support: Y  replay window size: 128
89    Status: ACTIVE
90
91  outbound ah sas:
92
93  outbound pcp sas:
```

For each tunnel interface, you should see both an *inbound esp sas* and *outbound esp sas*. Assuming an SA is listed ("spi: 0xF95D2F3C", for example) and the *Status* is ACTIVE, IPsec is configured correctly.

For further troubleshooting, use the following command to enable debugging.

```
1  router# debug crypto ipsec
```

Use the following command to disable debugging.

```
1  router# no debug crypto ipsec
```

Tunnel

First, check that you have the necessary firewall rules in place. For a list of the rules, see Configuring a Firewall Between the Internet and Your Customer Gateway.

If your firewall rules are set up correctly, then continue troubleshooting with the following command.

```
1  router# show interfaces tun1
```

```
1  Tunnel1 is up, line protocol is up
2    Hardware is Tunnel
3    Internet address is 169.254.255.2/30
4    MTU 17867 bytes, BW 100 Kbit/sec, DLY 50000 usec,
5      reliability 255/255, txload 2/255, rxload 1/255
6    Encapsulation TUNNEL, loopback not set
7    Keepalive not set
8    Tunnel source 174.78.144.73, destination 72.21.209.225
9    Tunnel protocol/transport IPSEC/IP
10   Tunnel TTL 255
11   Tunnel transport MTU 1427 bytes
12   Tunnel transmit bandwidth 8000 (kbps)
13   Tunnel receive bandwidth 8000 (kbps)
```

```
14  Tunnel protection via IPSec (profile "ipsec-vpn-92df3bfb-0")
15  Last input never, output never, output hang never
16  Last clearing of "show interface" counters never
17  Input queue: 0/75/0/0 (size/max/drops/flushes); Total output drops: 0
18  Queueing strategy: fifo
19  Output queue: 0/0 (size/max)
20  5 minute input rate 0 bits/sec, 1 packets/sec
21  5 minute output rate 1000 bits/sec, 1 packets/sec
22    407 packets input, 30010 bytes, 0 no buffer
23    Received 0 broadcasts, 0 runts, 0 giants, 0 throttles
```

Ensure the *line protocol* is up. Check that the tunnel source IP address, source interface and destination respectively match the tunnel configuration for the customer gateway outside IP address, interface, and virtual private gateway outside IP address. Ensure that *Tunnel protection via IPSec* is present. Make sure to run the command on both tunnel interfaces. To resolve any problems here, review the configuration.

Also use the following command, replacing 169.254.255.1 with the inside IP address of your virtual private gateway.

```
1  router# ping 169.254.255.1 df-bit size 1410
```

```
1  Type escape sequence to abort.
2  Sending 5, 1410-byte ICMP Echos to 169.254.255.1, timeout is 2 seconds:
3  Packet sent with the DF bit set
4  !!!!!
```

You should see 5 exclamation points.

For further troubleshooting, review the configuration.

BGP

Use the following command.

```
1  router# show ip bgp summary
```

```
1  BGP router identifier 192.168.37.160, local AS number 65000
2  BGP table version is 8, main routing table version 8
3  2 network entries using 312 bytes of memory
4  2 path entries using 136 bytes of memory
5  3/1 BGP path/bestpath attribute entries using 444 bytes of memory
6  1 BGP AS-PATH entries using 24 bytes of memory
7  0 BGP route-map cache entries using 0 bytes of memory
8  0 BGP filter-list cache entries using 0 bytes of memory
9  Bitfield cache entries: current 1 (at peak 2) using 32 bytes of memory
10 BGP using 948 total bytes of memory
11 BGP activity 4/1 prefixes, 4/1 paths, scan interval 15 secs
12
13 Neighbor       V    AS MsgRcvd MsgSent   TblVer  InQ OutQ Up/Down  State/PfxRcd
14 169.254.255.1  4  7224     363     323        8    0    0 00:54:21         1
15 169.254.255.5  4  7224     364     323        8    0    0 00:00:24         1
```

Here, both neighbors should be listed. For each, you should see a *State/PfxRcd* value of 1.

If the BGP peering is up, verify that your customer gateway router is advertising the default route (0.0.0.0/0) to the VPC.

```
1 router# show bgp all neighbors 169.254.255.1 advertised-routes

1 For address family: IPv4 Unicast
2 BGP table version is 3, local router ID is 174.78.144.73
3 Status codes: s suppressed, d damped, h history, * valid, > best, i - internal,
4     r RIB-failure, S Stale
5 Origin codes: i - IGP, e - EGP, ? - incomplete
6
7 Originating default network 0.0.0.0
8
9 Network          Next Hop          Metric   LocPrf Weight Path
10 *> 10.120.0.0/16   169.254.255.1        100         0   7224     i
11
12 Total number of prefixes 1
```

Additionally, ensure that you're receiving the prefix corresponding to your VPC from the virtual private gateway.

```
1 router# show ip route bgp

1     10.0.0.0/16 is subnetted, 1 subnets
2 B       10.255.0.0 [20/0] via 169.254.255.1, 00:00:20
```

For further troubleshooting, review the configuration.

Virtual Private Gateway Attachment

Make sure your virtual private gateway is attached to your VPC. Your integration team does this with the AWS Management Console.

If you have questions or need further assistance, please use the Amazon VPC forum.

Troubleshooting Cisco IOS Customer Gateway without Border Gateway Protocol Connectivity

When you troubleshoot the connectivity of a Cisco customer gateway, you need to consider three things: IKE, IPsec and tunnel. You can troubleshoot these areas in any order, but we recommend that you start with IKE (at the bottom of the network stack) and move up.

IKE

Use the following command. The response shows a customer gateway with IKE configured correctly.

```
1 router# show crypto isakmp sa
```

```
1 IPv4 Crypto ISAKMP SA
2 dst              src             state        conn-id slot status
3 174.78.144.73 205.251.233.121 QM_IDLE        2001    0 ACTIVE
4 174.78.144.73 205.251.233.122 QM_IDLE        2002    0 ACTIVE
```

You should see one or more lines containing an *src* of the remote gateway specified in the tunnels. The *state* should be QM_IDLE and *status* should be ACTIVE. The absence of an entry, or any entry in another state, indicates that IKE is not configured properly.

For further troubleshooting, run the following commands to enable log messages that provide diagnostic information.

```
1 router# term mon
2 router# debug crypto isakmp
```

To disable debugging, use the following command.

```
1 router# no debug crypto isakmp
```

IPsec

Use the following command. The response shows a customer gateway with IPsec configured correctly.

```
1 router# show crypto ipsec sa
```

```
1 interface: Tunnel1
2     Crypto map tag: Tunnel1-head-0, local addr 174.78.144.73
3
4     protected vrf: (none)
5     local  ident (addr/mask/prot/port): (0.0.0.0/0.0.0.0/0/0)
6     remote ident (addr/mask/prot/port): (0.0.0.0/0.0.0.0/0/0)
7     current_peer 72.21.209.225 port 500
8      PERMIT, flags={origin_is_acl,}
9      #pkts encaps: 149, #pkts encrypt: 149, #pkts digest: 149
10     #pkts decaps: 146, #pkts decrypt: 146, #pkts verify: 146
11     #pkts compressed: 0, #pkts decompressed: 0
12     #pkts not compressed: 0, #pkts compr. failed: 0
13     #pkts not decompressed: 0, #pkts decompress failed: 0
14     #send errors 0, #recv errors 0
15
16     local crypto endpt.: 174.78.144.73, remote crypto endpt.:205.251.233.121
```

```
 17     path mtu 1500, ip mtu 1500, ip mtu idb FastEthernet0
 18     current outbound spi: 0xB8357C22(3090512930)
 19
 20     inbound esp sas:
 21      spi: 0x6ADB173(112046451)
 22       transform: esp-aes esp-sha-hmac ,
 23       in use settings ={Tunnel, }
 24       conn id: 1, flow_id: Motorola SEC 2.0:1, crypto map: Tunnel1-head-0
 25       sa timing: remaining key lifetime (k/sec): (4467148/3189)
 26       IV size: 16 bytes
 27       replay detection support: Y  replay window size: 128
 28       Status: ACTIVE
 29
 30     inbound ah sas:
 31
 32     inbound pcp sas:
 33
 34     outbound esp sas:
 35      spi: 0xB8357C22(3090512930)
 36       transform: esp-aes esp-sha-hmac ,
 37       in use settings ={Tunnel, }
 38       conn id: 2, flow_id: Motorola SEC 2.0:2, crypto map: Tunnel1-head-0
 39       sa timing: remaining key lifetime (k/sec): (4467148/3189)
 40       IV size: 16 bytes
 41       replay detection support: Y  replay window size: 128
 42       Status: ACTIVE
 43
 44     outbound ah sas:
 45
 46     outbound pcp sas:
 47
 48   interface: Tunnel2
 49     Crypto map tag: Tunnel2-head-0, local addr 205.251.233.122
 50
 51     protected vrf: (none)
 52     local  ident (addr/mask/prot/port): (0.0.0.0/0.0.0.0/0/0)
 53     remote ident (addr/mask/prot/port): (0.0.0.0/0.0.0.0/0/0)
 54     current_peer 72.21.209.193 port 500
 55      PERMIT, flags={origin_is_acl,}
 56     #pkts encaps: 26, #pkts encrypt: 26, #pkts digest: 26
 57     #pkts decaps: 24, #pkts decrypt: 24, #pkts verify: 24
 58     #pkts compressed: 0, #pkts decompressed: 0
 59     #pkts not compressed: 0, #pkts compr. failed: 0
 60     #pkts not decompressed: 0, #pkts decompress failed: 0
 61     #send errors 0, #recv errors 0
 62
 63     local crypto endpt.: 174.78.144.73, remote crypto endpt.:205.251.233.122
 64     path mtu 1500, ip mtu 1500, ip mtu idb FastEthernet0
 65     current outbound spi: 0xF59A3FF6(4120526838)
 66
 67     inbound esp sas:
 68      spi: 0xB6720137(3060924727)
 69       transform: esp-aes esp-sha-hmac ,
 70       in use settings ={Tunnel, }
```

```
71      conn id: 3, flow_id: Motorola SEC 2.0:3, crypto map: Tunnel2-head-0
72      sa timing: remaining key lifetime (k/sec): (4387273/3492)
73      IV size: 16 bytes
74      replay detection support: Y  replay window size: 128
75      Status: ACTIVE
76
77   inbound ah sas:
78
79   inbound pcp sas:
80
81   outbound esp sas:
82    spi: 0xF59A3FF6(4120526838)
83      transform: esp-aes esp-sha-hmac ,
84      in use settings ={Tunnel, }
85      conn id: 4, flow_id: Motorola SEC 2.0:4, crypto map: Tunnel2-head-0
86      sa timing: remaining key lifetime (k/sec): (4387273/3492)
87      IV size: 16 bytes
88      replay detection support: Y  replay window size: 128
89      Status: ACTIVE
90
91   outbound ah sas:
92
93   outbound pcp sas:
```

For each tunnel interface, you should see both an inbound esp sas and outbound esp sas. This assumes that an SA is listed (for example, spi: 0x48B456A6), the status is ACTIVE, and IPsec is configured correctly.

For further troubleshooting, use the following command to enable debugging.

```
1 router# debug crypto ipsec
```

To disable debugging, use the following command.

```
1 router# no debug crypto ipsec
```

Tunnel

First, check that you have the necessary firewall rules in place. For a list of the rules, see Configuring a Firewall Between the Internet and Your Customer Gateway.

If your firewall rules are set up correctly, then continue troubleshooting with the following command.

```
1 router# show interfaces tun1
```

```
1 Tunnel1 is up, line protocol is up
2   Hardware is Tunnel
3   Internet address is 169.254.249.18/30
4   MTU 17867 bytes, BW 100 Kbit/sec, DLY 50000 usec,
5     reliability 255/255, txload 2/255, rxload 1/255
6   Encapsulation TUNNEL, loopback not set
7   Keepalive not set
8   Tunnel source 174.78.144.73, destination 205.251.233.121
9   Tunnel protocol/transport IPSEC/IP
10  Tunnel TTL 255
11  Tunnel transport MTU 1427 bytes
12  Tunnel transmit bandwidth 8000 (kbps)
```

```
13   Tunnel receive bandwidth 8000 (kbps)
14   Tunnel protection via IPSec (profile "ipsec-vpn-92df3bfb-0")
15   Last input never, output never, output hang never
16   Last clearing of "show interface" counters never
17   Input queue: 0/75/0/0 (size/max/drops/flushes); Total output drops: 0
18   Queueing strategy: fifo
19   Output queue: 0/0 (size/max)
20   5 minute input rate 0 bits/sec, 1 packets/sec
21   5 minute output rate 1000 bits/sec, 1 packets/sec
22     407 packets input, 30010 bytes, 0 no buffer
23     Received 0 broadcasts, 0 runts, 0 giants, 0 throttles
```

Ensure the line protocol is up. Check that the tunnel source IP address, source interface, and destination respectively match the tunnel configuration for the customer gateway outside IP address, interface, and virtual private gateway outside IP address. Ensure that Tunnel protection through IPSec is present. Make sure to run the command on both tunnel interfaces. To resolve any problems, review the configuration.

You can also use the following command, replacing 169.254.249.18 with the inside IP address of your virtual private gateway.

```
1 router# ping 169.254.249.18 df-bit size 1410
```

```
1 Type escape sequence to abort.
2 Sending 5, 1410-byte ICMP Echos to 169.254.249.18, timeout is 2 seconds:
3 Packet sent with the DF bit set
4 !!!!!
```

You should see five exclamation points.

Routing

To see your static route table, use the following command.

```
1 router# sh ip route static
```

```
1      1.0.0.0/8 is variably subnetted
2 S        10.0.0.0/16 is directly connected, Tunnel1
3 is directly connected, Tunnel2
```

You should see that the static route for the VPC CIDR through both tunnels exists. If it does not exist, add the static routes as shown here.

```
1 router# ip route 10.0.0.0 255.255.0.0 Tunnel1 track 100
2 router# ip route 10.0.0.0 255.255.0.0 Tunnel2 track 200
```

Checking the SLA Monitor

```
1 router# show ip sla statistics 100
```

```
1 IPSLAs Latest Operation Statistics
2
3 IPSLA operation id: 100
4      Latest RTT: 128 milliseconds
5 Latest operation start time: *18:08:02.155 UTC Wed Jul  15 2012
6 Latest operation return code: OK
```

```
7 Number of successes: 3
8 Number of failures: 0
9 Operation time to live: Forever
```

```
1 router# show ip sla statistics 200
```

```
1 IPSLAs Latest Operation Statistics
2
3 IPSLA operation id: 200
4        Latest RTT: 128 milliseconds
5 Latest operation start time: *18:08:02.155 UTC Wed Jul  15 2012
6 Latest operation return code: OK
7 Number of successes: 3
8 Number of failures: 0
9 Operation time to live: Forever
```

The value of "Number of successes" indicates whether the SLA monitor has been set up successfully.

For further troubleshooting, review the configuration.

Virtual Private Gateway Attachment

Verify that your virtual private gateway is attached to your VPC. Your integration team does this with the AWS Management Console.

If you have questions or need further assistance, please use the Amazon VPC forum.

Troubleshooting Juniper JunOS Customer Gateway Connectivity

When you troubleshoot the connectivity of a Juniper customer gateway you need to consider four things: IKE, IPsec, tunnel, and BGP. You can troubleshoot these areas in any order, but we recommend that you start with IKE (at the bottom of the network stack) and move up.

IKE

Use the following command. The response shows a customer gateway with IKE configured correctly.

```
1 user@router> show security ike security-associations
```

```
1 Index    Remote Address  State  Initiator cookie  Responder cookie  Mode
2 4        72.21.209.225   UP     c4cd953602568b74  0d6d194993328b02  Main
3 3        72.21.209.193   UP     b8c8fb7dc68d9173  ca7cb0abaedeb4bb  Main
```

You should see one or more lines containing a Remote Address of the Remote Gateway specified in the tunnels. The *State* should be UP. The absence of an entry, or any entry in another state (such as DOWN) is an indication that IKE is not configured properly.

For further troubleshooting, enable the IKE trace options (as recommended in the example configuration information (see Example: Juniper J-Series JunOS Device). Then run the following command to print a variety of debugging messages to the screen.

```
1 user@router> monitor start kmd
```

From an external host, you can retrieve the entire log file with the following command.

```
1 scp username@router.hostname:/var/log/kmd
```

IPsec

Use the following command. The response shows a customer gateway with IPsec configured correctly.

```
1 user@router> show security ipsec security-associations
```

```
1 Total active tunnels: 2
2 ID        Gateway        Port  Algorithm      SPI       Life:sec/kb  Mon vsys
3 <131073 72.21.209.225   500   ESP:aes-128/sha1 df27aae4 326/ unlim   -   0
4 >131073 72.21.209.225   500   ESP:aes-128/sha1 5de29aa1 326/ unlim   -   0
5 <131074 72.21.209.193   500   ESP:aes-128/sha1 dd16c453 300/ unlim   -   0
6 >131074 72.21.209.193   500   ESP:aes-128/sha1 c1e0eb29 300/ unlim   -   0
```

Specifically, you should see at least two lines per Gateway address (corresponding to the Remote Gateway). Note the carets at the beginning of each line (< >) which indicate the direction of traffic for the particular entry. The output has separate lines for inbound traffic ("<", traffic from the virtual private gateway to this customer gateway) and outbound traffic (">").

For further troubleshooting, enable the IKE traceoptions (for more information, see the preceding section about IKE).

Tunnel

First, double-check that you have the necessary firewall rules in place. For a list of the rules, see Configuring a Firewall Between the Internet and Your Customer Gateway.

If your firewall rules are set up correctly, then continue troubleshooting with the following command.

```
1 user@router> show interfaces st0.1
```

```
1  Logical interface st0.1 (Index 70) (SNMP ifIndex 126)
2      Flags: Point-To-Point SNMP-Traps Encapsulation: Secure-Tunnel
3      Input packets : 8719
4      Output packets: 41841
5      Security: Zone: Trust
6      Allowed host-inbound traffic : bgp ping ssh traceroute
7      Protocol inet, MTU: 9192
8       Flags: None
9       Addresses, Flags: Is-Preferred Is-Primary
10       Destination: 169.254.255.0/30, Local: 169.254.255.2
```

Make sure that the *Security: Zone* is correct, and that the *Local* address matches the customer gateway tunnel inside address.

Next, use the following command, replacing 169.254.255.1 with the inside IP address of your virtual private gateway. Your results should look like the response shown here.

```
1 user@router> ping 169.254.255.1 size 1382 do-not-fragment
```

```
1 PING 169.254.255.1 (169.254.255.1): 1410 data bytes
2 64 bytes from 169.254.255.1: icmp_seq=0 ttl=64 time=71.080 ms
3 64 bytes from 169.254.255.1: icmp_seq=1 ttl=64 time=70.585 ms
```

For further troubleshooting, review the configuration.

BGP

Use the following command.

```
1 user@router> show bgp summary
```

```
1 Groups: 1 Peers: 2 Down peers: 0
2 Table          Tot Paths  Act Paths Suppressed   History Damp State   Pending
3 inet.0             2          1         0            0        0           0
4 Peer                    AS      InPkt     OutPkt    OutQ   Flaps Last Up/Dwn State|#Active/
      Received/Accepted/Damped...
5 169.254.255.1        7224        9         10        0       0     1:00 1/1/1/0
             0/0/0/0
6 169.254.255.5        7224        8          9        0       0       56 0/1/1/0
             0/0/0/0
```

For further troubleshooting, use the following command, replacing 169.254.255.1 with the inside IP address of your virtual private gateway.

```
1 user@router> show bgp neighbor 169.254.255.1
```

```
 1 Peer: 169.254.255.1+179 AS 7224 Local: 169.254.255.2+57175 AS 65000
 2   Type: External     State: Established     Flags: <ImportEval Sync>
 3   Last State: OpenConfirm   Last Event: RecvKeepAlive
 4   Last Error: None
 5   Export: [ EXPORT-DEFAULT ]
 6   Options: <Preference HoldTime PeerAS LocalAS Refresh>
 7   Holdtime: 30 Preference: 170 Local AS: 65000 Local System AS: 0
 8   Number of flaps: 0
 9   Peer ID: 169.254.255.1    Local ID: 10.50.0.10       Active Holdtime: 30
10   Keepalive Interval: 10         Peer index: 0
11   BFD: disabled, down
12   Local Interface: st0.1
13   NLRI for restart configured on peer: inet-unicast
14   NLRI advertised by peer: inet-unicast
15   NLRI for this session: inet-unicast
16   Peer supports Refresh capability (2)
17   Restart time configured on the peer: 120
18   Stale routes from peer are kept for: 300
19   Restart time requested by this peer: 120
20   NLRI that peer supports restart for: inet-unicast
21   NLRI that restart is negotiated for: inet-unicast
22   NLRI of received end-of-rib markers: inet-unicast
23   NLRI of all end-of-rib markers sent: inet-unicast
24   Peer supports 4 byte AS extension (peer-as 7224)
25   Table inet.0 Bit: 10000
26     RIB State: BGP restart is complete
27     Send state: in sync
28     Active prefixes:             1
29     Received prefixes:           1
30     Accepted prefixes:           1
31     Suppressed due to damping:   0
32     Advertised prefixes:         1
33 Last traffic (seconds): Received 4     Sent 8     Checked 4
34 Input messages:  Total 24     Updates 2      Refreshes 0     Octets 505
35 Output messages: Total 26     Updates 1      Refreshes 0     Octets 582
36 Output Queue[0]: 0
```

Here you should see *Received prefixes* and *Advertised prefixes* listed at 1 each. This should be within the *Table inet.0* section.

If the *State* is not `Established`, check the *Last State* and *Last Error* for details of what is required to correct the problem.

If the BGP peering is up, verify that your customer gateway router is advertising the default route (0.0.0.0/0) to the VPC.

```
 1 user@router> show route advertising-protocol bgp 169.254.255.1
```

```
 1 inet.0: 10 destinations, 11 routes (10 active, 0 holddown, 0 hidden)
 2   Prefix              Nexthop          MED     Lclpref     AS path
 3 * 0.0.0.0/0           Self                                 I
```

Additionally, ensure that you're receiving the prefix corresponding to your VPC from the virtual private gateway.

```
 1 user@router> show route receive-protocol bgp 169.254.255.1
```

```
1 inet.0: 10 destinations, 11 routes (10 active, 0 holddown, 0 hidden)
2   Prefix              Nexthop            MED     Lclpref    AS path
3 * 10.110.0.0/16       169.254.255.1      100                7224 I
```

Virtual Private Gateway Attachment

Make sure your virtual private gateway is attached to your VPC. Your integration team does this with the AWS Management Console.

If you have questions or need further assistance, please use the Amazon VPC forum.

Troubleshooting Juniper ScreenOS Customer Gateway Connectivity

When you troubleshoot the connectivity of a Juniper ScreenOS-based customer gateway you need to consider four things: IKE, IPsec, tunnel, and BGP. You can troubleshoot these areas in any order, but we recommend that you start with IKE (at the bottom of the network stack) and move up.

IKE and IPsec

Use the following command. The response shows a customer gateway with IKE configured correctly.

```
1 ssg5-serial-> get sa
```

```
1 total configured sa: 2
2 HEX ID      Gateway        Port Algorithm      SPI        Life:sec kb Sta    PID vsys
3 00000002<   72.21.209.225  500 esp:a128/sha1   80041ca4   3385 unlim A/-    -1 0
4 00000002>   72.21.209.225  500 esp:a128/sha1   8cdd274a   3385 unlim A/-    -1 0
5 00000001<   72.21.209.193  500 esp:a128/sha1   ecf0bec7   3580 unlim A/-    -1 0
6 00000001>   72.21.209.193  500 esp:a128/sha1   14bf7894   3580 unlim A/-    -1 0
```

You should see one or more lines containing a Remote Address of the Remote Gateway specified in the tunnels. The *Sta* should be `A/-` and the *SPI* should be a hexadecimal number other than 00000000. Entries in other states indicate that IKE is not configured properly.

For further troubleshooting, enable the IKE trace options (as recommended in the example configuration information (see Example: Juniper ScreenOS Device).

Tunnel

First, double-check that you have the necessary firewall rules in place. For a list of the rules, see Configuring a Firewall Between the Internet and Your Customer Gateway.

If your firewall rules are set up correctly, then continue troubleshooting with the following command.

```
1 ssg5-serial-> get interface tunnel.1
```

```
1    Interface tunnel.1:
2    description tunnel.1
3    number 20, if_info 1768, if_index 1, mode route
4    link ready
5    vsys Root, zone Trust, vr trust-vr
6    admin mtu 1500, operating mtu 1500, default mtu 1500
7    *ip 169.254.255.2/30
8    *manage ip 169.254.255.2
9    route-deny disable
10   bound vpn:
11     IPSEC-1
12
13   Next-Hop Tunnel Binding table
14   Flag Status Next-Hop(IP)    tunnel-id  VPN
15
16   pmtu-v4 disabled
17   ping disabled, telnet disabled, SSH disabled, SNMP disabled
18   web disabled, ident-reset disabled, SSL disabled
19
```

```
20   OSPF disabled  BGP enabled  RIP disabled  RIPng disabled  mtrace disabled
21   PIM: not configured  IGMP not configured
22   NHRP disabled
23   bandwidth: physical 0kbps, configured egress [gbw 0kbps mbw 0kbps]
24            configured ingress mbw 0kbps, current bw 0kbps
25            total allocated gbw 0kbps
```

Make sure that you see *link:ready*, and that the *IP* address matches the customer gateway tunnel inside address.

Next, use the following command, replacing 169.254.255.1 with the inside IP address of your virtual private gateway. Your results should look like the response shown here.

```
1 ssg5-serial-> ping 169.254.255.1
```

```
1 Type escape sequence to abort
2
3 Sending 5, 100-byte ICMP Echos to 169.254.255.1, timeout is 1 seconds
4 !!!!!
5 Success Rate is 100 percent (5/5), round-trip time min/avg/max=32/32/33 ms
```

For further troubleshooting, review the configuration.

BGP

Use the following command.

```
1 ssg5-serial-> get vrouter trust-vr protocol bgp neighbor
```

```
1 Peer AS Remote IP       Local IP       Wt Status   State     ConnID Up/Down
2 ------------------------------------------------------------------------------
3   7224 169.254.255.1  169.254.255.2   100 Enabled  ESTABLISH    10 00:01:01
4   7224 169.254.255.5  169.254.255.6   100 Enabled  ESTABLISH    11 00:00:59
```

Both BGP peers should be listed as State: ESTABLISH, which means the BGP connection to the virtual private gateway is active.

For further troubleshooting, use the following command, replacing 169.254.255.1 with the inside IP address of your virtual private gateway.

```
1 ssg5-serial-> get vr trust-vr prot bgp neigh 169.254.255.1
```

```
 1 peer: 169.254.255.1,  remote AS: 7224, admin status: enable
 2 type: EBGP, multihop: 0(disable), MED: node default(0)
 3 connection state: ESTABLISH, connection id: 18 retry interval: node default(120s), cur retry
     time 15s
 4 configured hold time: node default(90s), configured keepalive: node default(30s)
 5 configured adv-interval: default(30s)
 6 designated local IP: n/a
 7 local IP address/port: 169.254.255.2/13946, remote IP address/port: 169.254.255.1/179
 8 router ID of peer: 169.254.255.1, remote AS: 7224
 9 negotiated hold time: 30s, negotiated keepalive interval: 10s
10 route map in name: , route map out name:
11 weight: 100 (default)
12 self as next hop: disable
13 send default route to peer: disable
14 ignore default route from peer: disable
```

```
15 send community path attribute: no
16 reflector client: no
17 Neighbor Capabilities:
18    Route refresh: advertised and received
19    Address family IPv4 Unicast:   advertised and received
20 force reconnect is disable
21 total messages to peer: 106, from peer: 106
22 update messages to peer: 6, from peer: 4
23 Tx queue length 0, Tx queue HWM: 1
24 route-refresh messages to peer: 0, from peer: 0
25 last reset 00:05:33 ago, due to BGP send Notification(Hold Timer Expired)(code 4 : subcode 0)
26 number of total successful connections: 4
27 connected: 2 minutes 6 seconds
28 Elapsed time since last update: 2 minutes 6 seconds
```

If the BGP peering is up, verify that your customer gateway router is advertising the default route (0.0.0.0/0) to the VPC. Note that this command applies to ScreenOS version 6.2.0 and higher.

```
1 ssg5-serial-> get vr trust-vr protocol bgp  rib neighbor 169.254.255.1 advertised

1 i: IBGP route, e: EBGP route, >: best route, *: valid route
2              Prefix         Nexthop    Wt  Pref   Med Orig   AS-Path
3 --------------------------------------------------------------------------
4 >i          0.0.0.0/0       0.0.0.0 32768   100     0 IGP
5 Total IPv4 routes advertised: 1
```

Additionally, ensure that you're receiving the prefix corresponding to your VPC from the virtual private gateway. Note that this command applies to ScreenOS version 6.2.0 and higher.

```
1 ssg5-serial-> get vr trust-vr protocol bgp  rib neighbor 169.254.255.1 received

1 i: IBGP route, e: EBGP route, >: best route, *: valid route
2              Prefix         Nexthop    Wt  Pref   Med Orig   AS-Path
3 --------------------------------------------------------------------------
4 >e*     10.0.0.0/16   169.254.255.1   100   100   100 IGP    7224
5 Total IPv4 routes received: 1
```

Virtual Private Gateway Attachment

Make sure your virtual private gateway is attached to your VPC. Your integration team does this with the AWS Management Console.

If you have questions or need further assistance, please use the Amazon VPC forum.

Troubleshooting Yamaha Customer Gateway Connectivity

When you troubleshoot the connectivity of a Yamaha customer gateway you need to consider four things: IKE, IPsec, tunnel, and BGP. You can troubleshoot these areas in any order, but we recommend that you start with IKE (at the bottom of the network stack) and move up.

IKE

Use the following command. The response shows a customer gateway with IKE configured correctly.

```
1 # show ipsec sa gateway 1
```

```
1 sgw  flags local-id                    remote-id        # of sa
2 ----------------------------------------------------------------------
3 1    U K   YOUR_LOCAL_NETWORK_ADDRESS   72.21.209.225    i:2 s:1 r:1
```

You should see a line containing a *remote-id* of the Remote Gateway specified in the tunnels. You can list all the security associations (SAs) by omitting the tunnel number.

For further troubleshooting, run the following commands to enable DEBUG level log messages that provide diagnostic information.

```
1 # syslog debug on
2 # ipsec ike log message-info payload-info key-info
```

To cancel the logged items, use the following command.

```
1 # no ipsec ike log
2 # no syslog debug on
```

IPsec

Use the following command. The response shows a customer gateway with IPsec configured correctly.

```
1 # show ipsec sa gateway 1 detail
```

```
1  SA[1] Duration: 10675s
2  Local ID: YOUR_LOCAL_NETWORK_ADDRESS
3  Remote ID: 72.21.209.225
4  Protocol: IKE
5  Algorithm: AES-CBC, SHA-1, MODP 1024bit
6
7  SPI: 6b ce fd 8a d5 30 9b 02 0c f3 87 52 4a 87 6e 77
8  Key: ** ** ** ** **  (confidential)   ** ** ** ** **
9  -------------------------------------------------------
10 SA[2] Duration: 1719s
11 Local ID: YOUR_LOCAL_NETWORK_ADDRESS
12 Remote ID: 72.21.209.225
13 Direction: send
14 Protocol: ESP (Mode: tunnel)
15 Algorithm: AES-CBC (for Auth.: HMAC-SHA)
16 SPI: a6 67 47 47
17 Key: ** ** ** ** **  (confidential)   ** ** ** ** **
18 -------------------------------------------------------
```

```
19  SA[3] Duration: 1719s
20  Local ID: YOUR_LOCAL_NETWORK_ADDRESS
21  Remote ID: 72.21.209.225
22  Direction: receive
23  Protocol: ESP (Mode: tunnel)
24  Algorithm: AES-CBC (for Auth.: HMAC-SHA)
25  SPI: 6b 98 69 2b
26  Key: ** ** ** ** **  (confidential)   ** ** ** ** **
27  ---------------------------------------------------
28  SA[4] Duration: 10681s
29  Local ID: YOUR_LOCAL_NETWORK_ADDRESS
30  Remote ID: 72.21.209.225
31  Protocol: IKE
32  Algorithm: AES-CBC, SHA-1, MODP 1024bit
33  SPI: e8 45 55 38 90 45 3f 67 a8 74 ca 71 ba bb 75 ee
34  Key: ** ** ** ** **  (confidential)   ** ** ** ** **
35  ---------------------------------------------------
```

For each tunnel interface, you should see both *receive sas* and *send sas*.

For further troubleshooting, use the following command to enable debugging.

```
1  # syslog debug on
2  # ipsec ike log message-info payload-info key-info
```

Use the following command to disable debugging.

```
1  # no ipsec ike log
2  # no syslog debug on
```

Tunnel

First, check that you have the necessary firewall rules in place. For a list of the rules, see Configuring a Firewall Between the Internet and Your Customer Gateway.

If your firewall rules are set up correctly, then continue troubleshooting with the following command.

```
1  # show status tunnel 1
```

```
1  TUNNEL[1]:
2  Description:
3    Interface type: IPsec
4    Current status is Online.
5    from 2011/08/15 18:19:45.
6    5 hours 7 minutes 58 seconds  connection.
7    Received:    (IPv4) 3933 packets [244941 octets]
8                 (IPv6) 0 packet [0 octet]
9    Transmitted: (IPv4) 3933 packets [241407 octets]
10               (IPv6) 0 packet [0 octet]
```

Ensure the *current status* is online. Also, ensure that *Interface type* is IPsec. Make sure to run the command on both tunnel interfaces. To resolve any problems here, review the configuration.

BGP

Use the following command.

```
1 # show status bgp neighbor
```

```
1 BGP neighbor is 169.254.255.1, remote AS 7224, local AS 65000, external link
2   BGP version 0, remote router ID 0.0.0.0
3   BGP state = Active
4   Last read 00:00:00, hold time is 0, keepalive interval is 0 seconds
5   Received 0 messages, 0 notifications, 0 in queue
6   Sent 0 messages, 0 notifications, 0 in queue
7   Connection established 0; dropped 0
8   Last reset never
9 Local host: unspecified
10 Foreign host: 169.254.255.1, Foreign port: 0
11
12 BGP neighbor is 169.254.255.5, remote AS 7224, local AS 65000, external link
13   BGP version 0, remote router ID 0.0.0.0
14   BGP state = Active
15   Last read 00:00:00, hold time is 0, keepalive interval is 0 seconds
16   Received 0 messages, 0 notifications, 0 in queue
17   Sent 0 messages, 0 notifications, 0 in queue
18   Connection established 0; dropped 0
19   Last reset never
20 Local host: unspecified
21 Foreign host: 169.254.255.5, Foreign port:
```

Here, both neighbors should be listed. For each, you should see a *BGP state* value of Active.

If the BGP peering is up, verify that your customer gateway router is advertising the default route (0.0.0.0/0) to the VPC.

```
1 # show status bgp neighbor 169.254.255.1 advertised-routes
```

```
1 Total routes: 1
2 *: valid route
3   Network           Next Hop         Metric LocPrf Path
4 * default           0.0.0.0               0      IGP
```

Additionally, ensure that you're receiving the prefix corresponding to your VPC from the virtual private gateway.

```
1 # show ip route
```

```
1 Destination          Gateway          Interface      Kind  Additional Info.
2 default              ***.***.***.***  LAN3(DHCP)     static
3 10.0.0.0/16          169.254.255.1    TUNNEL[1]      BGP   path=10124
```

For further troubleshooting, review the configuration.

Virtual Private Gateway Attachment

Make sure your virtual private gateway is attached to your VPC. Your integration team does this with the AWS Management Console.

If you have questions or need further assistance, please use the Amazon VPC forum.

Troubleshooting Generic Device Customer Gateway Connectivity Using Border Gateway Protocol

The following diagram and table provide general instructions for troubleshooting a customer gateway that uses Border Gateway Protocol for devices other than those listed in this guide.

Tip
When troubleshooting problems, you might find it useful to enable the debug features of your gateway device. Consult your gateway device vendor for details.

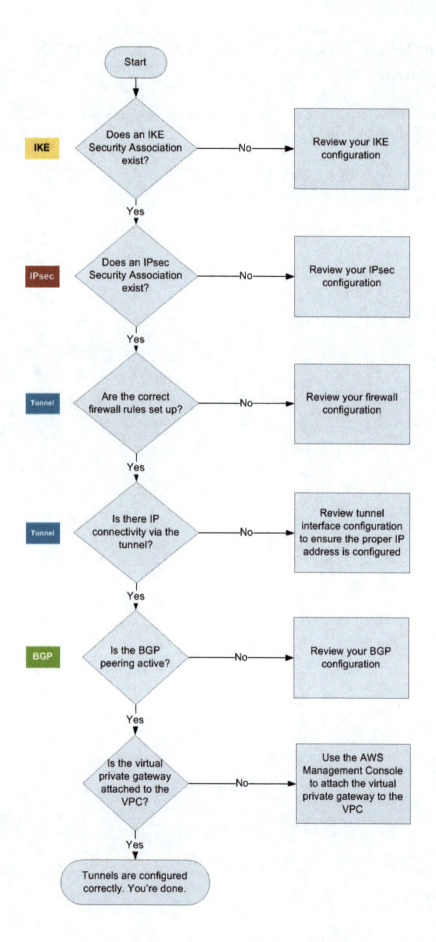

IKE

Determine if an IKE Security Association exists. An IKE security association is required to exchange keys that are used to establish the IPsec Security Association. If no IKE security association exists, review your IKE configuration settings. You must configure the encryption, authentication, perfect-forward-secrecy, and mode parameters as listed in the customer gateway configuration. If an IKE security association exists, move on to IPsec.

IPsec

Determine if an IPsec Security Association exists. An IPsec security association is the tunnel itself. Query your customer gateway to determine if an IPsec Security Association is active. Proper configuration of the IPsec SA is critical. You must configure the encryption, authentication, perfect-forward-secrecy, and mode parameters as listed in the customer gateway configuration. If no IPsec Security Association exists, review your IPsec configuration. If an IPsec Security Association exists, move on to the tunnel.

Tunnel

Confirm the required firewall rules are set up (for a list of the rules, see Configuring a Firewall Between the Internet and Your Customer Gateway). If they are, move forward. Determine if there is IP connectivity via the tunnel. Each side of the tunnel has an IP address as specified in the customer gateway configuration. The virtual private gateway address is the address used as the BGP neighbor address. From your customer gateway, ping this address to determine if IP traffic is being properly encrypted and decrypted. If the ping isn't successful, review your tunnel interface configuration to ensure the proper IP address is configured. If the ping is successful, move on to BGP.

BGP

Determine if the BGP peering is active. For each tunnel, do the following: [See the AWS documentation website for more details] If the tunnels are not in this state, review your BGP configuration. If the BGP peering is established, you are receiving a prefix, and you are advertising a prefix, your tunnel is configured correctly. Ensure both tunnels are in this state, and you're done.

> Make sure your virtual private gateway is attached to your VPC. Your integration team does this with the AWS Management Console.

For general testing instructions applicable to all customer gateways, see How to Test the Customer Gateway Configuration.

If you have questions or need further assistance, please use the Amazon VPC forum.

Troubleshooting Generic Device Customer Gateway without Border Gateway Protocol Connectivity

The following diagram and table provide general instructions for troubleshooting a customer gateway device that does not use Border Gateway Protocol.

Tip
When troubleshooting problems, you might find it useful to enable the debug features of your gateway device. Consult your gateway device vendor for details.

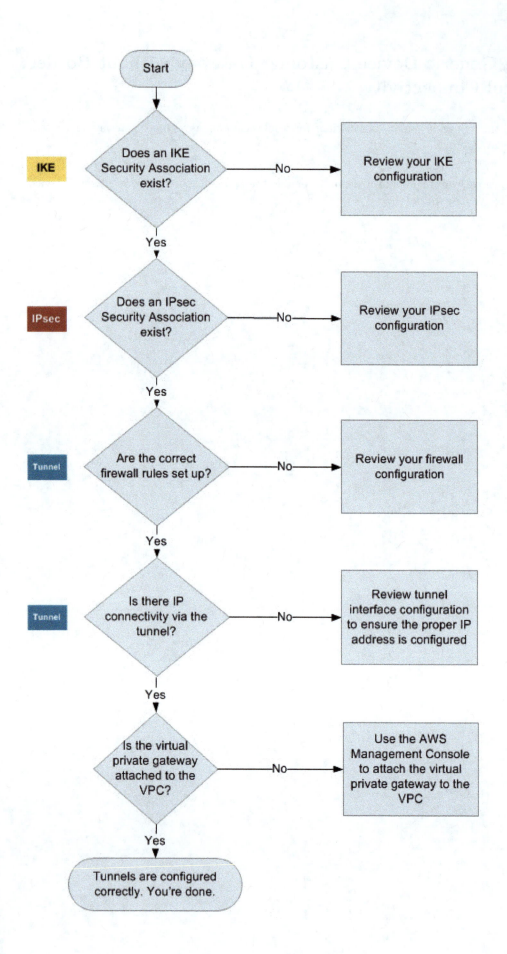

IKE	Determine if an IKE Security Association exists. An IKE security association is required to exchange keys that are used to establish the IPsec Security Association. If no IKE security association exists, review your IKE configuration settings. You must configure the encryption, authentication, perfect-forward-secrecy, and mode parameters as listed in the customer gateway configuration. If an IKE security association exists, move on to IPsec.
IPsec	Determine if an IPsec Security Association exists. An IPsec security association is the tunnel itself. Query your customer gateway to determine if an IPsec Security Association is active. Proper configuration of the IPsec SA is critical. You must configure the encryption, authentication, perfect-forward-secrecy, and mode parameters as listed in the customer gateway configuration. If no IPsec Security Association exists, review your IPsec configuration. If an IPsec Security Association exists, move on to the tunnel.
Tunnel	Confirm the required firewall rules are set up (for a list of the rules, see Configuring a Firewall Between the Internet and Your Customer Gateway). If they are, move forward. Determine if there is IP connectivity via the tunnel. Each side of the tunnel has an IP address as specified in the customer gateway configuration. The virtual private gateway address is the address used as the BGP neighbor address. From your customer gateway, ping this address to determine if IP traffic is being properly encrypted and decrypted. If the ping isn't successful, review your tunnel interface configuration to ensure the proper IP address is configured. If the ping is successful, move on to Routing.
Static routes	Routing: For each tunnel, do the following: [See the AWS documentation website for more details] If the tunnels are not in this state, review your device configuration. Ensure both tunnels are in this state, and you're done.
	Make sure your virtual private gateway is attached to your VPC. Your integration team does this with the AWS Management Console.

If you have questions or need further assistance, please use the Amazon VPC forum.

Configuring Windows Server 2008 R2 as a Customer Gateway

You can configure Windows Server 2008 R2 as a customer gateway for your VPC. Use the following process whether you are running Windows Server 2008 R2 on an EC2 instance in a VPC, or on your own server.

Topics

- Configuring Your Windows Server
- Step 1: Create a VPN Connection and Configure Your VPC
- Step 2: Download the Configuration File for the VPN Connection
- Step 3: Configure the Windows Server
- Step 4: Set Up the VPN Tunnel
- Step 5: Enable Dead Gateway Detection
- Step 6: Test the VPN Connection

Configuring Your Windows Server

To configure Windows Server as a customer gateway, ensure that you have Windows Server 2008 R2 on your own network, or on an EC2 instance in a VPC. If you use an EC2 instance that you launched from a Windows AMI, do the following:

- Disable source/destination checking for the instance:

  1. Open the Amazon EC2 console at https://console.aws.amazon.com/ec2/.

  2. Select your Windows Server instance, and choose **Actions, Networking, Change Source/Dest. Check**. Choose **Yes, Disable**.

- Update your adapter settings so that you can route traffic from other instances:

  1. Connect to your Windows instance. For more information, see Connecting to Your Windows Instance.

  2. Open the Control Panel, and start the Device Manager.

  3. Expand the **Network adapters** node.

  4. Right-click the Citrix or AWS PV network adapter, and then click **Properties**.

  5. On the **Advanced** tab, disable the **IPv4 Checksum Offload, TCP Checksum Offload (IPv4)**, and **UDP Checksum Offload (IPv4)** properties, and then choose **OK**.

- Associate an Elastic IP address with the instance:

  1. Open the Amazon EC2 console at https://console.aws.amazon.com/ec2/.

  2. In the navigation pane, choose **Elastic IPs**. Choose **Allocate new address**.

  3. Select the Elastic IP address, and choose **Actions, Associate Address**.

  4. For **Instance**, select your Windows Server instance. Choose **Associate**.

  Take note of this address — you will need it when you create the customer gateway in your VPC.

- Ensure the instance's security group rules allow outbound IPsec traffic. By default, a security group allows all outbound traffic; however, if the security group's outbound rules have been modified from their original state, you must create the following outbound custom protocol rules for IPsec traffic: IP protocol 50, IP protocol 51, and UDP 500.

Take note of the CIDR range for your network in which the Windows server is located, for example, 172.31.0.0/16 .

Step 1: Create a VPN Connection and Configure Your VPC

To create a VPN connection from your VPC, you must first create a virtual private gateway and attach it to your VPC. Then you can create a VPN connection and configure your VPC. You must also have the CIDR range for your network in which the Windows server is located, for example, 172.31.0.0/16.

To create a virtual private gateway

1. Open the Amazon VPC console at https://console.aws.amazon.com/vpc/.

2. In the navigation pane, choose **Virtual Private Gateways**, and then **Create Virtual Private Gateway**.

3. You can optionally enter a name for your virtual private gateway, and then choose **Yes, Create**.

4. Select the virtual private gateway that you created, and then choose **Attach to VPC**.

5. In the **Attach to VPC** dialog box, select your VPC from the list, and then choose **Yes, Attach**.

To create a VPN connection

1. Open the Amazon VPC console at https://console.aws.amazon.com/vpc/.

2. In the navigation pane, choose **VPN Connections**, and then **Create VPN Connection**.

3. Select the virtual private gateway from the list.

4. For **Customer Gateway**, choose **New**. For **IP address**, specify the public IP address of your Windows Server. **Note**
   The IP address must be static and may be behind a device performing network address translation (NAT). To ensure that NAT traversal (NAT-T) can function, you must adjust your firewall rules to unblock UDP port 4500. If your customer gateway is an EC2 Windows Server instance, use its Elastic IP address.

5. Select the **Static** routing option, enter the **Static IP Prefixes** values for your network in CIDR notation, and then choose **Yes, Create**.

To configure your VPC

- Create a private subnet in your VPC (if you don't have one already) for launching instances that will communicate with the Windows server. For more information, see Adding a Subnet to Your VPC. **Note**
  A private subnet is a subnet that does not have a route to an Internet gateway. The routing for this subnet is described in the next item.
- Update your route tables for the VPN connection:
  - Add a route to your private subnet's route table with the virtual private gateway as the target, and the Windows server's network (CIDR range) as the destination.
  - Enable route propagation for the virtual private gateway. For more information, see Route Tables in the *Amazon VPC User Guide*.
- Create a security group configuration for your instances that allows communication between your VPC and network:
  - Add rules that allow inbound RDP or SSH access from your network. This enables you to connect to instances in your VPC from your network. For example, to allow computers in your network to access Linux instances in your VPC, create an inbound rule with a type of SSH, and the source set to the CIDR range of your network; for example, 172.31.0.0/16. For more information, see Security Groups for Your VPC in the *Amazon VPC User Guide*.
  - Add a rule that allows inbound ICMP access from your network. This enables you to test your VPN connection by pinging an instance in your VPC from your Windows server.

Step 2: Download the Configuration File for the VPN Connection

You can use the Amazon VPC console to download a Windows server configuration file for your VPN connection.

209

To download the configuration file

1. Open the Amazon VPC console at https://console.aws.amazon.com/vpc/.

2. In the navigation pane, click **VPN Connections**.

3. Select your VPN connection, and then click **Download Configuration**.

4. Select **Microsoft** as the vendor, **Windows Server** as the platform, and **2008 R2** as the software. Click **Yes, Download**. You can open the file or save it.

The configuration file contains a section of information similar to the following example. You'll see this information presented twice, one time for each tunnel. You'll use this information when configuring the Windows Server 2008 R2 server.

```
1 vgw-1a2b3c4d Tunnel1
2 --------------------------------------------------------------------
3 Local Tunnel Endpoint:          203.0.113.1
4 Remote Tunnel Endpoint:         203.83.222.237
5 Endpoint 1:                     [Your_Static_Route_IP_Prefix]
6 Endpoint 2:                     [Your_VPC_CIDR_Block]
7 Preshared key:                  xCjNLsLoCmKsakwcdoR9yX6GsEXAMPLE
```

`Local Tunnel Endpoint`
The IP address for the customer gateway—in this case, your Windows server—that terminates the VPN connection on your network's side. If your customer gateway is a Windows server instance, this is the instance's private IP address.

`Remote Tunnel Endpoint`
One of two IP addresses for the virtual private gateway that terminates the VPN connection on the AWS side.

`Endpoint 1`
The IP prefix that you specified as a static route when you created the VPN connection. These are the IP addresses on your network that are allowed to use the VPN connection to access your VPC.

`Endpoint 2`
The IP address range (CIDR block) of the VPC attached to the virtual private gateway (for example 10.0.0.0/16).

`Preshared key`
The pre-shared key that is used to establish the IPsec VPN connection between `Local Tunnel Endpoint` and `Remote Tunnel Endpoint`.

We suggest that you configure both tunnels as part of the VPN connection. Each tunnel connects to a separate VPN concentrator on the Amazon side of the VPN connection. Although only one tunnel at a time is up, the second tunnel automatically establishes itself if the first tunnel goes down. Having redundant tunnels ensure continuous availability in the case of a device failure. Because only one tunnel is available at a time, the Amazon VPC console indicates that one tunnel is down. This is expected behavior, so there's no action required from you.

With two tunnels configured, if a device failure occurs within AWS, your VPN connection automatically fails over to the second tunnel of the AWS virtual private gateway within a matter of minutes. When you configure your customer gateway, it's important that you configure both tunnels.

Note
From time to time, AWS performs routine maintenance on the virtual private gateway. This maintenance may disable one of the two tunnels of your VPN connection for a brief period of time. Your VPN connection automatically fails over to the second tunnel while we perform this maintenance.

Additional information regarding the Internet Key Exchange (IKE) and IPsec Security Associations (SA) is presented in the downloaded configuration file. Because the AWS VPC VPN suggested settings are the same as the Windows Server 2008 R2 default IPsec configuration settings, minimal work is needed on your part.

```
1 MainModeSecMethods:        DHGroup2-AES128-SHA1,DHGroup2-3DES-SHA1
2 MainModeKeyLifetime:       480min,0sec
3 QuickModeSecMethods:       ESP:SHA1-AES128+60min+100000kb,
4                            ESP:SHA1-3D ES+60min+100000kb
5 QuickModePFS:              DHGroup2
```

MainModeSecMethods

The encryption and authentication algorithms for the IKE SA. These are the suggested settings for the VPN connection, and are the default settings for Windows Server 2008 R2 IPsec VPN connections.

MainModeKeyLifetime

The IKE SA key lifetime. This is the suggested setting for the VPN connection, and is the default setting for Windows Server 2008 R2 IPsec VPN connections.

QuickModeSecMethods

The encryption and authentication algorithms for the IPsec SA. These are the suggested settings for the VPN connection, and are the default settings for Windows Server 2008 R2 IPsec VPN connections.

QuickModePFS

We suggest the use of master key perfect forward secrecy (PFS) for your IPsec sessions.

Step 3: Configure the Windows Server

Before you set up the VPN tunnel, you must install and configure Routing and Remote Access Services on your Windows server to allow remote users to access resources on your network.

To install Routing and Remote Access Services on Windows Server 2008 R2

1. Log on to the Windows Server 2008 R2 server.

2. Click **Start**, point to **All Programs**, point to **Administrative Tools**, and then click **Server Manager**.

3. Install Routing and Remote Access Services:

    1. In the Server Manager navigation pane, click **Roles**.

    2. In the **Roles** pane, click **Add Roles**.

    3. On the **Before You Begin** page, verify that your server meets the prerequisites and then click **Next**.

    4. On the **Select Server Roles** page, click **Network Policy and Access Services**, and then click **Next**.

    5. On the **Network Policy and Access Services** page, click **Next**.

    6. On the **Select Role Services** page, click **Routing and Remote Access Services**, leave **Remote Access Service** and **Routing** selected, and then click **Next**.

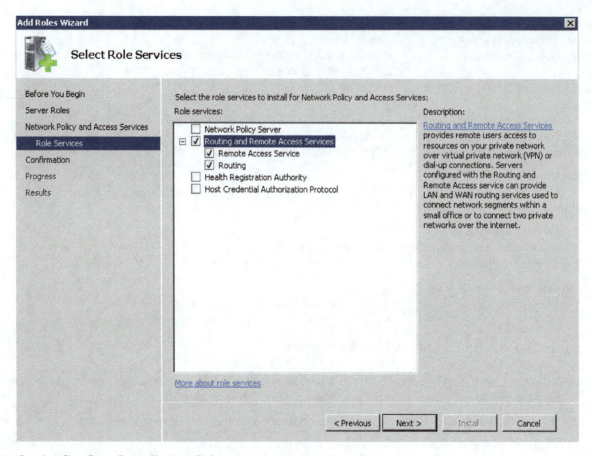

7. On the **Confirm Installation Selections** page, click **Install**.

8. When the wizard completes, click **Close**.

To configure and enable Routing and Remote Access Server

1. In the Server Manager navigation pane, expand **Roles**, and then expand **Network Policy and Access**.

2. Right-click **Routing and Remote Access Server**, and then click **Configure and Enable Routing and Remote Access**.

3. In the **Routing and Remote Access Setup Wizard**, on the **Welcome** page, click **Next**.

4. On the **Configuration** page, click **Custom Configuration**, and then click **Next**.

5. Click **LAN routing**, and then click **Next**.

6. Click **Finish**.

7. When prompted by the **Routing and Remote Access** dialog box, click **Start service**.

Step 4: Set Up the VPN Tunnel

You can configure the VPN tunnel by running the netsh scripts included in the downloaded configuration file, or by using the New Connection Security Rule Wizard on the Windows server.

Important

We suggest that you use master key perfect forward secrecy (PFS) for your IPsec sessions. However, you can't enable PFS using the Windows Server 2008 R2 user interface; you can only enable this setting by running the netsh script with qmpfs=dhgroup2. Therefore, you should consider your requirements before you pick an option.

Option 1: Run netsh Script

Copy the netsh script from the downloaded configuration file and replace the variables. The following is an example script.

```
1 netsh advfirewall consec add rule Name="VGW-1a2b3c4d Tunnel 1" Enable=Yes ^
2 Profile=any Type=Static Mode=Tunnel
3 LocalTunnelEndpoint=Windows_Server_Private_IP_address ^
4 RemoteTunnelEndpoint=203.83.222.236 Endpoint1=Static_Route_IP_Prefix ^
5 Endpoint2=VPC_CIDR_Block Protocol=Any Action=RequireInClearOut ^
6 Auth1=ComputerPSK Auth1PSK=xCjNLsLoCmKsakwcdoR9yX6Gsexample ^
7 QMSecMethods=ESP:SHA1-AES128+60min+100000kb ^
8 ExemptIPsecProtectedConnections=No ApplyAuthz=No QMPFS=dhgroup2
```

Name: You can replace the suggested name (`VGW-1a2b3c4d Tunnel 1`) with a name of your choice.

LocalTunnelEndpoint: Enter the private IP address of the Windows server on your network.

Endpoint1: The CIDR block of your network on which the Windows server resides, for example, `172.31.0.0/16`.

Endpoint2: The CIDR block of your VPC or a subnet in your VPC, for example, `10.0.0.0/16`.

Run the updated script in a command prompt window. (The ^ enables you to cut and paste wrapped text at the command line.) To set up the second VPN tunnel for this VPN connection, repeat the process using the second netsh script in the configuration file.

When you are done, go to 2.4: Configure the Windows Firewall.

For more information about the netsh parameters, go to Netsh AdvFirewall Consec Commands in the *Microsoft TechNet Library*.

Option 2: Use the Windows Server User Interface

You can also use the Windows server user interface to set up the VPN tunnel. This section guides you through the steps.

Important
You can't enable master key perfect forward secrecy (PFS) using the Windows Server 2008 R2 user interface. Therefore, if you decide to use PFS, you must use the netsh scripts described in option 1 instead of the user interface described in this option.

- 2.1: Configure a Security Rule for a VPN Tunnel
- 2.3: Confirm the Tunnel Configuration
- 2.4: Configure the Windows Firewall

2.1: Configure a Security Rule for a VPN Tunnel

In this section, you configure a security rule on your Windows server to create a VPN tunnel.

To configure a security rule for a VPN tunnel

1. In the Server Manager navigation pane, expand **Configuration**, and then expand **Windows Firewall with Advanced Security**.

2. Right-click **Connection Security Rules**, and then click **New Rule**.

3. In the **New Connection Security Rule** wizard, on the **Rule Type** page, click **Tunnel**, and then click **Next**.

4. On the **Tunnel Type** page, under **What type of tunnel would you like to create**, click **Custom Configuration**. Under **Would you like to exempt IPsec-protected connections from this tunnel**, leave the default value checked (**No. Send all network traffic that matches this connection security rule through the tunnel**), and then click **Next**.

5. On the **Requirements** page, click **Require authentication for inbound connections. Do not establish tunnels for outbound connections**, and then click **Next**.

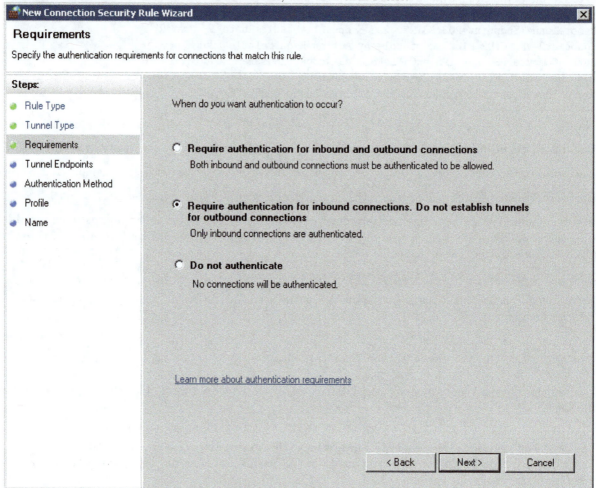

6. On **Tunnel Endpoints** page, under **Which computers are in Endpoint 1**, click **Add**. Enter the CIDR range of your network (behind your Windows server customer gateway), and then click **OK**. (Note that the range can include the IP address of your customer gateway.)

7. Under **What is the local tunnel endpoint (closest to computer in Endpoint 1)**, click **Edit**. Enter the private IP address of your Windows server, and then click **OK**.

8. Under **What is the remote tunnel endpoint (closest to computers in Endpoint 2)**, click **Edit**. Enter the IP address of the virtual private gateway for Tunnel 1 from the configuration file (see `Remote Tunnel Endpoint`), and then click **OK**. **Important**
   If you are repeating this procedure for Tunnel 2, be sure to select the endpoint for Tunnel 2.

9. Under **Which computers are in Endpoint 2**, click **Add**. Enter the CIDR block of your VPC, and then click **OK**. **Important**
   You must scroll in the dialog box until you locate **Which computers are in Endpoint 2**. Do not click **Next** until you have completed this step, or you won't be able to connect to your server.

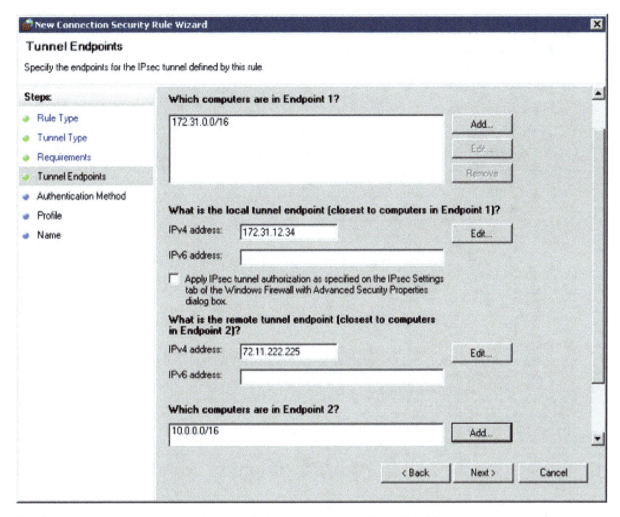

10. Confirm that all the settings you've specified are correct, and then click **Next**.

11. On the **Authentication Method** page, select **Advanced**, and then click **Customize**.

12. Under **First authentication methods**, click **Add**.

13. Select **Pre-Shared key**, enter the pre-shared key value from the configuration file, and click **OK**. Important
If you are repeating this procedure for Tunnel 2, be sure to select the pre-shared key for Tunnel 2.

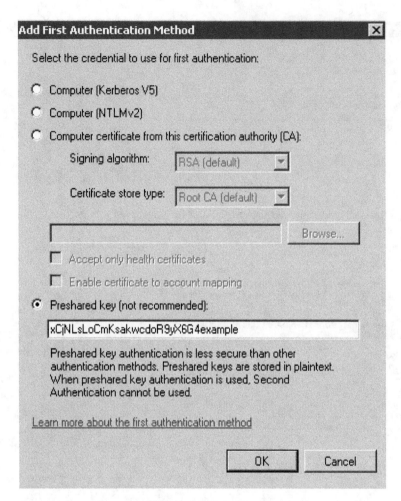

14. Ensure that **First authentication is optional** is not selected, and click **OK**.

15. On the **Authentication Method** page, click **Next**.

16. On the **Profile** page, select all three check boxes: **Domain**, **Private**, and **Public**, and then click **Next**.

17. On the **Name** page, enter a name for your connection rule, and then click **Finish**.

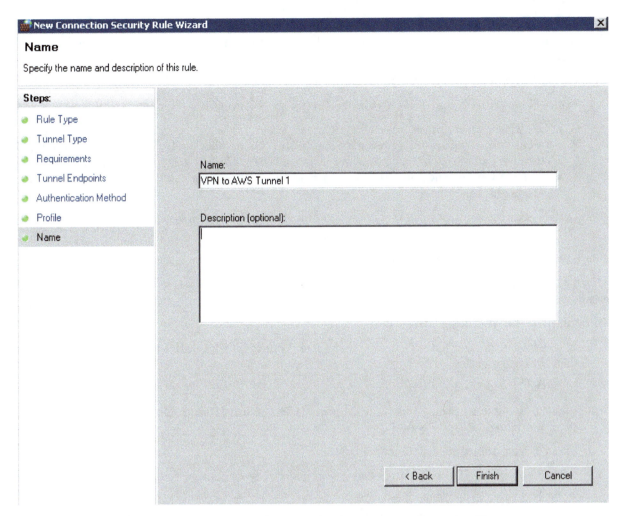

Repeat the above procedure, specifying the data for Tunnel 2 from your configuration file.

After you've finished, you'll have two tunnels configured for your VPN connection.

2.3: Confirm the Tunnel Configuration

To confirm the tunnel configuration

1. In the Server Manager navigation pane, expand the **Configuration** node, expand **Windows Firewall with Advanced Security**, and then click **Connection Security Rules**.

2. Verify the following for both tunnels:

   - **Enabled** is Yes
   - **Authentication mode** is Require inbound and clear outbound
   - **Authentication method** is Custom
   - **Endpoint 1 port** is Any
   - **Endpoint 2 port** is Any
   - **Protocol** is Any

3. Double-click the security rule for your first tunnel.

4. On the **Computers** tab, verify the following:

   - Under **Endpoint 1**, the CIDR block range shown matches the CIDR block range of your network.
   - Under **Endpoint 2**, the CIDR block range shown matches the CIDR block range of your VPC.

5. On the **Authentication** tab, under **Method**, click **Customize**, and verify that **First authentication methods** contains the correct pre-shared key from your configuration file for the tunnel, and then click **OK**.

6. On the **Advanced** tab, verify that **Domain**, **Private**, and **Public** are all selected.

7. Under **IPsec tunneling**, click **Customize**. Verify the following IPsec tunneling settings.

   - **Use IPsec tunneling** is selected.
   - **Local tunnel endpoint (closest to Endpoint 1)** contains the IP address of your server. If your customer gateway is a Windows server instance, this is the instance's private IP address.
   - **Remote tunnel endpoint (closest to Endpoint 2)** contains the IP address of the virtual private gateway for this tunnel.

8. Double-click the security rule for your second tunnel. Repeat steps 4 to 7 for this tunnel.

2.4: Configure the Windows Firewall

After setting up your security rules on your server, configure some basic IPsec settings to work with the virtual private gateway.

To configure the Windows firewall

1. In the Server Manager navigation pane, right-click **Windows Firewall with Advanced Security**, and then click **Properties**.

2. Click the **IPsec Settings** tab.

3. Under **IPsec exemptions**, verify that **Exempt ICMP from IPsec** is **No (default)**. Verify that **IPsec tunnel authorization** is **None**.

4. Under **IPsec defaults**, click **Customize**.

5. In the **Customize IPsec Settings** dialog box, under **Key exchange (Main Mode)**, select **Advanced** and then click **Customize**.

6. In **Customize Advanced Key Exchange Settings**, under **Security methods**, verify that these default values are used for the first entry.

   - Integrity: SHA-1
   - Encryption: AES-CBC 128
   - Key exchange algorithm: Diffie-Hellman Group 2
   - Under **Key lifetimes**, verify that **Minutes** is 480 and **Sessions** is 0.

These settings correspond to these entries in the configuration file:

```
1 MainModeSecMethods: DHGroup2-AES128-SHA1,DHGroup2-3DES-SHA1
2 MainModeKeyLifetime: 480min,0sec
```

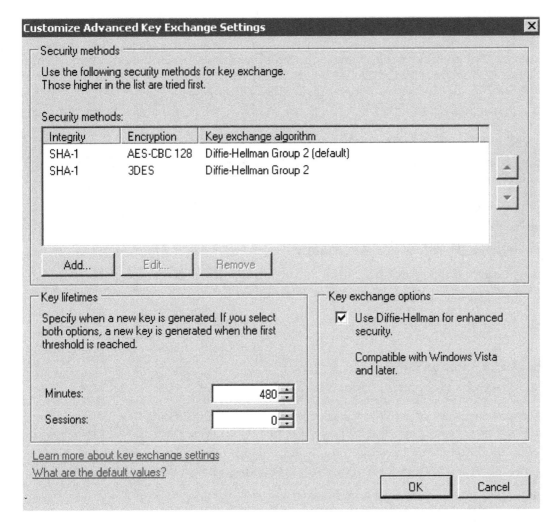

1. Under **Key exchange options**, select **Use Diffie-Hellman for enhanced security**, and then click **OK**.

2. Under **Data protection (Quick Mode)**, click **Advanced**, and then click **Customize**.

3. Click **Require encryption for all connection security rules that use these settings**.

4. Under **Data integrity and encryption algorithms**, leave the default values:

   - Protocol: ESP
   - Integrity: SHA-1
   - Encryption: AES-CBC 128
   - Lifetime: 60 minutes

   These value correspond to the following entries from the configuration file.

   ```
   1 QuickModeSecMethods:
   2 ESP:SHA1-AES128+60min+100000kb,ESP:SHA1-3D ES+60min+100000kb
   ```

5. Click **OK** to return to the **Customize IPsec Settings** dialog box and click **OK** again to save the configuration .

Step 5: Enable Dead Gateway Detection

Next, you need to configure TCP to detect when a gateway becomes unavailable. You can do this by modifying this registry key: HKLM\SYSTEM\CurrentControlSet\Services\Tcpip\Parameters. Do not perform this step until you've completed the preceding sections. After you change the registry key, you must reboot the server.

To enable dead gateway detection

1. On the server, click **Start**, and then type **regedit** to start Registry Editor.

2. Expand **HKEY_LOCAL_MACHINE**, expand **SYSTEM**, expand **CurrentControlSet**, expand **Services**, expand **Tcpip**, and then expand **Parameters**.

3. In the other pane, right-click, point to **New**, and select **DWORD (32-bit) Value**.

4. Enter the name **EnableDeadGWDetect**.

5. Right-click **EnableDeadGWDetect**, and click **Modify**.

6. In **Value data**, enter **1**, and then click **OK**.

7. Close Registry Editor and reboot the server.

For more information, go to EnableDeadGWDetect in the *Microsoft TechNet Library*.

Step 6: Test the VPN Connection

To test that the VPN connection is working correctly, launch an instance into your VPC, and ensure that it does not have an Internet connection. After you've launched the instance, ping its private IP address from your Windows server. The VPN tunnel comes up when traffic is generated from the customer gateway, therefore the ping command also initiates the VPN connection.

To launch an instance in your VPC and get its private IP address

1. Open the Amazon EC2 console, and click **Launch Instance**.

2. Select an Amazon Linux AMI, and select an instance type.

3. On the **Step3: Configure Instance Details** page, select your VPC from the **Network** list, and select a subnet from the **Subnet** list. Ensure that you select the private subnet that you configured in Step 1: Create a VPN Connection and Configure Your VPC.

4. In the **Auto-assign Public IP** list, ensure that the setting is set to **Disable**.

5. Click **Next** until you get to the** Step 6: Configure Security Group** page. You can either select an existing security group that you configured in Step 1: Create a VPN Connection and Configure Your VPC, or you can create a new security group and ensure that it has a rule that allows all ICMP traffic from the IP address of your Windows server.

6. Complete the rest of the steps in the wizard, and launch your instance.

7. On the **Instances** page, select your instance. Get the private IP address in the **Private IPs** field on the details pane.

Connect to or log on to your Windows server, open the command prompt, and then use the `ping` command to ping your instance using its private IP address; for example:

```
1 ping 10.0.0.4
```

```
1 Pinging 10.0.0.4 with 32 bytes of data:
2 Reply from 10.0.0.4: bytes=32 time=2ms TTL=62
3 Reply from 10.0.0.4: bytes=32 time=2ms TTL=62
4 Reply from 10.0.0.4: bytes=32 time=2ms TTL=62
```

```
5 Reply from 10.0.0.4: bytes=32 time=2ms TTL=62
6
7 Ping statistics for 10.0.0.4:
8     Packets: Sent = 4, Received = 4, Lost = 0 (0% loss),
9 Approximate round trip times in milli-seconds:
10     Minimum = 2ms, Maximum = 2ms, Average = 2ms
```

If the `ping` command fails, check the following information:

- Ensure that you have configured your security group rules to allow ICMP to the instance in your VPC. If your Windows server is an EC2 instance, ensure that its security group's outbound rules allow IPsec traffic. For more information, see Configuring Your Windows Server.
- Ensure that the operating system on the instance you are pinging is configured to respond to ICMP. We recommend that you use one of the Amazon Linux AMIs.
- If the instance you are pinging is a Windows instance, log in to the instance and enable inbound ICMPv4 on the Windows firewall.
- Ensure that you have configured the route tables for your VPC or your subnet correctly. For more information, see Step 1: Create a VPN Connection and Configure Your VPC.
- If your customer gateway is a Windows server instance, ensure that you've disabled source/destination checking for the instance. For more information, see Configuring Your Windows Server.

In the Amazon VPC console, on the **VPN Connections** page, select your VPN connection. The first tunnel is in the UP state. The second tunnel should be configured, but it won't be used unless the first tunnel goes down. It may take a few moments to establish the encrypted tunnels.

Configuring Windows Server 2012 R2 as a Customer Gateway

You can configure Windows Server 2012 R2 as a customer gateway for your VPC. Use the following process whether you are running Windows Server 2012 R2 on an EC2 instance in a VPC, or on your own server.

Topics

- Configuring Your Windows Server
- Step 1: Create a VPN Connection and Configure Your VPC
- Step 2: Download the Configuration File for the VPN Connection
- Step 3: Configure the Windows Server
- Step 4: Set Up the VPN Tunnel
- Step 5: Enable Dead Gateway Detection
- Step 6: Test the VPN Connection

Configuring Your Windows Server

To configure Windows Server as a customer gateway, ensure that you have Windows Server 2012 R2 on your own network, or on an EC2 instance in a VPC. If you use an EC2 instance that you launched from a Windows AMI, do the following:

- Disable source/destination checking for the instance:

    1. Open the Amazon EC2 console at https://console.aws.amazon.com/ec2/.

    2. Select your Windows Server instance, and choose **Actions**, **Networking**, **Change Source/Dest. Check**. Choose **Yes, Disable**.

- Update your adapter settings so that you can route traffic from other instances:

    1. Connect to your Windows instance. For more information, see Connecting to Your Windows Instance.

    2. Open the Control Panel, and start the Device Manager.

    3. Expand the **Network adapters** node.

    4. Select the AWS PV network device, choose **Action**, **Properties**.

    5. On the **Advanced** tab, disable the **IPv4 Checksum Offload**, **TCP Checksum Offload (IPv4)**, and **UDP Checksum Offload (IPv4)** properties, and then choose **OK**.

- Associate an Elastic IP address with the instance:

    1. Open the Amazon EC2 console at https://console.aws.amazon.com/ec2/.

    2. In the navigation pane, choose **Elastic IPs**. Choose **Allocate new address**.

    3. Select the Elastic IP address, and choose **Actions**, **Associate Address**.

    4. For **Instance**, select your Windows Server instance. Choose **Associate**.

    Take note of this address — you will need it when you create the customer gateway in your VPC.

- Ensure the instance's security group rules allow outbound IPsec traffic. By default, a security group allows all outbound traffic; however, if the security group's outbound rules have been modified from their original state, you must create the following outbound custom protocol rules for IPsec traffic: IP protocol 50, IP protocol 51, and UDP 500.

Take note of the CIDR range for your network in which the Windows server is located, for example, 172.31.0.0/16

Step 1: Create a VPN Connection and Configure Your VPC

To create a VPN connection from your VPC, you must first create a virtual private gateway and attach it to your VPC. Then you can create a VPN connection and configure your VPC. You must also have the CIDR range for your network in which the Windows server is located, for example, `172.31.0.0/16`.

To create a virtual private gateway

1. Open the Amazon VPC console at https://console.aws.amazon.com/vpc/.

2. In the navigation pane, choose **Virtual Private Gateways**, and then **Create Virtual Private Gateway**.

3. You can optionally enter a name for your virtual private gateway, and then choose **Yes, Create**.

4. Select the virtual private gateway that you created, and then choose **Attach to VPC**.

5. In the **Attach to VPC** dialog box, select your VPC from the list, and then choose **Yes, Attach**.

To create a VPN connection

1. Open the Amazon VPC console at https://console.aws.amazon.com/vpc/.

2. In the navigation pane, choose **VPN Connections**, and then **Create VPN Connection**.

3. Select the virtual private gateway from the list.

4. For **Customer Gateway**, choose **New**. For **IP address**, specify the public IP address of your Windows Server. **Note**
The IP address must be static and may be behind a device performing network address translation (NAT). To ensure that NAT traversal (NAT-T) can function, you must adjust your firewall rules to unblock UDP port 4500. If your customer gateway is an EC2 Windows Server instance, use its Elastic IP address.

5. Select the **Static** routing option, enter the **Static IP Prefixes** values for your network in CIDR notation, and then choose **Yes, Create**.

To configure your VPC

- Create a private subnet in your VPC (if you don't have one already) for launching instances that will communicate with the Windows server. For more information, see Adding a Subnet to Your VPC. **Note**
A private subnet is a subnet that does not have a route to an Internet gateway. The routing for this subnet is described in the next item.
- Update your route tables for the VPN connection:
  - Add a route to your private subnet's route table with the virtual private gateway as the target, and the Windows server's network (CIDR range) as the destination.
  - Enable route propagation for the virtual private gateway. For more information, see Route Tables in the *Amazon VPC User Guide*.
- Create a security group configuration for your instances that allows communication between your VPC and network:
  - Add rules that allow inbound RDP or SSH access from your network. This enables you to connect to instances in your VPC from your network. For example, to allow computers in your network to access Linux instances in your VPC, create an inbound rule with a type of SSH, and the source set to the CIDR range of your network; for example, `172.31.0.0/16`. For more information, see Security Groups for Your VPC in the *Amazon VPC User Guide*.
  - Add a rule that allows inbound ICMP access from your network. This enables you to test your VPN connection by pinging an instance in your VPC from your Windows server.

Step 2: Download the Configuration File for the VPN Connection

You can use the Amazon VPC console to download a Windows server configuration file for your VPN connection.

To download the configuration file

1. Open the Amazon VPC console at https://console.aws.amazon.com/vpc/.

2. In the navigation pane, choose **VPN Connections**.

3. Select your VPN connection, and then choose **Download Configuration**.

4. Select **Microsoft** as the vendor, **Windows Server** as the platform, and **2012 R2** as the software. Choose **Yes, Download**. You can open the file or save it.

The configuration file contains a section of information similar to the following example. You'll see this information presented twice, one time for each tunnel. You'll use this information when configuring the Windows Server 2012 R2 server.

```
1 vgw-1a2b3c4d Tunnel1
2 ------------------------------------------------------------------
3 Local Tunnel Endpoint:        203.0.113.1
4 Remote Tunnel Endpoint:       203.83.222.237
5 Endpoint 1:                   [Your_Static_Route_IP_Prefix]
6 Endpoint 2:                   [Your_VPC_CIDR_Block]
7 Preshared key:                xCjNLsLoCmKsakwcdoR9yX6GsEXAMPLE
```

Local Tunnel Endpoint
The IP address for the customer gateway—in this case, your Windows server—that terminates the VPN connection on your network's side. If your customer gateway is a Windows server instance, this is the instance's private IP address.

Remote Tunnel Endpoint
One of two IP addresses for the virtual private gateway that terminates the VPN connection on the AWS side of the connection.

Endpoint 1
The IP prefix that you specified as a static route when you created the VPN connection. These are the IP addresses in your network that are allowed to use the VPN connection to access your VPC.

Endpoint 2
The IP address range (CIDR block) of the VPC attached to the virtual private gateway (for example 10.0.0.0/16).

Preshared key
The pre-shared key that is used to establish the IPsec VPN connection between `Local Tunnel Endpoint` and `Remote Tunnel Endpoint`.

We suggest that you configure both tunnels as part of the VPN connection. Each tunnel connects to a separate VPN concentrator on the Amazon side of the VPN connection. Although only one tunnel at a time is up, the second tunnel automatically establishes itself if the first tunnel goes down. Having redundant tunnels ensure continuous availability in the case of a device failure. Because only one tunnel is available at a time, the Amazon VPC console indicates that one tunnel is down. This is expected behavior, so there's no action required from you.

With two tunnels configured, if a device failure occurs within AWS, your VPN connection automatically fails over to the second tunnel of the AWS virtual private gateway within a matter of minutes. When you configure your customer gateway, it's important that you configure both tunnels.

Note
From time to time, AWS performs routine maintenance on the virtual private gateway. This maintenance may disable one of the two tunnels of your VPN connection for a brief period of time. Your VPN connection automatically fails over to the second tunnel while we perform this maintenance.

Additional information regarding the Internet Key Exchange (IKE) and IPsec Security Associations (SA) is presented in the downloaded configuration file. Because the VPC VPN suggested settings are the same as the Windows Server 2012 R2 default IPsec configuration settings, minimal work is needed on your part.

```
1 MainModeSecMethods:      DHGroup2-AES128-SHA1
2 MainModeKeyLifetime:     480min,0sess
3 QuickModeSecMethods:     ESP:SHA1-AES128+60min+100000kb
4 QuickModePFS:            DHGroup2
```

MainModeSecMethods
The encryption and authentication algorithms for the IKE SA. These are the suggested settings for the VPN connection, and are the default settings for Windows Server 2012 R2 IPsec VPN connections.

MainModeKeyLifetime
The IKE SA key lifetime. This is the suggested setting for the VPN connection, and is the default setting for Windows Server 2012 R2 IPsec VPN connections.

QuickModeSecMethods
The encryption and authentication algorithms for the IPsec SA. These are the suggested settings for the VPN connection, and are the default settings for Windows Server 2012 R2 IPsec VPN connections.

QuickModePFS
We suggest that you use master key perfect forward secrecy (PFS) for your IPsec sessions.

Step 3: Configure the Windows Server

Before you set up the VPN tunnel, you must install and configure Routing and Remote Access Services on your Windows server to allow remote users to access resources on your network.

To install Routing and Remote Access Services on Windows Server 2012 R2

1. Log on to the Windows Server 2012 R2 server.

2. Go to the **Start** menu, and choose **Server Manager**.

3. Install Routing and Remote Access Services:

    1. From the **Manage** menu, choose **Add Roles and Features**.

    2. On the **Before You Begin** page, verify that your server meets the prerequisites, and then choose **Next**.

    3. Choose **Role-based or feature-based installation**, and then choose **Next**.

    4. Choose **Select a server from the server pool**, select your Windows 2012 R2 server, and then choose **Next**.

    5. Select **Network Policy and Access Services** in the list. In the dialog box that displays, choose **Add Features** to confirm the features that are required for this role.

    6. In the same list, choose **Remote Access**, and then choose **Next**.

    7. On the **Select features** page, choose **Next**.

    8. On the **Network Policy and Access Services** page, choose **Next**. Leave **Network Policy Server** selected, and choose **Next**.

    9. On the **Remote Access** page, choose **Next**. On the next page, select **DirectAccess and VPN (RAS)**. In the dialog box that displays, choose **Add Features** to confirm the features that are required for this role service. In the same list, select **Routing**, and then choose **Next**.

    10. On the **Web Server Role (IIS)** page, choose **Next**. Leave the default selection, and choose **Next**.

    11. Choose **Install**. When the installation completes, choose **Close**.

To configure and enable Routing and Remote Access Server

1. On the dashboard, choose **Notifications** (the flag icon). There should be a task to complete the post-deployment configuration. Choose the **Open the Getting Started Wizard** link.

2. Choose **Deploy VPN only**.

3. In the **Routing and Remote Access** dialog box, choose the server name, choose **Action**, and select **Configure and Enable Routing and Remote Access**.

4. In the **Routing and Remote Access Server Setup Wizard**, on the first page, choose **Next**.

5. On the **Configuration** page, choose **Custom Configuration** and **Next**.

6. Choose **LAN routing**, **Next**, and **Finish**.

7. When prompted by the **Routing and Remote Access** dialog box, choose **Start service**.

Step 4: Set Up the VPN Tunnel

You can configure the VPN tunnel by running the netsh scripts included in the downloaded configuration file, or by using the New Connection Security Rule wizard on the Windows server.

Important
We suggest that you use master key perfect forward secrecy (PFS) for your IPsec sessions. If you choose to run the netsh script, it includes a parameter to enable PFS (`qmpfs=dhgroup2`). You cannot enable PFS using the Windows Server 2012 R2 user interface — you must enable it using the command line.

Option 1: Run netsh Script

Copy the netsh script from the downloaded configuration file and replace the variables. The following is an example script.

```
1 netsh advfirewall consec add rule Name="vgw-1a2b3c4d Tunnel 1" ^
2 Enable=Yes Profile=any Type=Static Mode=Tunnel ^
3 LocalTunnelEndpoint=Windows_Server_Private_IP_address ^
4 RemoteTunnelEndpoint=203.83.222.236 Endpoint1=Your_Static_Route_IP_Prefix ^
5 Endpoint2=Your_VPC_CIDR_Block Protocol=Any Action=RequireInClearOut ^
6 Auth1=ComputerPSK Auth1PSK=xCjNLsLoCmKsakwcdoR9yX6GsEXAMPLE ^
7 QMSecMethods=ESP:SHA1-AES128+60min+100000kb ^
8 ExemptIPsecProtectedConnections=No ApplyAuthz=No QMPFS=dhgroup2
```

Name: You can replace the suggested name (vgw-1a2b3c4d Tunnel 1) with a name of your choice.

LocalTunnelEndpoint: Enter the private IP address of the Windows server on your network.

Endpoint1: The CIDR block of your network on which the Windows server resides, for example, 172.31.0.0/16.

Endpoint2: The CIDR block of your VPC or a subnet in your VPC, for example, 10.0.0.0/16.

Run the updated script in a command prompt window on your Windows server. (The ^ enables you to cut and paste wrapped text at the command line.) To set up the second VPN tunnel for this VPN connection, repeat the process using the second netsh script in the configuration file.

When you are done, go to 2.4: Configure the Windows Firewall.

For more information about the netsh parameters, go to Netsh AdvFirewall Consec Commands in the *Microsoft TechNet Library*.

Option 2: Use the Windows Server User Interface

You can also use the Windows server user interface to set up the VPN tunnel. This section guides you through the steps.

Important
You can't enable master key perfect forward secrecy (PFS) using the Windows Server 2012 R2 user interface. You must enable PFS using the command line, as described in Enable Master Key Perfect Forward Secrecy.

Topics

- 2.1: Configure a Security Rule for a VPN Tunnel
- 2.3: Confirm the Tunnel Configuration
- Enable Master Key Perfect Forward Secrecy

2.1: Configure a Security Rule for a VPN Tunnel

In this section, you configure a security rule on your Windows server to create a VPN tunnel.

To configure a security rule for a VPN tunnel

1. Open Server Manager, choose **Tools**, and select **Windows Firewall with Advanced Security**.

2. Select **Connection Security Rules**, choose **Action**, and then **New Rule**.

3. In the **New Connection Security Rule** wizard, on the **Rule Type** page, choose **Tunnel**, and then choose **Next**.

4. On the **Tunnel Type** page, under **What type of tunnel would you like to create**, choose **Custom configuration**. Under **Would you like to exempt IPsec-protected connections from this tunnel**, leave the default value checked (**No. Send all network traffic that matches this connection security rule through the tunnel**), and then choose **Next**.

5. On the **Requirements** page, choose **Require authentication for inbound connections. Do not establish tunnels for outbound connections**, and then choose **Next**.

6. On **Tunnel Endpoints** page, under **Which computers are in Endpoint 1**, choose **Add**. Enter the CIDR range of your network (behind your Windows server customer gateway; for example, `172.31.0.0/16`), and then choose **OK**. (Note that the range can include the IP address of your customer gateway.)

7. Under **What is the local tunnel endpoint (closest to computer in Endpoint 1)**, choose **Edit**. In the **IPv4 address** field, enter the private IP address of your Windows server, and then choose **OK**.

8. Under **What is the remote tunnel endpoint (closest to computers in Endpoint 2)**, choose **Edit**. In the **IPv4 address** field, enter the IP address of the virtual private gateway for Tunnel 1 from the configuration file (see `Remote Tunnel Endpoint`), and then choose **OK**. **Important**
If you are repeating this procedure for Tunnel 2, be sure to select the endpoint for Tunnel 2.

9. Under **Which computers are in Endpoint 2**, choose **Add**. In the **This IP address or subnet field**, enter the CIDR block of your VPC, and then choose **OK**. **Important**
You must scroll in the dialog box until you locate **Which computers are in Endpoint 2**. Do not choose **Next** until you have completed this step, or you won't be able to connect to your server.

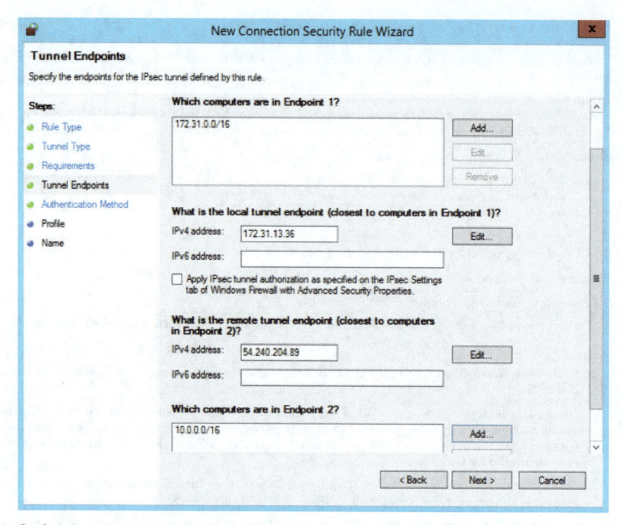

10. Confirm that all the settings you've specified are correct, and then choose **Next**.

11. On the **Authentication Method** page, select **Advanced**, and then choose **Customize**.

12. Under **First authentication methods**, choose **Add**.

13. Select **Preshared key**, enter the pre-shared key value from the configuration file, and choose **OK**.
    Important
    If you are repeating this procedure for Tunnel 2, be sure to select the pre-shared key for Tunnel 2.

14. Ensure that **First authentication is optional** is not selected, and choose **OK**.

15. Choose **Next**.

16. On the **Profile** page, select all three checkboxes: **Domain**, **Private**, and **Public**, and then choose **Next**.

17. On the **Name** page, enter a name for your connection rule; for example, VPN to AWS Tunnel 1, and then choose **Finish**.

Repeat the above procedure, specifying the data for Tunnel 2 from your configuration file.

After you've finished, you'll have two tunnels configured for your VPN connection.

2.3: Confirm the Tunnel Configuration

To confirm the tunnel configuration

1. Open Server Manager, choose **Tools**, select **Windows Firewall with Advanced Security**, and then select **Connection Security Rules**.

2. Verify the following for both tunnels:

   - **Enabled** is `Yes`
   - **Endpoint 1** is the CIDR block for your network
   - **Endpoint 2** is the CIDR block of your VPC
   - **Authentication mode** is `Require inbound and clear outbound`
   - **Authentication method** is `Custom`
   - **Endpoint 1 port** is `Any`
   - **Endpoint 2 port** is `Any`
   - **Protocol** is `Any`

3. Select the first rule and choose **Properties**.

4. On the **Authentication** tab, under **Method**, choose **Customize**, and verify that **First authentication methods** contains the correct pre-shared key from your configuration file for the tunnel, and then choose **OK**.

5. On the **Advanced** tab, verify that **Domain**, **Private**, and **Public** are all selected.

6. Under **IPsec tunneling**, choose **Customize**. Verify the following IPsec tunneling settings, and then choose **OK** and **OK** again to close the dialog box.

   - **Use IPsec tunneling** is selected.
   - **Local tunnel endpoint (closest to Endpoint 1)** contains the IP address of your Windows server. If your customer gateway is an EC2 instance, this is the instance's private IP address.
   - **Remote tunnel endpoint (closest to Endpoint 2)** contains the IP address of the virtual private gateway for this tunnel.

7. Open the properties for your second tunnel. Repeat steps 4 to 7 for this tunnel.

Enable Master Key Perfect Forward Secrecy

You can enable master key perfect forward secrecy by using the command line. You cannot enable this feature using the user interface.

To enable master key perfect forward secrecy

1. In your Windows server, open a new command prompt window.

2. Type the following command, replacing `rule_name` with the name you gave the first connection rule.

```
1 netsh advfirewall consec set rule name="rule_name" new QMPFS=dhgroup2 QMSecMethods=ESP:SHA1
    -AES128+60min+100000kb
```

3. Repeat step 2 for the second tunnel, this time replacing `rule_name` with the name that you gave the second connection rule.

2.4: Configure the Windows Firewall

After setting up your security rules on your server, configure some basic IPsec settings to work with the virtual private gateway.

To configure the Windows firewall

1. Open Server Manager, choose **Tools**, select **Windows Firewall with Advanced Security**, and then choose **Properties**.

229

2. On the **IPsec Settings** tab, under **IPsec exemptions**, verify that **Exempt ICMP from IPsec** is **No (default)**. Verify that **IPsec tunnel authorization** is **None**.

3. Under **IPsec defaults**, choose **Customize**.

4. Under **Key exchange (Main Mode)**, select **Advanced** and then choose **Customize**.

5. In **Customize Advanced Key Exchange Settings**, under **Security methods**, verify that these default values are used for the first entry.

   - Integrity: SHA-1
   - Encryption: AES-CBC 128
   - Key exchange algorithm: Diffie-Hellman Group 2
   - Under **Key lifetimes**, verify that **Minutes** is 480 and **Sessions** is 0.

   These settings correspond to these entries in the configuration file:

   ```
   1 MainModeSecMethods: DHGroup2-AES128-SHA1,DHGroup2-3DES-SHA1
   2 MainModeKeyLifetime: 480min,0sec
   ```

6. Under **Key exchange options**, select **Use Diffie-Hellman for enhanced security**, and then choose **OK**.

7. Under **Data protection (Quick Mode)**, select **Advanced**, and then choose **Customize**.

8. Select **Require encryption for all connection security rules that use these settings**.

9. Under **Data integrity and encryption**, leave the default values:

   - Protocol: ESP
   - Integrity: SHA-1
   - Encryption: AES-CBC 128
   - Lifetime: 60 minutes

   These value correspond to the following entry from the configuration file.

   ```
   1 QuickModeSecMethods:
   2 ESP:SHA1-AES128+60min+100000kb
   ```

10. Choose **OK** to return to the **Customize IPsec Settings** dialog box and choose **OK** again to save the configuration .

Step 5: Enable Dead Gateway Detection

Next, you need to configure TCP to detect when a gateway becomes unavailable. You can do this by modifying this registry key: HKLM\SYSTEM\CurrentControlSet\Services\Tcpip\Parameters. Do not perform this step until you've completed the preceding sections. After you change the registry key, you must reboot the server.

To enable dead gateway detection

1. From your Windows server, launch the command prompt or a PowerShell session, and type **regedit** to start Registry Editor.

2. Expand **HKEY_LOCAL_MACHINE**, expand **SYSTEM**, expand **CurrentControlSet**, expand **Services**, expand **Tcpip**, and then expand **Parameters**.

3. From the **Edit** menu, select **New** and select **DWORD (32-bit) Value**.

4. Enter the name **EnableDeadGWDetect**.

5. Select **EnableDeadGWDetect**, and choose **Modify** from the **Edit** menu.

6. In **Value data**, enter **1**, and then choose **OK**.

7. Close the Registry Editor and reboot the server.

For more information, go to EnableDeadGWDetect in the *Microsoft TechNet Library*.

Step 6: Test the VPN Connection

To test that the VPN connection is working correctly, launch an instance into your VPC, and ensure that it does not have an Internet connection. After you've launched the instance, ping its private IP address from your Windows server. The VPN tunnel comes up when traffic is generated from the customer gateway, therefore the ping command also initiates the VPN connection.

To launch an instance in your VPC and get its private IP address

1. Open the Amazon EC2 console, and choose **Launch Instance**.

2. Select an Amazon Linux AMI, and select an instance type.

3. On the **Step 3: Configure Instance Details** page, select your VPC from the **Network** list, and select a subnet from the **Subnet** list. Ensure that you select the private subnet that you configured in Step 1: Create a VPN Connection and Configure Your VPC.

4. In the **Auto-assign Public IP** list, ensure that the setting is set to **Disable**.

5. Choose **Next** until you get to the** Step 6: Configure Security Group** page. You can either select an existing security group that you configured in Step 1: Create a VPN Connection and Configure Your VPC, or you can create a new security group and ensure that it has a rule that allows all ICMP traffic from the IP address of your Windows server.

6. Complete the rest of the steps in the wizard, and launch your instance.

7. On the **Instances** page, select your instance. Get the private IP address in the **Private IPs** field on the details pane.

Connect to or log on to your Windows server, open the command prompt, and then use the `ping` command to ping your instance using its private IP address; for example:

```
1 ping 10.0.0.4
```

```
1 Pinging 10.0.0.4 with 32 bytes of data:
2 Reply from 10.0.0.4: bytes=32 time=2ms TTL=62
3 Reply from 10.0.0.4: bytes=32 time=2ms TTL=62
4 Reply from 10.0.0.4: bytes=32 time=2ms TTL=62
5 Reply from 10.0.0.4: bytes=32 time=2ms TTL=62
6
7 Ping statistics for 10.0.0.4:
8     Packets: Sent = 4, Received = 4, Lost = 0 (0% loss),
9 Approximate round trip times in milli-seconds:
10     Minimum = 2ms, Maximum = 2ms, Average = 2ms
```

If the `ping` command fails, check the following information:

- Ensure that you have configured your security group rules to allow ICMP to the instance in your VPC. If your Windows server is an EC2 instance, ensure that its security group's outbound rules allow IPsec traffic. For more information, see Configuring Your Windows Server.
- Ensure that the operating system on the instance you are pinging is configured to respond to ICMP. We recommend that you use one of the Amazon Linux AMIs.
- If the instance you are pinging is a Windows instance, connect to the instance and enable inbound ICMPv4 on the Windows firewall.
- Ensure that you have configured the route tables correctly for your VPC or your subnet . For more information, see Step 1: Create a VPN Connection and Configure Your VPC.

- If your customer gateway is a Windows server instance, ensure that you've disabled source/destination checking for the instance. For more information, see Configuring Your Windows Server.

In the Amazon VPC console, on the **VPN Connections** page, select your VPN connection. The first tunnel is in the UP state. The second tunnel should be configured, but it won't be used unless the first tunnel goes down. It may take a few moments to establish the encrypted tunnels.

Document History

For more information about the important changes in each release of the *Amazon VPC Network Administrator Guide*, see Document History in the *Amazon VPC User Guide*.